Christian Faith and University Life

T. Laine Scales · Jennifer L. Howell
Editors

Christian Faith and University Life

Stewards of the Academy

Editors
T. Laine Scales
Baylor University
Waco, TX, USA

Jennifer L. Howell
Baylor University
Waco, TX, USA

ISBN 978-3-319-87151-6 ISBN 978-3-319-61744-2 (eBook)
DOI 10.1007/978-3-319-61744-2

Softcover reprint of the hardcover 1st edition 2017

Printed on acid-free paper

This Palgrave Macmillan imprint is published by Springer Nature
The registered company is Springer International Publishing AG
The registered company address is: Gewerbestrasse 11, 6330 Cham, Switzerland

In memory of Susan E. Colón
1973–2012

Acknowledgements

This project has been a cooperative endeavor from the beginning. We are grateful to our colleagues in the community of learning at Baylor University who challenged us to think through the question of graduate student formation and Christian faith. Darin Davis, Vice President of University Mission and Director of the Institute of Faith and Learning and Larry Lyon, Dean of the Graduate School have encouraged us, supported us, and offered their insights.

We are particularly indebted to the doctoral students, faculty, and pastors who took time to help us shape the practice that came to be known as the Conyers Scholars Program at Baylor. In particular, we are grateful to Bruce Longenecker, Rev. Dorisanne Cooper, Ian Gravagne, Darin Davis, Rev. Matt Snowden, Robert Kruschwitz, Rev. Eric Howell, B.J. Parker, Michael DePalma, Nathan Alleman, Michael Beaty, Rev. Robert Creech, Rebecca Hays, Nathan Hays, and Katie Robbins for their efforts in leading the program.

While we both tend to live in the world of ideas, producing an edited volume requires close attention to detail. For that set of skills, we relied upon Nathan Hays and Alanna Martinez who helped us with manuscript preparation. We appreciated the guidance of Milana Vernikova and the editorial staff at Palgrave for their technical assistance and encouragement at several stages of this project. Several anonymous Conyers Scholars offered blind review, providing helpful feedback for our contributors.

Finally, we are especially grateful for the investment of time, wisdom, and heart the late Susan E. Colón provided in the first years of the Conyers Scholars project. Susan was a true steward of the academy and of the faith; we dedicate this volume to her memory.

Contents

Part II Faithful Teachers and Pedagogical Practices

Part III Church and Academy: Stewarding our Faith and our Universities

Editors and Contributors

About the Editors

T. Laine Scales is Professor of Higher Education and Associate Dean of Graduate Studies at Baylor University, Waco, TX. She earned a B.A. from University of North Carolina, MSW from The Southern Baptist Theological Seminary, and Ph.D. from University of Kentucky. Dr. Scales served 15 years with social work faculties of three universities before joining Baylor's School of Education in 2008. In 2016, she was honored with Baylor's most prestigious teaching award, Master Teacher. Dr. Scales' research has resulted in over 40 articles and chapters in social work education, history of women in higher education, and doctoral education. Her ten books include *Doing the Word: Southern Baptists' Carver School of Church Social Work and its Predecessors,* 1907–1997. Co-authored with Melody Maxwell (University of Tennessee Press, forthcoming 2018) *Social Environments & Human Behavior: Contexts for Practice with Groups, Organizations, Communities, & Social Movements* (Oxford University Press, 2016), and *All That Fits a Woman: Training Southern Baptist Women for Charity and Mission, 1907–1926* (Mercer University Press, 2000). Dr. Scales is founder of Good Neighbor Settlement House, a Christian nonprofit in Waco, TX established in 2013.

Jennifer L. Howell recently completed her Ph.D. in Theology at Baylor University. She earned her B.A. in English Literature from Texas A&M University and her M.Div. from Duke Divinity School in Durham, NC. After completing her M.Div., she spent several years on ministerial staff at Broadus Memorial Baptist Church in Charlottesville, VA. Her areas of interest include the works of Dietrich Bonhoeffer and Maximus the Confessor. Her essays and reviews have appeared in *The Christian Century*, *The Other Journal*, *The Journal of Church and State*, and *Christian Reflections*. She teaches courses in the Great Texts program at Baylor University. Jennifer and her husband Eric have three children: Lara, Lily, and Jimmy.

Contributors

Karl Aho is an instructor of Philosophy at Tarleton State University. His academic journey is somewhat unusual, in that he has been both student and teacher at public and church-related institutions. After semesters at Michigan Technological University and Keweenaw Bay Ojibwa Community College, he earned a B.A. in Philosophy and Humanities from Valparaiso University, an M.A. from Boston College, and a Ph.D. from Baylor University. Dr. Aho's scholarship engages the history of philosophy to address contemporary ethical and pedagogical concerns. While his main research interest is Søren Kierkegaard, he has a long-standing appreciation of classical philosophy and a burgeoning interest in American philosophers such as William James.

Nathan Alleman is Associate Professor of Higher Education Studies at Baylor University. He earned a B.A. from Messiah College in Philosophy, an M.A. in Higher Education from Geneva College, and a Ph.D. in Educational Policy, Planning, and Leadership, with an emphasis in Higher Education from the College in William and Mary. He studies marginal and marginalized groups and institutions in higher education. Foci include sociological studies of faculty subgroups (nontenure track, religious minorities, faculty denied tenure), faith-based college and universities, and the collegiate identity of student subgroups (undocumented, community college, food insecure students). He recently coauthored the book *Restoring the Soul of the University: Unifying Christian Higher Education in a Fragmented Age* (2017).

Jack R. Baker is Associate Professor of English at Spring Arbor University. Baker hails from rural Shelby, Michigan and earned his B.A. in Philosophy from Cornerstone University, his M.A. from The Medieval Institute at Western Michigan University, and his Ph.D. in English from Purdue University. Baker draws upon his training in language, the liberal arts, and philosophy in his teaching. He has studied and taught Wendell

Berry's works, especially his fiction, alongside those of J.R.R. Tolkien, C.S. Lewis, Dana Gioia, Frederick Buechner, and Marilyn Robinson. He and Jeffrey Bilbro have enjoyed collaborating on several publications—their book, *Wendell Berry and Higher Education: Cultivating Virtues of Place*, was released with the University Press of Kentucky in June 2017. He and his wife Kelly have three wonderful children—Owen, Silvia, and Griffin.

Jeffrey Bilbro is Assistant Professor of English at Spring Arbor University in Southern Michigan. He grew up in the mountainous state of Washington and earned his B.A. in Writing and Literature from George Fox University in Oregon and his Ph.D. in English from Baylor University. He is the author of *Loving God's Wildness: The Christian Roots of Ecological Ethics in American Literature* (University of Alabama Press, 2015) and the coauthor, with Jack Baker, of *Wendell Berry and Higher Education: Cultivating Virtues of Place* (University Press of Kentucky, 2017).

João Chaves is originally from Recife, Brazil. He serves as a lecturer in Religion and Human Behavior at the Baptist University of the Américas in San Antonio, Texas. João has a B.Th. from CEBESP (São Paulo, Brazil), a B.A. from the Baptist University of the Américas, a M.T.S. from the G.W. Truett Theological Seminary of Baylor University, and is currently a Ph.D. candidate in the Religion Department of Baylor University. João authored several book reviews, peer-reviewed articles, book chapters, and the book *Evangelicals and Liberation Revisited* (Wipf & Stock, 2013). His dissertation explores the effects of transnational relationships and migration on religious communal identity.

Rev. Kyle Childress has been the pastor of the Austin Heights Baptist Church in Nacogdoches, Texas since 1989. Located near Stephen F. Austin University, the congregation has long had numerous faculty and students as members. A graduate of Baylor University (B.A.) and Southern Baptist Theological Seminary (M.Div.) Kyle is a writer of over 50 articles, has contributed chapters to nine books and is the author with Rodney Kennedy of *Will Campbell, Preacher Man: Essays in the Spirit of a Divine Provocateur* (Cascade, 2016). He is also a frequent guest preacher and lecturer and in 2008 was named one of the preachers of the Great Preaching Series at Andover Newton Theological School in Boston during the school's 200th anniversary celebration. Kyle is married to Jane, a poet and they have two adult daughters, Emily and Callie.

David C. Cramer is teaching pastor at Keller Park Church in South Bend, Indiana. He earned a B.A. in Biblical Studies and Philosophy from Bethel College (Indiana), M.Div. and M.A. in Philosophy of Religion from Trinity Evangelical Divinity School, and Ph.D. in Religion from Baylor University. He has taught courses in religion at Bethel College and Baylor University and worked as a theological editor at Baker Academic and Brazos Press. His research interests include theological ethics and Anabaptist theology, and he has published in *Christian Century*, *Christian Scholar's Review*, *Sojourners*, and elsewhere. He is the coeditor of *The Activist Impulse: Essays on the Intersection of Evangelicalism and Anabaptism* (Pickwick, 2012) and is currently coauthoring a book tentatively titled, *A Field Guide to Christian Nonviolence*.

Darin H. Davis is Vice President for University Mission and Director of the Institute for Faith and Learning (IFL) at Baylor University. He earned degrees at the University of Texas (B.A. in English and Philosophy), Baylor (M.A. in Philosophy), and Saint Louis University (Ph.D. in Philosophy). As IFL's director, he oversees the annual Baylor Symposium on Faith and Culture, various faculty and staff development efforts, and programs for Baylor students, including the Crane Scholars Program and Conyers Scholars Program. His scholarly research focuses on the history of moral philosophy, virtue ethics, and higher education. His articles have appeared in the *American Catholic Philosophical Quarterly*, *Christian Reflection*, *International Journal of Christianity and Education*, and *The Southern Journal of Philosophy*. He is the editor and coauthor of *Educating for Wisdom in the Twenty-First Century* (St. Augustine's Press, 2017). Davis also teaches at Baylor as a faculty member in the Honors Program.

David T. Echelbarger is Assistant Professor of Philosophy at The University of Mary, where he is also a faculty mentor for the Gregorian Scholars Honors Program. He earned his B.A. in Philosophy and Religious studies from St. Norbert College and his M.A. and Ph.D. in Philosophy from Baylor University. He has published on the passions' role in practical reasoning and has additional research interests in ethical theory and moral education.

Perry L. Glanzer is Professor of Educational Foundations at Baylor University and a resident scholar with Baylor Institute for Studies of Religion. He earned a B.A. in History and Political Science from Rice

University, an M.A. in Church-State Studies from Baylor University and a Ph.D. in Social Ethics from the University of Southern California. His primarily scholarly interests pertain to moral education and Christian higher education, and he has authored or coauthored over 70 journal articles and book chapters on these topics. He recently coauthored *Restoring the Soul of the University: Unifying Christian Higher Education in a Fragmented Age (Intervarsity Press)* and *The Quest for Purpose: The Collegiate Search for a Meaningful Life* (SUNY Press). He also recently coedited *Christian Higher Education: A Global Reconnaissance* (Eerdmans).

Rachel B. Griffis is Assistant Professor of English at Sterling College, where she teaches literature and writing. She received her Ph.D. in English from Baylor University in 2016, and her scholarly interests include colonial and nineteenth-century American literature, women writers, and religion and literature. Her writing has appeared in *Pacific Coast Philology, Women's Studies, Teaching American Literature, International Journal of Christianity and Education*, *Religions*, and elsewhere. At the onset of her doctoral studies, she was selected for the Lilly Graduate Fellows Program, and in 2012 she became a Conyers Scholar at Baylor. These experiences deepened and shaped her commitment to the integration of faith and learning within her discipline. She now serves as the Lilly Faculty Representative at Sterling College.

David Guthrie is Associate Professor of Higher Education at Penn State University. He received a B.A. in Sociology and in Religion from Grove City College, an M.A. in Religion from Pittsburgh Theological Seminary, and a Ph.D. in Higher Education from Penn State University. He previously served as a dean in both student affairs and academic affairs, and directed a multiyear grant from the Lilly Endowment that explored the topic of vocation in higher education, particularly at church-related institutions. Dave is the author of two monographs, several journal articles, and numerous conference presentations. His intellectual interests include foundations of US higher education, church-related colleges and universities, and connections among religion, society, and higher education.

Emily Hunt serves as a senior research analyst at the Baylor Center for Community Research and Development and is a research fellow at the Institute for Advanced Studies in Culture focusing on Moral Foundations of Education Project. She is a Ph.D. candidate in the Department of

Sociology at Baylor University specializing in education, culture, and religion. Before joining the program at Baylor she earned a Master of Arts in Higher Education and Student Affairs from Taylor University and was the Cortina Service Program Director at Creighton University. Emily's dissertation examines how moral cultures influence high school student achievement and shape aspirations for higher education.

L. Gregory Jones is the founder and currently serves as a senior fellow at Leadership Education at Duke Divinity School, Williams Professor of Theology and Ministry and senior fellow at the Fuqua-Coach K Center for Leadership and Ethics, all at Duke University, Durham, NC. He earned his B.A. and MPA degrees from University of Denver and M.Div. and Ph.D. degrees from Duke University. Jones previously served in several capacities at Duke, including chief international strategist, and Dean of Duke Divinity School. In 2016–17 Jones served as executive president and provost at Baylor University, helping the university through several leadership transitions. Jones is the author or editor of over 17 books, including Christian Social Innovation (2016) and Embodying forgiveness (1995), and more than 200 articles. He serves on the editorial board of the journal *Modern Theology* and is an editor-at-large for *The Christian Century*.

Matthew A. Rothaus Moser is Visiting Assistant Professor of Theology at Loyola University of Maryland. He earned his Ph.D. from Baylor University and M. Div. from Lutheran Theological Seminary at Gettysburg. He is the author of *Love Itself is Understanding: Hans Urs von Balthasar's Theology of the Saints* (Fortress Press, 2016) and the forthcoming *Dante: Poet of the Christian Life* (Wipf & Stock Publishers). His work focuses on contemplation, religious epistemology, and the spirituality of prayer. He has won two awards for teaching excellence (Baylor University, 2013 and Loyola University Maryland, 2016). Outside the academy, he devotes himself to spending time with his wife, Kaitlyn, and serving at St. John's Episcopal Church in Glyndon, Maryland.

Jane Kelley Rodeheffer is a philosopher who currently holds the Fletcher Jones Chair in Great Books at Pepperdine University in California. Professor Rodeheffer received degrees from Boston College, Harvard, and Vanderbilt. She has published a range of articles in philosophy, literature, and great books, and she is the coeditor of three collections of essays. She is currently at work on a project involving the use of narrative Icons in the work of Dostoevsky. Professor Rodeheffer was instrumental in the founding of the Lilly Graduate Fellows Program and served as Faculty Mentor to Cohorts 1 and 6. Professor Rodeheffer collaborates frequently with Professors of Studio Arts to engage her own students in the visual language of Dante, Milton, Confucius, Lao Tzu, and Zen Buddhism. A potter and calligrapher in the Asian tradition, she served as artist in residence at the St. John's University pottery in Collegeville, MN for the summer of 2016.

Mark Schwehn is Professor of Humanities in Christ College, the Honors College of Valparaiso University. He served as Dean of Christ College from 1990–2003 and as Provost of Valparaiso University from 2009–2014. He received his B.A. from Valparaiso University, and his Ph.D. in History and Humanities from Stanford University. He has written widely about Henry Adams and William James, including a volume that he edited and to which he contributed an essay, *A William James Renaissance* (Harvard, 1983). He has published several books and articles on religion and higher learning, including *Exiles from Eden: Religion and the Academic Vocation in America* (Oxford, 1993) and *Everyone A Teacher* (Notre Dame, 2000). With Dorothy Bass, he is the editor of *Leading Lives That Matter: What We Should Do and Who We Should Be* (Eerdmans, 2006). In 2005–2006 he was a Fellow at the Institute for Ecumenical and Cultural Studies at St. John's University (MN). Schwehn is Project Director of the Lilly Fellows Program in Humanities and the Arts at Valparaiso, and serves on the boards of several major institutions addressing religion, education, and American public life.

David I. Smith is Director of the Kuyers Institute for Christian Teaching and Learning and Director of Graduate Studies in Education at Calvin College in Grand Rapids, Michigan. He serves as a senior editor of the *International Journal of Christianity and Education.* He has received awards for innovative teaching and for multicultural teaching. Some of his writing has focused on world language education and intercultural learning, including the books *The Gift of the Stranger: Faith, Hospitality, and Foreign Language Learning* (2000, with Barbara Carvill), *Learning from the Stranger: Christian Faith and Cultural Diversity* (2009) and *Christians and Cultural Difference* (2016, with Pennylyn Dykstra-Pruim). His broader work on Christian education includes the recent volumes *Teaching and Christian Practices* (2011, edited by James K.A. Smith) and *Teaching and Christian Imagination* (2016, with Susan M. Felch, Barbara M. Carvill, Kurt C. Schaefer, Timothy H. Steele, and John D. Witvliet).

List of Tables

CHAPTER 1

Introduction—Stewardship Reconsidered: Academic Work and the Faithful Christian

T. Laine Scales and Jennifer L. Howell

Think of us in this way, as servants of Christ and stewards of God's mysteries. Moreover, it is required of stewards that they be found trustworthy.
(1 Corinthians 4:1–2, NRSV).

The academy is a foreign land for the uninitiated. Misjudged and misunderstood by critics, admirers, and those who aspire to join its ranks, life in academic communities must be lived for awhile, and even then, the foreign customs, habits, and practices often make little sense, even to the academy's own inhabitants. Doctoral students, attempting to join academic communities during their studies, often express confusion and surprise at the start of their graduate work. Is the academic community really this competitive? Why do my undergraduate students only care about getting jobs? How can the subject I love so much seem so boring to my students? Christian graduate students may struggle even further to understand how the values and habits of an increasingly secularized academy may align with their faith. They may experience value conflicts and find themselves resisting what they see as pointless habits and unhappy

T. Laine Scales (✉) · J.L. Howell
Baylor University, Waco, TX, USA

T.L. Scales and J.L. Howell (eds.), *Christian Faith and University Life*,
DOI 10.1007/978-3-319-61744-2_1

dispositions of their professors. Or, they may avoid their conflicted feelings by abandoning their usual Christian practices and church communities for a time, seeing the doctoral years as a season to focus solely on one thing: finishing the degree.

Given the confusing and overwhelming season of doctoral study, would it be helpful if Christian doctoral students (and the faculty who mentor them) understood themselves as "servants of Christ and stewards of the mysteries God has revealed" (1 Cor. 4:1)? As scholars in the academy, if we were to view our task as *stewardship*, a careful tending and sharing of the intellectual gifts God has given to us, what difference would that make to our daily lives as Christian academics? In this introductory chapter we will explain how this question has impacted our professional and personal lives and eventually led us to create the community of respondents that would produce this volume. Drawing from recent work in each of our disciplines, higher education and theology, we will consider how stewardship might serve as a useful framework for our academic lives. How might we practice stewardship with humility and gratitude, while learning hard lessons from theological distortions that led the church into dangerous misuses of stewardship language? Throughout the chapter we will reflect on our own experiences of gathering with other Christian academics to "practice the practices" intended to form us into better stewards of our academic gifts.

As editors of this volume, the two of us lived with these ideas of stewardship and formation for about three years, met weekly to discuss them, and engaged other Christian academics in conversation. Together, we represent the current and future generations of faculty life. From our different vantage points we found this framework of stewardship prompted us to think more deeply and critically about the promises of doctoral education for Christian scholars.

Jennifer Howell (Jenny) was completing her doctoral studies at Baylor University while our conversations were ongoing. Like the other doctoral students writing essays for this volume, she faced important questions about the academy's future. Our universities are driven by fear as our nation falls in the global economic and social rankings when we compare ourselves to the rest of the world. We are forced to adjust quickly to shifts in technology that are drastically changing how higher education is offered. In an intellectual era that prioritizes specialization and intellectual property rights, education is often discussed as a commodity, where the end goal is to "out-expertise" other experts in the field. As a theologian, she wondered, in particular, how Christian faith, pedagogy, and vocation fit together in light of these trends. Jenny spoke often with her doctoral student colleagues about how Christians in the academy might respond to some of these challenges. She desired to create communities of support that would help her think through how to counteract some of these worrisome trends. In addition to the creation of the Conyers Scholars program, which we will turn to briefly, she helped form a writing group of friends who met weekly to read one another's work and offer constructive feedback, and she participated in a group with other graduate students and faculty to discuss approaches to pedagogy that challenge students to think of education in an integrated, holistic way. By the time she graduated, Jenny had gathered several intellectual communities around her to consider the academy's future as she entered the job market.

Terisa Laine Scales (Laine) is Professor and administrator at Baylor University and, like the other faculty mentors writing essays for this volume, works with doctoral students learning to navigate the rocky terrain of the academy. Looking toward the future, she reminds her doctoral students regularly: "You are the next generation of Christian faculty and administrators who will inherit these universities with their problems and opportunities." Rather than letting graduate students get stuck in their criticism or their fears of university life, she asks them, "What will you do to make it better, when you are leading the way?" When doctoral students think in these terms, they begin planning as stewards: they consider what they hope to preserve and what they want to change about the academy in years to come. Imagining themselves in charge, these future faculty and administrators explore in conversation with others how to steward both the academy and their Christian faith in light of our current challenges. Laine collaborates with other leaders to facilitate regular student gatherings to talk seriously about the academy and its future. In these gatherings, Christian doctoral students form habits and practices of community dialogue that transcend disciplinary boundaries. Laine's hope is that doctoral students will carry these practices into their faculty roles after graduation, creating their own transdisciplinary communities. Several essays in this volume are extensions of conversations graduate students started within these gatherings. Now the authors take the dialogue outward in new directions as they live into their new faculty positions.

Stewardship and the Educational Process

Appropriating the word *stewardship* as an ideal for doctoral education is not original to us. We were inspired by the work of the Carnegie Initiative on the Doctorate (CID), a forward-thinking research group conducting a five-year study as the twenty-first century began. The CID concluded that forming "stewards of the disciplines" is an essential goal for doctoral education. Their study goes on to provide data and examples from a diverse group of programs in the study. The CID researchers explain this "provocative framework" of stewardship in their book, *Formation of Scholars: Rethinking Doctoral Education for the Twenty-First Century*; their conclusions present a bold call for reexamination of our traditional practices.[1] The academic steward, according to the authors, is "not simply manager of her own career," rather she "embraces a larger sense of purpose" and has been entrusted with the care of her discipline "on behalf of those in and beyond it."[2] The authors are candid about their intent when borrowing ecclesiastical language to express their ideas:

> We do not choose the language of "formation" or "stewardship" capriciously. The doctorate carries with it both a sense of intellectual mastery and of moral responsibility. That the entire process concludes with all members of the community dressed in religious robes and engaged in an act of ordination of the novice by the master with a priestly hood is no accident.[3]

For Christians, the call to embrace a larger sense of purpose in our work is not new; discussions of *vocation* have flourished in the past two decades within Christian circles, particularly within undergraduate education. Using religious language to speak specifically about doctoral education, however, was rather novel in our experience, and we wanted to dig deeper into ideas like vocation, formation, and stewardship to see if we might discern their relevance for Christian academics. There were many resources available. During the same years that CID researchers combed the nation's universities for promising practices in doctoral education, Christian universities were piloting new programs to prepare future faculty. Sponsored in large part by the Lilly Endowment, these programs focused particularly on how graduates might bring their faith to bear on their work as scholars and teachers. For example, the Lilly Graduate Fellows Program, described by Jane Kelley Rodeheffer (Chap. 8), offers opportunities for mentoring and dialogue to prepare doctoral students for faith-informed faculty life. The Lilly postdoctoral fellows at Valparaiso offers practical opportunities for Christian scholar-teachers in the years between their doctoral work and first faculty appointments. Baylor University's Conyers Scholars program, described later in this introduction, focuses on cultivating particular practices aimed at shaping Christian scholar-teachers. Each of these programs aims to form the next generation of Christian faculty, but with different methods and emphases. This volume engages members of these and other groups as it weaves together threads of discussion among doctoral students, faculty mentors, and clergy. Together we consider the question of how we might envision and inhabit a Christian understanding of the concept of stewardship within the academy.

Listening to the Carnegie Initiative on the Doctorate (CID)

What convinced us that the voices of the CID were the right ones for us to hear? Was this really a conversation we wanted to join? We found the CID's conclusions compelling as they came from a multidisciplinary group of experts and were backed up by a long-term research project of both public and private universities. While carrying the Carnegie imprimatur, well-known for educational innovation, the CID challenged the status quo in ways we found courageous. Project leaders demonstrated what they challenged other academics to do, namely, to "preserve the best of the past for those who will follow," and to consider how to "prepare and initiate the next generation of stewards."[4] The CIDs progressive and creative recommendations appealed to us and gave would-be reformers a rationale for rethinking doctoral education while still showing respect for the traditions that should endure.

The CID's work was also appealing to us for its practical examples derived from real programs. While our dialogue would eventually expand to other universities and programs, it began within the walls of Baylor University. Baylor is relatively new to larger scale doctoral education. The work of the CID appeared just as we were exploring ways in which Baylor's graduate programs could be aligned with the university's commitment to being distinctively Christian as a research university. Since an overwhelming majority of Christian colleges and universities serve undergraduates, models for Christian research universities with robust graduate programs were few. The CID's practical examples of graduate student formation inspired our own thinking regarding possibilities.

Finally, the familiarity of the CID's metaphors, while startling at first, drew us in and made us feel "at home." Words like *formation* and *stewardship* were "church words" that we had been exposed to in congregational life. We were surprised to find this language in a field like higher education that can sometimes be allergic to its Christian roots. Beyond the CID's work, we had access in our immediate circles to theological and historical resources for exploring these terms more deeply and in different directions than the CID had done. What might we contribute to the formation of future faculty if we expanded upon the work of the CID and carefully considered with our graduate students the academy's future? Drawn toward this orientation that combines past, present, and future, we began our exploration with the idea of the steward.

According to the CID, stewards engage in three interrelated tasks: generation, conservation, and transformation. *Generation* is often the first thing we imagine when we think of a scholar: conducting original and important research. Scholars move their fields forward by posing significant questions, developing strategies to investigate these questions, analyzing the results of their investigations, and then communicating their results. Related to generation, is *conservation*, the task of preserving the prior groundwork of researchers that have gone before us. Scholars practice conservation when they successfully judge which ideas are worth keeping and which should be discarded. To succeed at conservation, a scholar must understand relationships between a particular area of expertise and the discipline as a whole. Then, she must be able to articulate how her research contributes to the larger intellectual landscape. The third task, *transformation,* speaks to the scholar's teaching responsibilities, and much more besides. By passing on ideas that one has generated or conserved, a steward engages in "a dynamic process of transforming knowledge so that new learners can meaningfully engage with it."[5] Since learners are found everywhere (not just in classrooms), the CID ambitiously imagines the steward as one who shares knowledge broadly to transform the entire world in which we live. While performing these three interrelated tasks, the steward lives out a commitment to moral responsibility as a scholar and "embraces a larger sense of purpose."[6]

Firm in our conviction that the work of the CID was the right place to start listening, the Baylor Graduate School asked some of its doctoral students to read *Formation of Scholars* when it was hot off the presses in 2008 and suggest some actions they would like to take in response. The rich ideas the students presented to the Graduate School indicated the resonance they found with the authors' arguments and the practical applications began to flow. These graduate student readers appreciated the CID's emphasis on student responsibility and resolved to get more involved in their departments. They were motivated by the CID's practical list of ideas to create their own dissertation writing groups, invite their faculty to dialogue with them more outside the seminar walls, and to pursue family friendly policies through their graduate student association. As the Baylor Graduate School began trying out some of the graduate students' ideas for new and improved programs, the two of us began conversations about a larger project: we wondered what might happen if Christian doctoral students and faculty were to spend a year or two developing a set of practices to deepen our understanding of and commitments to academic life. What would happen if we carefully built and lovingly maintained a solid spiritual and intellectual community to explore important questions about the academy's past, present, and future? Would stewardship then take root within this set of practices?

Creating an Intellectual and Faith Community

Over the next few months, through many planning discussions with students, pastors, professors, and administrators, we formulated what would become the Conyers Scholars program. Darin Davis and Baylor's Institute for Faith and Learning (IFL) agreed to partner with the Graduate School in sponsorship and suggested that we name the program in memory of one of Baylor's most serious thinkers about vocation and the academic life: A.J. "Chip" Conyers. By the Fall of 2010, we held our first gathering in Laine's home of 14 Conyers Scholars and leaders. We began our practices of praying together, sharing a meal, enjoying conversation, and discussing a common reading. This group would meet faithfully each month to carry out these practices for the next two years. If we were successful, our Conyers community would take root and bear fruit in the graduate student years, but it would not stop there. Our scholars would take the seeds of this experience with them to their new academic positions after graduation and plant them in new soil.

Gathering a group to explore the idea of Christian scholarship and teaching also appealed to our desire for intellectual community, a notion put forth by the CID as an essential component of a robust doctoral experience. If these communities are multigenerational, so much the better, argues the CID.[7] Our group of students and faculty was indeed multigenerational and multidisciplinary, which required each of us to practice clarifying our ideas for one another patiently and charitably. We still, however, shared much in common with one another as we each drew our primary identities from beyond the academy. That is, we were all part of a faith community expressed in the church universal. Honoring that common commitment, we thought it was important to invite pastors into the conversation as well. Our goal was to develop both an intellectual and a faith community to explore three essential areas: scholarship, teaching, and church–academy relationships. Employing the stewardship framework and expanding upon it to include our responsibilities to shepherd both field and faith became the scaffolding we used to organize our process.

Stewardship and the Church

As the group's organizers, both of us quickly realized that before we could speak further about stewardship in our own context, we needed to listen and learn more about the term and its uses in Christian traditions and in the church. Thus began our weekly readings and side conversations about ownership, stewardship, and the relationships between a doctoral student, her subject, and the undergraduate students she teaches. *Steward* is a centuries-old term that combined the Old English words for "hall" [stig] and "warden" [weard] to describe the servant providing oversight for the lord's estate. Over time, a steward was seen as "an administrator and dispenser of wealth, favours, etc.; esp. one regarded as the servant of God or of the people" (Oxford English Dictionary). John Wesley and others brought theological overtones to the term in the seventeenth-century England, resulting in an understanding of stewardship as "the responsible use of resources, esp. money, time, and talents, in the service of God" (OED). In modern times, the steward (or stewardess) of a ship, plane, or train is responsible for safeguarding the passengers and their valuables.

The theological uses of the term interested us most so we started with reflection on what we had been taught as children in church. Jenny's church celebrated "Stewardship Sunday" when the special sermon called for church members to give generously of their own wealth for the sake of God's kingdom. Laine recalled growing up Baptist, placing a dime in the little white envelope (the required ten percent tithe from a one dollar allowance) and checking off the box for stewardship, which was listed along with Bible reading, church attendance, and daily prayer as actions for which children were accountable. Surely stewardship of our very lives means more than a check mark in a box?

By understanding how the church used the term stewardship throughout its history, we hoped to discover new ways of applying the concept of stewardship to our academic pursuits. We learned from Kelly Johnson's book *The Fear of Beggars: Stewardship and Poverty in Christian Ethics* that the use of the term in the ecclesial world seemed to be particular to the English language. John Wesley developed the term widely in the seventeenth-century England by developing a "rhetoric of money" that encouraged Christians to seek wealth, but only for the purpose of giving more away. "Gain all you can, save all you can, and give all you can." was the watchword.[8] As Protestant churches separated themselves from established religious institutions and infrastructure, churches had to rely on the personal commitment of their members to pay the salaries of clergy, maintain their buildings, and carry out mission work. The biblical metaphor of "the good steward" was used to motivate this monetary commitment to one's own church community.[9]

Within the American context, the idea of stewardship flourished in a "great stewardship awakening" as clergy raised financial support for missions and for their own congregations.[10] A common narrative of the "generous man" who grows wealthier after making a commitment to give generously drove members to contribute. This rhetoric, however, ignored the important question of where the wealth came from or how it was obtained.[11]

The de-emphasis on *how* wealth was achieved led to distorted views of ownership and property. Perhaps the most pernicious example was the use of stewardship to justify human slavery. While most Christians might condemn slavery as a distortion of relationship with fellow humans, some used the rhetoric of stewardship to articulate a theological defense of slavery, believing that a Christian master who kept slaves and Christianized them would be rewarded with greater material profit: the slaves would become better slaves, more obedient, and more industrious.[12]

Along with this distorted conception of stewardship, a new and inverted account of humility emerged. The humility associated with penance, contemplation, the crucified Christ, and dependence on God was replaced with an account of humility understood as the benevolent act of a successful owner who shared from his abundance to provide for the needs of others, a misrepresentation Johnson describes as "theological vocabulary run amok."[13] Without an emphasis on God as the source of all that is, the claim that wealth is a gift loses contact with the scriptural cautions about how wealth might be accumulated and no one questions ownership and the right to claim something as one's own.

Ownership in the Academy

As we continued to explore how the concept of stewardship had been used in the church over the centuries, we developed some deep concerns about ownership in the academy. If stewardship language is to be used, we must avoid misusing it as a disguise for ownership. Our academic cultures support ownership goals when our ranking systems and vocabularies focus on goods (such as our knowledge, our ideas, even our disciplines) as commodities to be collected, branded as ours, and even sold to others. A Christian can easily rationalize that using one's wealth of knowledge or one's "intellectual property" for the greater good might even lead to more wealth to spend, regardless of how such wealth was acquired. A distorted vision of stewardship within the academy claims ownership over a body of knowledge and chooses how much (if any) to share with others and for what purposes. As a scientist and faculty leader in the Conyers Scholars program explained to us, an extreme sense of ownership leads to near-paranoia in his field. Scholars go through the motions of presenting their research at annual conferences, but rather than sharing openly about new findings, presenters intentionally muddle or hide their results from the other scholars in the audience. These vague reports represent the opposite of stewardship. Scholars are not gratefully and excitedly passing on the gifts of knowledge they received to move the discipline forward. Instead, they are appearing on the program as contributors, but focused on hiding essential information to prevent others from "stealing" their research.

While this example may represent an extreme, the language and habits of ownership, rather than stewardship, pervade academic life. To correct these distortions and reclaim for the academy a useful understanding of stewardship, Christians must return to the forgotten question: What is the source of our knowledge? When we remember that we are not owners of intellectual goods, but rather participants in the blessed gifts of God, then our relation to these academic goods must change. In order to embrace stewardship as a disposition of gratitude we would need to reject the language of "using" and "commodity," and instead practice using vocabulary that celebrates God's sharing with us God's abundant gifts.[14]

This notion of sharing what has been given is central to the Christian faith and can be found in pages of Scripture from beginning to end. As Smith and Scales explored the stewardship theme in the creation stories of Genesis and Luke's parable of "the ten talents," they reminded us that the Christian academic is stewarding two things at once: the academy and, more importantly, the faith.

> If, as scholars, we are stewards of our academic disciplines, we are also stewards of much more besides.... For those scholars who identify ourselves as Christians, we are moreover stewards of a two-thousand-year-old tradition handed down to us through the church and entrusted to us for future generations. Our stewardship of the Christian faith is prior to and more important than any of the other things en-trusted to our care. It is the compass by which we orient and order all our other commitments.[15]

It is in this sense that we began to formulate our thinking about how the idea of stewardship might shape an account of Christian vocation within the academy. Such an account would entail particular practices and commitments. We next turned to the question of what those practices and commitments might be.

Stewardship and Christian Practices

As we began to consider academic stewardship as a specifically Christian practice, we explored recent thinking on practices, led by Craig Dykstra and Dorothy Bass. What could we expect from meeting regularly to enact a chosen set of practices together such as prayer, sharing a meal, charitable reading, and hospitable dialogue? In practice, we are rehearsing. As these authors describe rehearsal, "It is 'practicing' the practices in the same way a child practices catching a ball or playing scales. You may not think you need this skill, we tell the child, but stay in the game and the time will probably come when you do."[16] These rehearsals are most effective as an interrelated group of practices, rather than in isolation. So the combination of these practices, rehearsed over and over again with the same people, brought the powerful experience of God's presence to our Conyers Scholars group. "After a time," says Dykstra, "the primary point about the practices is no longer that they are something we do. Instead they become arenas in which something is done *to us,* in us, and through us that we could not of ourselves do, that is beyond what we do."[17]

Dykstra reminds Christians that our story ought to be different from the predominant and competing story of mastery and control.

> Christian practices are different. And that is because their story is different. While human achievement is valued in the Christian story, it has a different place and meaning. The human task [in the Christian story] is not fundamentally mastery. It is rather the right use of gifts graciously bestowed by a loving God for the sake of the good that God intends–*and ultimately assures*.... So our basic task is not mastery and control. It is instead trust and grateful receptivity. Our exemplars are not heroes; they are saints. Our epitome is not excellence; our honor is in faithfulness.[18]

Christian practices cultivate virtues. When considering the shape of virtues as they relate to the academic life, we soon saw the centrality of humility as a Christian virtue and scholarly disposition. As we looked for examples of humility among our fellow academics, we did find a few. Unfortunately, we quickly realized that the current culture of American higher education does not naturally support this virtue. In the midst of a university culture that values competition, ranking, ownership of ideas, and the mandate to distinguish one's thinking as "original," the virtue of humility, would indeed be countercultural. We believed that the liminal space of doctoral education, not fully student, not fully faculty, would be a great context for a free and open discussion, and we hoped, formation as it relates to humility.

Sharing What We Learned

After wrestling with the idea of stewardship in our side conversations and participating in the Conyers Scholars group for over two years, it was time to open the conversation beyond our group and speak of what we had learned. We invited some of our doctoral students and leaders from the Conyers group, along with faculty mentors and pastors from other institutions, to consider with us the practice of stewardship within the academic life. This volume is the result of that invitation. We asked authors to draw something from our common readings and shared conversations and filter their ideas through the lenses of their own disciplines and academic work. Our essayists integrated these conversations into a narrative of their journeys toward embracing stewardship as a teacher, scholar, and Christian. We wrestled with three core questions that have shaped and guided us:

1. How does the Christian life of faith and stewardship guide the way in which I pursue scholarship in my discipline?
2. How does my faith and my commitment to cultivate the next generation of scholars affect my pedagogical practices?
3. If we conceive of stewardship as the task of both the academy and the church, then what is the academy's relationship to the church and what is the church's relationship to the academy?

These questions organize and shape this volume. The result is a collection of essays that reframe contemporary higher education to consider stewardship of our intellectual disciplines as part and parcel of our Christian faith. The distinct purpose of this academic life is different from what we typically find expressed in higher education The end, as we see it, is worshiping the Christian God and delighting in "the mysteries God has revealed" (1 Corinthians 4:1).

The ensuing essays explore how these questions might be answered and how the vision of Christian stewardship in the academy might be achieved. Authors share their commitments and criticisms of an academy they love while raising further questions to be explored. David Smith, a trusted companion in this Conyers Scholars journey, reflects in his concluding essay on the "heartening sign of movement" he sees within this discussion and raises additional questions to challenge us in healthy ways.

* * *

The life of a doctoral student or a new faculty member, at its worst, can be isolating, competitive, and soul-crushing. As we have seen through the Conyers program, however, these early years of joining the academy can provide an opportunity for Christians to prepare, within a caring community, for long-term commitments to their disciplines and to their faith. Christian academics must pay particular attention to this opportunity for creating communities and cultivating practices that will point to God as the source of our gifts. We hope our readers will be inspired to create their own communities for cultivating stewardship. Perhaps these essays will offer insight for that preparation and provide encouragement and inspiration for those who seek to be stewards of the academy.

Notes

1. George E. Walker et al., *The Formation of Scholars Rethinking Doctoral Education for the Twenty-First Century* (San Francisco: Jossey-Bass, 2008), 12–13.
2. Ibid., 12.
3. Ibid., x.
4. Ibid., 10.
5. Ibid., 12.
6. Ibid.
7. Walker et al., *The Formation of Scholars Rethinking Doctoral Education for the Twenty-First Century.*
8. Kelly S Johnson, *The Fear of Beggars: Stewardship and Poverty in Christian Ethics* (Grand Rapids: Eerdmans, 2007), 86.
9. Ibid., 84–87.
10. Ibid., 91.
11. Johnson, *The Fear of Beggars.*
12. Ibid., 95.
13. Ibid., 97.
14. Here we learned a great deal from Paul Griffiths who came to dialogue with our Conyers Scholars group twice. While he brought his own personal stories and examples to our meetings together, many of these ideas are presented in his work *Intellectual Appetite: A Theological Grammar* (The Catholic University of America Press: Washington, DC, 2009).
15. J.C.H. Smith and T.L. Scales, "Stewardship: A Biblical Model for the Formation of Christian Scholars." *Journal of Education and Christian Belief*, Vol. 17, no. 1 (2013): 82. Julien Smith represents a steward who began this conversation with us when he was a doctoral student at Baylor, using his intellectual gifts to interpret these passages in light of the academic world he would soon enter. Years later, Julien has opportunities

to demonstrate stewardship at Valparaiso University, where he mentors future faculty in the Lilly Fellows Program for postdoctoral students.

16. Dorothy Bass, *Practicing Our Faith: A Way of Life for a Searching People*, 2nd ed. (San Francisco: Jossey-Bass, 2010), 10.
17. Craig Dykstra, *Growing in the Life of Faith* (Louisville, KY: Westminster John Knox, 2005), 56.
18. Ibid., 76.

PART I

Vocation and a Scholarly Life of Stewardship

CHAPTER 2

Toward a Vision of Vocation

Darin H. Davis

American higher education is in the midst of profound challenge and transformation.[1] The cost of pursuing a college degree continues to increase by leaps and bounds as students assume enormous student loan debt.[2] Not long ago a college education almost guaranteed some measure of financial success and career stability, but those days seem long gone. Some wonder if the days of traditional classroom teaching and learning are over as well, as sweeping technological change, especially online instruction, is now forcing colleges and universities to reenvision how they can offer course content to students.[3] These issues are by no means the only signs that the academy is experiencing change and stress.

Amid these challenges is growing confusion about what colleges and universities are supposed to do in the first place. Should they be primarily devoted to preparing their graduates to enter the workforce? Should they at the same time advance research across the disciplines in ways that expand the frontiers of knowledge? Should they seek to form their

The opening and concluding portions of this chapter are adapted from Darin Davis, "The University in Crisis and the Ways of Wisdom," in *Educating for Wisdom in the 21st Century* (St. Augustine Press: forthcoming).

D.H. Davis (✉)
Baylor University, Waco, TX, USA

T.L. Scales and J.L. Howell (eds.), *Christian Faith and University Life*,
DOI 10.1007/978-3-319-61744-2_2

students intellectually, morally, and even spiritually while preparing them for responsible citizenship and civic engagement? Should they also be the places where passionate sports fans gather in grand arenas and stadiums to watch athletes pursue victory? The answer seems to be a resounding "yes" to all of these; with so many competing expectations from so many constituencies, however, the contemporary academy seems to be suffering an *identity* crisis, or perhaps something akin to cognitive dissonance. It is becoming increasingly difficult for colleges and universities to navigate these challenges.

Christian higher education in the twenty-first century is by no means immune from these difficulties. Even as colleges and universities point to mission statements steeped in the theological tradition of their founders, clarity of identity and purpose do not always follow. Still, there are things that Christian colleges and universities can do to help themselves better understand and lead from their mission, even as they navigate the challenges of the present. One of the essential things they can do is foster a *vision of vocation* whereby the goals and purposes of teaching, learning, research, and the like are motivated by and oriented toward a divine calling. In what follows, I explore three questions that may help illuminate what the phrase "vision of vocation" suggests. First, how might vocation be described as a summons from God, a calling that makes claims upon those who are called and yet promises them ultimate blessing? Second, how might the project of Christian higher learning be described in a way that captures well this commitment to vocation? Third, what practical efforts can colleges and universities make to cultivate a vision of vocation?

A Vision of Vocation

In my view, the most helpful and insightful single essay on vocation was written by A.J. Conyers. Entitled "The Meaning of Vocation," Conyers's essay is both an attempt to rescue the notion of vocation from some religious and secular misunderstandings and an effort to reimagine the notion of "calling" in an authentically Christian way.[4] Conyers's essay is steeped in theological and biblical insight; it is, likewise, a graceful articulation of vocation that suggests how calling is most fundamentally a summons from God requiring obedience from those who hear the call yet promising ultimate blessing. For all those reasons, Conyers's essay is a rich resource for those seeking a clear, compelling, and faithful account of vocation.

Conyers sees the notion of vocation as particularly vulnerable to misunderstanding. On one hand, vocation seen through the lens of monastic life implies that calling pertains only to those who hear and respond to the divine summons to religious life. Those who become priests, pastors, and the like are the only ones for whom the notion of vocation applies. On the other hand, Luther and other Protestant Reformers tried to reorient vocation to apply to everyone. The effect was to broaden the notion of calling beyond religious life; the unforeseen consequence, however, was to make vocation more about being called into particular occupations—even bakers, boot makers, and farmers could be "called." These two misunderstandings obscure a more powerful conception of vocation. Vocation does indeed matter to everyone, but it is much more than being called into a particular task or job. Being called is, as Conyers puts it, "life affirming."[5] Rooted in the Latin *vocatio,* vocation is a call, summons, or invitation to an entire life of faithfulness. The church, comprised of those who are "called out" both individually and collectively, expresses concretely the way that God speaks and God's people respond. This conception of vocation leaves room for meaningful talk about how God calls people to service in particular times and particular roles, but it also affirms the view that God invites all of his people to follow the leading of God to lives of purpose, meaning, and fidelity.

The meaning of vocation, Conyers goes on to explain, must be dislodged from several Enlightenment assumptions that twist its true meaning. Toward this end, Conyers offers four corrective statements about the meaning of vocation that are worthy of reflection.

First, being called implies an agent outside of the one who is subject to the call. A calling implies a caller; a calling cannot come from nowhere or no one. Such an understanding of summons and response does not in the least undermine freedom, though it certainly challenges the modern conception of freedom as merely "freedom from." As Conyers puts it, a Christian conception of freedom "is not an inner-directed impulse, but the use of the will to respond to an unforeseen and perhaps unknown reality."[6] The biblical tradition is replete with examples of such callings. Abraham, Moses, Isaiah, Hannah, Mary, and Paul among many others are summoned by one who calls them into fullness of life.

Second, vocation is often against the will of the one who is called. Reflection on the biblical tradition again reveals that callings are often not what those who are called always wish for or want. The example of Jeremiah is powerful. Not only did Jeremiah struggle with God's summons to be a prophet to the nations (he thought himself too young and without words to speak), he likewise complained that the wicked, whom he has been called to rebuke, seemed to prosper while God's calling on his life had rendered him like a lamb being led to slaughter. Yet, God's calling remained. The summons was clear, though it conflicted with Jeremiah's own will. Conyers maintains that modern conceptions of reason do not account well for this kind of "contrary to the will" summons. For Kant and other Enlightenment figures, the guide of human action is not an external source (a law given by God or the state) but reason, an internal source of normativity that legislates with universal necessity what is to be done. As Conyers explains, "While vocation contradicts the will of the person being called, reason is the instrument by which the modern person thought his will could be enforced."[7]

Third, calling frequently involves great difficulties that must be overcome if the summons is to be answered. Vocation perhaps is too often idealized; the hard truth is that answering a calling can involve risk, injury, and even death. Jeremiah, Ezekiel, Paul, and a host of Christian martyrs answered God's calling even as they realized the threat and reality of losing their lives. As Conyers points out, the life and ministry of Jesus is the most profound example of how vocation makes incredible demands on those who are called, for it is Jesus, willing to die for the sake of all others, who likewise asks his followers to take up their own crosses and follow him.

Finally, vocation is made difficult not simply because those who answer may encounter great struggle but because those who seek to follow their vocation must be ever on guard to becoming diverted or distracted from achieving the task set before them. Following one's vocation, Conyers explains, is fraught with opportunities to lose one's way, to become disillusioned, to succumb to temptation. Jesus's prayer "Lead us not into temptation, but deliver us from evil," expresses the deep truth that following the summons of God may well be full of twists and turns—obstacles and distractions encountered along the way, some of our making.

These four features of a Christian inspired conception of vocation challenge the view that callings emanate from no one in particular, make few claims upon the called, and are easy to discern and follow. Nothing could be further from the truth. For those who seek to cultivate a culture of authentic vocation, a right understanding of calling is required.

Yet there is another aspect of Conyers's treatment of vocation that is particularly insightful. Beginning in the New Testament, the notion of vocation makes a key transition. While Old Testament figures respond to the call of God, their response is also toward a covenant nation. In the New Testament, those who respond to God's summons are called to an entirely new kind of community, one that is above and beyond any particular historical nation and one that resists the divisions of race, creed, color, and the like.

More importantly, as Conyers describes it, Christian vocation does not trade in the legacies of the past but in the hope-filled promise of the future. For Christians, Jesus's life, death, and resurrection call them toward a new destiny—namely, to become a part of the redemptive and reconciling work of Christ. While our eternal goal is fixed, it would be a mistake to envision vocation as something akin to having a roadmap or travel itinerary always before us, charting each move we need to make as we live our lives. Here is the power and indeed the mystery of God's calling and a brute fact that any Christian vision of vocation must embrace: as Conyers puts it, "vocation is something that happens to us. It is an experience. Its truth is captured in the words 'we are his workmanship'" (Eph 2:5, 10 RSV).

Faith *Animating* Learning

Conyers's effort to disentangle vocation from various modern assumptions helps to show the mystery and power of a distinctively Christian account of calling. Now allow me to focus on an image that Conyers employs to envision how, as he puts it, vocation "happens to us." I find Conyers's image powerfully suggestive of how the project of Christian higher education might be described, especially when it is practiced through a faithful vision of vocation. Conyers writes:

> We might think of Jesus' raising of Lazarus as a rich image of the deepest meaning of vocation. Lazarus is not merely healed, but raised from the dead. From the isolation of death, he is called by Christ's powerful voice to the community of the living. His grave clothes, in which he is bound, are loosed and he is made free to respond as one living before God and in the power of God. Each of us is so called. Vocation, *vocatio*, is about being raised from the dead, made alive to the reality that we do not merely exist, but we are "called forth" to a divine purpose.[8]

Simply put, Lazarus is more than healed. He is brought back from the dead. But he also is more than "no longer dead." He is remade, his whole being repurposed to respond to God's calling, free to live out the summons that God has voiced through Christ. When Jesus tells Lazarus to come forth, to be alive again, it is toward something grander and fuller than just living. Lazarus is called to fulfill his God-given vocation, to realize the summons to be as he truly ought to be. Lazarus is quite literally *animated* by faith. The calling of God summons each of us toward new life.

The example of Lazarus, which Conyers so strikingly frames, suggests a different way of describing the task of Christian colleges and universities, especially when the project of Christian learning is envisioned through this account of vocation. Very often, the task of Christian higher education—which includes the wide scope of teaching, learning, research, mentoring, and student life—is described as the "integration of faith and learning." As Perry Glanzer observes, the exact origins of the phrase are difficult to trace, though Arthur Holmes and other influential Christian scholars used the term so often and with such great effect that it has become a foundational phrase in the vocabulary of the Christian academy, perhaps especially at Protestant institutions.[9] The image of the resurrected Lazarus, however, points helpfully to an alternative way of describing the task of Christian higher education. Beyond integration, faith actually *animates* the sacred task of learning. Put differently, when a vision of Christian vocation is embraced, the appropriate response to the divine summons is an expression of profound faith. When such a response is offered, those who are "called" are transformed. Vocation thus gives life to all we are, imagine, and do. Likewise, a vision of vocation, when cultivated in the context of Christian higher education, animates learning.

There are three advantages, I believe, in adopting this way of describing the project of Christian higher learning. First and foremost, *faith animating learning* envisions faith as the motivating force of learning; in Aristotelian terms, faith is the efficient cause. As such, faith inspires, directs, and moves the effort to seek knowledge, grasp truth, and cultivate wisdom. In this way, faith is not just one side of the conjunction "and," as in faith and learning, faith and work, faith and science, faith and economics, faith and politics, and so on. Nor is faith one category among others. It is at the heart of the mission of Christian higher learning, not a mere add-on or something to be imported so as to provide the effect of "baptizing" whatever it is linked to. The language of the integration of faith and learning does not accurately capture the primacy of faith.

Second, the notion of *faith animating learning* better captures both the challenge and promise of distinctively Christian learning. Consider, as an example, Jesus's injunction to "'Love the Lord your God with *all* your heart and with *all* your soul and with *all* your strength and with *all* your mind'; and, 'Love your neighbor as yourself'" (Luke 10:27, NIV). Jesus's words commend to his followers the necessity of total commitment. The summons to love God and neighbor is not taken up in a half-hearted way or according to terms that we negotiate with God. Likewise, when faith truly animates the pursuit of learning, it ought to engage the entire range of capacities that are a part of one's questioning, knowing, and understanding, including even one's emotional capacities, which are an important part of our perception. As Aristotle puts it, humans desire to know. When faith animates, the calling of God reorients our path and purposes and similarly renews us in heart, soul, strength, and mind. In this respect, the notion of faith animating learning may avoid simplistic accounts of the relationship between Christian faith, teaching, learning, and scholarship. If faith can motivate learning in the all-embracing way that the image of Lazarus suggests, it is likely inadequate to claim that the defining characteristic of a Christian college or university is that its faculty are attentive and kind to students during office hours or that such faculty may freely quote biblical passages during lectures. Both of these things are doubtlessly important, yet they do not go far enough.

Third, in a world in which fragmentation reigns, the language of *faith animating learning* captures in a more complete way the theology of a Christian institution of higher learning. While the contemporary academy is often described as a "multiversity" where fragmentation abounds and the various disciplines lack a common language with which to speak to one another, Christians have a special reason to resist this trend.[10] The reason that Christian teachers and scholars might realize relationships among their subjects is not simply a matter of referring to themselves as Christian economists or Christian sociologists or anything else. Instead, the reason is ontological in nature, built into the fabric of a Christian conception of reality. If faith is the very wellspring of all teaching and learning (i.e., if God is the creative source of all goodness, truth, and beauty), then each academic discipline, as it seeks to discover that source of truth, will in some way find relation to other lines of inquiry that seek the same end.[11] Indeed, if faith truly animates learning, there will be no part of a Christian college or university that is not an expression, each in its own way, of a vision of vocation, each revealing an aspect of the Divine.

Cultivating a Vision of Vocation

And yet the practical question remains: how might a vision of vocation be fostered so that it serves as a counterbalance to some of the present challenges facing Christian institutions of higher learning? How might the notion of faith animating learning function as more than a rhetorical device but as an apt description of the practices that sustain the lives of colleges and universities with a Christian identity? Allow me in closing to describe briefly one such project that now thrives at Baylor University.

In 2009, a discussion began at Baylor about how to encourage graduate students—particularly those seeking doctoral degrees—to think in broad and constructive ways about their faith commitments and their emerging vocations as teachers and scholars. The editors of the present volume led the discussion among several of us who began to think in these directions.

The centrality of Christian vocation was foundational in our initial discussion. We realized the powerful ways that graduate education, by its very nature as a training in academic specialization, often works against the kind of broader formation that we were hoping to support. I remember distinctly an early conversation that I had with Jenny Howell in which we agreed that the notion of a *practice* was key. No effort of formation, no attempt to deepen the theological understanding of vocation, could flourish absent some set of activities that intentionally tried to shape what people ought to care about most. A successful program already existed at Baylor for undergraduate students that had the overall shape we thought might work for graduate students.[12] What if we gathered a small group of students who cared about extending their understanding of their Christian vocation as emerging teachers, scholars, and researchers? What if we enlisted the help of talented and accomplished faculty mentors who were willing to host dinners at their homes and lead discussions around engaging readings that would lead to further reflection and conversations? After not much deliberation, we created a program that would be codirected by Baylor's Graduate School and Institute for Faith and Learning. But we needed to name the program.

That choice was easy. A.J. Conyers (1944–2004) had been a founding faculty member at Baylor's George W. Truett Theological Seminary. A beloved teacher whom students described as gentle, gracious, kind, yet challenging, Conyers and his theological writings were well-known and appreciated by a wide audience in both the academy and the church. He was a scholar whose writing resisted easy categories. He thought deeply, rooted in ancient texts and traditions.[13] Moreover, he loved the church and poured into its future by pouring into his seminary students. He himself was a powerful preacher.

With a small cohort of twelve doctoral students representing the disciplines of philosophy, religion, and English, the Conyers Graduate Scholars Program met for the first time in September 2010. In addition to faculty leaders, we included a local pastor to explore the importance of the relationship between the church and the academy. Nearly seven years later, the Conyers Scholars Program has blossomed into two cohorts, four leaders, and a diverse group of students from across the disciplines. Students in history and political theory are routinely joined by engineering students, chemists, and sociologists. Though there has been some variation in the reading selections over the years, one reading is a constant. Conyers's essay on "The Meaning of Vocation" is the first reading discussed with each new cohort.

The program has been remarkably successful. Its influence is palpable in the essays in this volume. The authors were shaped by their experiences as a Conyers Scholar. They read together. They discussed. They sometimes disagreed and challenged one another about very important matters, some intellectual, some theological, some having to do with matters of pedagogy. Yet they gathered around the table of fellowship and broke bread. They prayed for one another often. They have become not only colleagues but also friends. These various practices have nurtured a shared vision of vocation. Future academic leaders are being prepared in a significant way to steward the cause of Christian higher learning in the coming decades. This seems precisely the response that is needed in the present moment. In an age abounding with mission drift and institutional identity crises, the best response is to prepare those who will one day teach students, write books, and lead departments, programs, and entire institutions by nurturing in them a vision of vocation.

From the beginning, Conyers Scholars and their leaders have grasped the importance of educating for wisdom. I have in mind here the effort to engage fundamental questions of human meaning in a way that transcends technical learning, or credentialing, or other instrumentalist accounts of education. An education that cultivates wisdom—not mere knowledge—extends the horizon and reach of students, initiating them into a lifelong pursuit of excellence, helping them to make sense of who they are and should become.

Yet the Conyers Scholars and their leaders also have grasped the unique way that educating for wisdom might be pursued from the perspective of the Christian faith. Put simply, Christians embrace the idea that educating for wisdom is, at its core, a matter of seeking divine wisdom; seeking divine wisdom does not depend on the working of human reason alone. As Thomas Aquinas explained in the very first question of his *Summa Theologica,* it is necessary for human salvation that there should be a knowledge that is revealed by God instead of by reason.[14]

The Christian faith is deeply steeped, of course, in the wisdom tradition of the Old Testament, where the imagination of the good life extends to what orthodox Jews would call "the life to come." The book of Proverbs, most notably, is a sustained message about the necessity of discerning and following the wisdom of God and how those who do will find happiness.[15] Divine wisdom brings human beings a more distinct awareness of how God is not only manifest in all of creation but also of the particular ways that God calls each person to faithfulness. Such wisdom can never come from sheer intellectual effort alone because it surpasses what can ever be grasped through the power of cognition. This is not to say that reason plays no role in the discernment of divine wisdom. Rather, grace perfects reason, revealing a transcendent source of guidance that outstrips the powers of human understanding.

Educating for wisdom, from a Christian perspective, is inherently vocational. The divine wisdom we seek to understand and follow is the summons from God to flourish, to be the people that God intends us to be. Against the backdrop of contemporary higher education, nothing is more vital than preparing Christian teachers and scholars whose faith can animate all they do, whose vision is ever alive to the reality of vocation.

Notes

1. Among recent books that lament the present state of higher education are: Derek Bok, *Our Underachieving Colleges: A Candid Look at How Much Students Learn and Why They Should Be Learning More* (Princeton, Princeton University Press, 2006); Harry Lewis, *Excellence Without a Soul: How a Great University Forgot Education* (New York: Public Affairs, 2006); William G. Bowen, Matthew M. Chingos, and Michael S. McPherson, *Crossing the Finish Line: Completing College at America's Public Universities* (Princeton: Princeton University Press, 2011); and Richard Arum and Josipa Roksa, *Academically Adrift: Limited Learning on College Campuses* (Chicago: University of Chicago Press, 2011).
2. Glenn Harlan Reynolds, "Degrees of Value: Making College Pay Off: For Too Many Americans, College Today Isn't Worth It," *The Wall Street Journal* (15 January 2014), http://online.wsj.com/news/articles/SB10001424052702303870704579298302637802002?mg=reno64-wsj&url=http%3A%2F%2Fonline.wsj.com%2Farticle%2FSB10001424052702303870704579298302637802002.html (Accessed 21 December 2016).
3. See William G. Bowen, *Higher Education in the Digital Age* (Princeton: Princeton University Press, 2013) and Jeffrey J. Selingo, *College Unbound: The Future of Higher Education and What It Means for Students* (New York: Amazon Publishing, 2013).
4. A.J. Conyers, "The Meaning of Vocation," *Christian Reflection: Vocation* (2004): 11–19.
5. Ibid., 12.
6. Ibid.
7. Ibid., 13.
8. Ibid., 18.
9. Perry L. Glanzer, "Why We Should Discard 'the Integration of Faith and Learning': Rearticulating the Mission of the Christian Scholar," *Journal of Education and Christian Belief* 12.1 (2008): 42.
10. Wendell Berry, "The Loss of the University," in *Home Economics* (New York: North Point Press, 1987), 76–97.
11. A colleague of mine in Electrical Engineering frequently teaches a course on solar energy in an especially interesting way. Besides teaching principles and applications in electrical engineering, he also encourages students to reflect about matters involving God's creation, human consumption, and conservation, Christian views of stewardship, and so on. These questions seek engagement with other academic disciplines, including theology, philosophy, economics, and environmental science.

12. Named in honor of William Carey Crane, the fourth president of Baylor, the Crane Scholars Program is an intensive program for Baylor undergraduates sponsored by the Institute for Faith and Learning that encourages and supports gifted students who are interested in the connections between faith and reason. The program seeks to identify and mentor students who are considering graduate school and careers in academic life in particular, though not all Crane Scholars pursue a vocation in the academy.
13. I am grateful to my friend Rev. Dr. Jeff Raines for his reflections on Conyers. Dr. Raines was a member of the first graduating class of Baylor's George W. Truett Theological Seminary in 1997.
14. *Summa Theologica* I, Q.1, Art.1.
15. Prov 3:13 (NKJV).

CHAPTER 3

Vocation Is Something that Happens to You: Freedom, Education, and the American Literary Tradition

Rachel B. Griffis

American college students' approach to education, and the concept of vocation, tends to be informed by a definition of freedom that elevates the choice of an individual.[1] This definition of freedom has its roots in Protestantism, the Declaration of Independence, the American concept of the self-made man, and the strong connection between freedom and choice in American thought. Thus, as high school graduates consider selecting a college, a major, and a career trajectory, they begin from a mode of thinking that takes for granted their ability to choose where to go, what to study, and who to become. In contrast, the recurring story in the Christian tradition wherein a person is "called" to a task, lifestyle, or occupation by an external force appears unfamiliar, and perhaps even repugnant, to American students, including Christian students who were raised with such stories.

In *The Real American Dream: A Meditation on Hope* (1999), Andrew Delbanco explains why choice as an aspect of individualism has been so

R.B. Griffis (✉)
Sterling College, Sterling, KS, USA

T.L. Scales and J.L. Howell (eds.), *Christian Faith and University Life*,
DOI 10.1007/978-3-319-61744-2_3

important to Americans: "Here was the ground of hope," he writes, "the idea that Americans were not fixed in their circumstances of birth, but were free to become whatever they could imagine."[2] While the values of individualism and freedom have functioned as essential sources of hope in the United States, Delbanco's narrative of American life reaches a dark conclusion. He states that God and the nation itself initially functioned as symbolic sources of hope to Americans, symbols that directed responsible expressions of freedom and individualism. However, these external symbols for hope, God, and the nation were debunked around the time of the Civil War; consequently, Delbanco suggests, Americans gradually turned to the self for their source of hope. As he concludes his book, he looks into the twenty-first century and the country's future with trepidation. The story of hope he tells, and predicts, is one of "diminution."[3] The self, Delbanco argues, is an insufficient symbol of hope, and one of the primary reasons he observes and foresees the attenuation of American character and morals is that he anticipates no external symbols of hope on the horizon for the nation that has aimed to be the most free in the world.

While the Christian faith offers some students hope outside the self, many students have been influenced by distinctive Protestant-American values that Delbanco finds problematic. Within the American Christian university or college, students may hold a vague sense of calling or vocation, but such a sense grates against American values and definitions of freedom. This situation is taxing for young Christians who may have difficultly reconciling the solipsism of the age with an understanding of vocation gleaned from the Christian tradition.[4] It shall be my goal in the following pages to demonstrate how A.J. Conyers's representation of vocation may help students to gain a fuller, less self-centered understanding of vocation because of the way his thought challenges readers to define freedom. Conyers' understanding of vocation, though written for the present time, nevertheless draws upon a definition of freedom that recalls pre-Reformation ideas which are often unwelcome in a culture that equates freedom with choice and self-determination. By expanding upon Conyers' discussion of vocation, I hope to challenge stewards of the academy to address the melancholy of the present and future by helping students to recognize and revise their definitions of freedom. I believe that by investigating definitions of freedom in Christian history and in American culture, and furthermore bringing pre-Reformation ideas into these conversations, educators can support and illuminate the integrated and expansive definition of vocation that Conyers offers.

The Plight of College Students

One of the prominent outpourings of the elevation of the self, and the subsequent absence of external symbols for hope, is a consumerist approach to college education, which views this endeavor merely as a ticket to financial security or social prestige rather than a meaningful experience or an opportunity to grow in wisdom. In his more recent book *College* (2012), Delbanco points out that "We tend not to remember, or perhaps half deliberately to forget, that college was once conceived not as a road to wealth or as a screening service for a social club, but as a training ground for pastors, teachers, and, more broadly, public servants."[5] Although most parents and students are somewhat aware that spending four years working toward a Bachelor's degree is not solely about getting a job afterward, this purpose is nonetheless the prevailing one for sending children to college: so that they can do whatever they want with their lives, so that they can keep up with their peers, and have all possible advantages to forge a living for themselves. Currently, the vestiges of the "training ground" view that Delbanco mentions are often found in the way parents rationalize sending their children away from home upon completing high school. If an 18-year-old moves into a dormitory and commences her education at a university rather than staying home to attend a community college for two years, it is often because both the student and parents recognize that there are benefits to letting the student learn to live on her own, to do her own laundry and set her own bedtime. Yet to what end is this experience valuable? To form the 18-year-old into a responsible, functional, and, most importantly, employable adult.

As Delbanco acknowledges in the preface of *College*, the dichotomy between learning and acquiring skills for the job market is "a false one" and "not a question of either/or."[6] Although four years of serious study has the potential to transform minds and cultivate character, the necessities of life nevertheless are imminent and impossible to ignore. Thus, many students begin college hoping to grow and change but also feeling burdened with the realities of life, of which employment is often the most pressing burden. When I ask my first-year composition students to write about what they hope to accomplish during their collegiate years, they almost always refer to getting a job, but their responses are usually qualified by their desire to contribute to the world and to lead a meaningful life, thereby demonstrating the tension between a consumerist view of education and the concept of calling and vocation. Here are a few examples from their writing in their first semester at Baylor University:

- *While at Baylor, I need to think about how I can match a career with my interests. I would like to do this so that work will not be a chore to me, but rather something I enjoy doing.*
- *During my years at Baylor, I hope to think about, and hopefully figure out, whether the future I already have in mind for myself will actually be possible and if it's what I'm meant to do.*
- *The issue I need to think about while I am at Baylor is whether or not I want to be a nurse. Being a nurse is my dream job, the ability to help people is what makes me want to be a nurse.*

The fact that my students consistently refer to getting a job when prompted to write about the purpose of their own education indicates the centrality of this particular concern. Very few students respond to this question without articulating their plans for employment. In the economic downturn since the first few years of the millennium, literature about college, and education in general, has similarly tended to emphasize the importance of utilizing post-secondary education to get ahead financially and invest wisely. In 2012, *USA Today* issued an article titled, "Choose Your College, Major and Loans Wisely" which called attention to the fact that inflation is not keeping up with quickly increasing tuition costs.[7] The article consequently advised students either to select practical majors with high earning potential or to go to inexpensive schools if they are intent on studying philosophy. In 2016, an article in *Education News*, "Report Reveals Big Gaps Between the Degrees Students are Earning and In-Demand Jobs" implies that the intellectual development a student undergoes through a course of study is worthless if it cannot yield employment.[8]

However, as my students' responses demonstrate, many of them are not solely concerned with the cash return on their education, even if cash is the reason to get a college education. Most want their lives to be meaningful and enjoyable; they want their jobs to allow them to contribute to their communities in significant ways. For example, in a study published in 2012 of how students make decisions regarding their majors, Basit Zafar shows that the two most common determining factors are pleasing one's parents, who tend to favor majors that are likely to yield a high income, and having a sense of personal interest and delight in the subject itself.[9] Like Delbanco, students want their collegiate experiences to have both practical and transcendent outcomes. Christian students, no less torn between these two goals, are particularly prone to understand a "transcendent" outcome in terms of their faith. Like the student quoted above who writes that he needs to figure out if the future he wants is what he is "meant to do," most Christian students, Protestant and Catholic, have a post-Reformation perspective that assumes the validity of Martin Luther's "priesthood of all believers" assertion in one form or another.[10] Thus all legitimate endeavors and forms of employment—on a farm, in the home, at an office—are considered opportunities to serve God and further his kingdom. Christian students, for the most part, take joy in knowing that they should consider their professions as venues through which not only to please and provide for themselves but to serve God.

However, as students struggle with understanding how their choices relate to their vocation, many experience anxiety or even mental paralysis when faced with making decisions. They become preoccupied with making the right decision for their lives, which for Christians often entails considering what God wants for them. One of my students articulated this issue as a need "to answer the question of what kind of future God has planned for me." Many students similarly believe that God has a specific vocation in mind for the individual, but that the responsibility to decipher God's plan lies with the individual. Figuring out what God wants thus becomes an obligation to their Christian consciences and soon a form of enslavement as they continually look to themselves to provide an answer. Students believe that they have the freedom to decide the course of their lives, but their religious convictions add pressure to make the right choices, particularly in relation to their occupation, and this right choice is often understood as one's vocation.

Freedom and Vocation

William C. Placher succinctly articulates what is problematic about linking God's call and an individual's choice when he writes that the "vision of life as a sea of infinite choices is more like slavery than freedom," attributing Christians' struggles with vocation to a misconstrued understanding of freedom (10).[11] In Delbanco's words, as mentioned earlier, Americans have found hope in "the idea that [they] were not fixed in their circumstances of birth, but were free to become whatever they could imagine."[12] In contrast, a Christian view of freedom is not the ability to choose or determine one's future, nor to "become whatever [one] imagine[s]," but to internalize and live according to moral principles. In his account of freedom in the Christian tradition, Paul J. Wadell defines the word with the expression that "the freest people are good people, the people who have used the gift of freedom to grow in the goodness of God."[13] Conyers, commenting on the mistaken ideas of freedom Wadell corrects, illustrates what it means to separate individual choice from one's calling when he discusses several biblical examples of men who received external calls from God. He concludes that "We do not simply 'know' about our vocation as we would an itinerary on a travel schedule. Much less do we choose it! Instead, vocation is something that happens to us."[14] As he rejects the sovereignty of an individual's choice, Conyers demonstrates an understanding of vocation that has the potential to mollify students' self-consciousness and anxieties regarding their careers, freeing them to treat college less as a ticket to a better future and more as quest directed by a sovereign God.

Understanding vocation, therefore, as an occupation or profession to which one has been called by God for the purpose of service to God is to reduce the meaning of the word and all its manifestations. Conyers argues that vocation is neither limited to a job or a way of life, nor a monastic or clerical vow. Vocation means "being raised from the dead"; it means that "we are 'called forth' to a divine purpose."[15] Vocation, like conversion, encompasses all of life and all aspects of it. Furthermore, what seems to be most antithetical to current day thought about this issue is that an individual cannot choose his vocation. As is the case with biblical and church heroes like Abraham, Moses, Paul, and Joan of Arc, the individual receives a "summons" which is "*external* to the person who is called," and which may even be against her will.[16] For this reason, Conyers describes vocation as "something that happens to us" and as "an experience," echoing Margery Williams' Velveteen Rabbit who learns that becoming real is "something that happens to you" through the love of a child.[17]

Students, especially those who feel burdened with the "sea of infinite choices" at their fingertips, should consider Conyers' articulation of vocation and its implications for the meaning of freedom, the results of which may divert their preoccupation with themselves and their own choices and instead focus their attention on God and the life to which they have been called. Vocation is neither for them to figure out nor as simple as answering a question, and this idea may free students to make choices with less trepidation and within the comforting knowledge of God's omniscient grace. Vocation may happen, as with the Velveteen Rabbit, "bit by bit" or it may involve a clear external summons that was both uninvited and unexpected (17).[18] In either case, it is not for the student to choose or figure out, but to abide in God, to "run with perseverance the race marked out for" them, as St. Paul writes, and to "fix [their] eyes on Jesus" (Hebrews 12:1–2). The great challenge for a college student is to internalize and live under these countercultural definitions of freedom and vocation in a world where individual choice is sovereign and freedom means getting one's own way.[19]

In such a world, college students face a multitude of choices—which institution to attend, what to study, where to live, what classes to take and from whom, where to go to church, who to befriend, what jobs to pursue—and in this world, a Christian student should be challenged to make her choices according to the idea that God's sovereignty and grace not only transcend her choices but are also more powerful. God's sovereignty does not make one's choices meaningless, and neither does it signify that there is no wrong choice.[20] Instead, God's sovereignty draws attention to human beings' tendency to overestimate their own role in the cosmos, in God's work. The work we do, the choices we make, and the opportunities that come to us all occur by God's grace, and God similarly gives us the grace to respond to his summons. Like Calvin, who taught that human beings turn to God only by the grace of God, Conyers writes that the freedom to respond to the vocational call "is not an inner-directed impulse."[21] Choices, therefore, should be understood as a reality of modern life, a reality with which we struggle while employing various time-tested strategies—prayer, reason, the advice of friends and mentors—but ultimately, choices are made by God's grace whether or not we experience them that way. In Conyers' argument, vocation, like conversion, is the work of God alone. How to communicate these definitions of freedom and vocation to students stands as a challenge for Christian educators. Accordingly, what I have found to be most effective in encouraging students to think about their choices and vocational calling is to study how Americans present, discuss, and interact with definitions of freedom in my own discipline.[22]

Freedom in American Literature

The American literary tradition reveals a long and complicated history regarding Americans' understanding of freedom. While the Puritans and Pilgrims of the seventeenth century, who wrote much of our earliest literature, thought of freedom as serving God and submitting themselves to the authority of God and their community, these values, as Delbanco explains in *The Real American Dream*, gradually weakened for many reasons, of which the American Revolution had no small part. The Declaration of Independence assumes a definition of freedom that substantially differs from how the country's oldest fathers, such as Puritan John Winthrop or Pilgrim William Bradford, understood it. Eschewing the early Puritan-Calvinist definition of freedom, the Declaration of Independence is instead written under the assumptions of the Enlightenment and Scottish philosophy, which elevate the sovereignty of the individual. Just as the American colonies rejected the authority of the British king, so this document of liberty defines freedom as the right of an individual to control his own future, to have the freedom to make his own choices. Our country's most important document, the document that best defines what it means to be American, espouses a view of freedom that is incompatible with that of many Christians.[23] Therefore, challenging students of American literature to think about how such a historical and political document affects one's assumptions about freedom is a fruitful venue through which to convey an understanding of vocation as presented in Conyers' argument.

Taking their cue from the Declaration of Independence, American writers have explored the implications of these new ideas regarding freedom in ordinary life. Since the future of most American women until the twentieth century was marriage and family, Catharine Maria Sedgwick, one of the most popular writers of the early national period, defines freedom for women as the ability to choose a marriage partner. She believed that the choice to marry or remain single, and moreover to choose whom one married was tantamount to freedom and the pursuit of happiness, and she subsequently criticizes America in her fiction for falling short of this ideal. In her 1830 novel of manners, *Clarence*, a sort of American version of *Pride and Prejudice*, Emilie Layton's forced betrothal to a devious man named Pedrillo is conveyed in terms of enslavement. The narrative describes their engagement as a business transaction between Emilie's father and suitor, which settles a debt Mr. Layton owes to the suitor. Once Emilie has been informed of her engagement to Pedrillo, she laments, "*My price is paid*," and when the heroine, Gertrude Clarence, eventually negotiates with Mr. Layton on Emilie's behalf, she refers to her friend's "emancipation from this engagement," and tries to secure Emilie's "liberty" to marry whom she wants.[24]

At the end of the novel, both Emilie's father and her conniving suitor are dead, and the marriages that occur are entered into willingly and enthusiastically by both the men and women involved. This definition of freedom—the ability to choose one's own future—is elevated in this novel as the path to happiness, and, most importantly, virtue. As one minor, yet admirable, character puts it, "no virtue could have much vigor or merit, that was not free and independent in its operation."[25] Being a virtuous person and a good citizen is thus contingent on being able to control one's own destiny. Perhaps Sedgwick's view of freedom could be best encapsulated by a line in the novel of hers that is most studied today, *Hope Leslie* (1827): "this having our own way, is what everybody likes; it's the privilege we came to this wilderness world for."[26] Although Sedgwick's works are the earliest of the literary examples included here, and thus the furthest from contemporary readers in terms of time, her representation of the suffering young people endure for having their futures determined by their elders is remarkably redolent of the feelings of youth today as expressed in popular culture.[27]

Herman Melville, a canonical author who was influenced by Sedgwick, also explores the consequences of an individual's ability to choose one's own future, though less optimistically than Sedgwick. For Sedgwick, liberty and virtue are linked, but Melville's famous short story, "Bartleby, the Scrivener" (1853), which is known for generating the phrase "I would prefer not to," conveys skepticism toward the sovereignty of individual choice. Similar to famous movie quotations like "I'm going to make him an offer he can't refuse" and "May the Force be with you," Bartleby's "I would prefer not to" frequently serves as fodder for English department antics and humorous expressions, yet this very phrase unlocks how this story comments on the interconnected issues of freedom and vocation. Bartleby's "preferences" are what Melville uses to place his story in the American conversation about freedom and the individual's choice of a profession.

As its subtitle, "A Story of Wall-Street" indicates, "Bartleby, the Scrivener" is a story about modern life, featuring a thoroughly urban setting. The characters have almost no contact with nature, animals, or America's wild and bucolic past. The window that graces Bartleby's workspace gives him a view of another building, as he sees no trees, sky, or even other people walking along the street. Furthermore, the characters have modern professions that distance them from nature and manual labor: the narrator is a lawyer and Bartleby's job is to sit at a desk and to copy documents. Many literary critics have argued that this story is Melville's indictment of capitalism and industrialization, for it attributes Bartleby's "cadaverous" demeanor to the dehumanizing monotony and alienation of modern life.[28] As a result, Bartleby, a superb copyist, randomly decides to stop working one day and becomes, metaphorically, paralyzed. He refuses to copy any more documents or to leave his workspace, even at night when the offices close, and the only answer given for his behavior is the infamous phrase, "I would prefer not to." Eventually, the lawyer for whom Bartleby works is forced to relocate his law office, for Bartleby will not leave his workspace even after being fired, and the poor scrivener is subsequently incarcerated and dies in prison after spending a few days standing and staring at the prison yard wall.

Critics who point out the futility of modern life in this story are correct in their readings, though I would expand their thoughts to point to a conversation Melville enters regarding the concept of vocation, and its relationship to choice and freedom. Melville's contribution to this conversation lies in Bartleby's "preferences." Modern life—industrialization, capitalism, the Enlightenment elevation of the individual and reason—birthed not only the type of profession in which Bartleby finds himself but also his choice, or his preference, to do or not to do it. In the post-Puritan world in which he lives, where Christianity has acclimated to the Enlightenment and consequently relinquished God's sovereignty for a more elevated view of human will, Bartleby's paralysis comes from his ability-turned-inability to choose his own future. The lawyer, accordingly, provides him with several options to determine his own future: to copy documents for another employer, to become a clerk or a bartender, to collect bills for businessmen in the country, or to go Europe as a gentleman's companion. Bartleby rejects all of these options, giving one reason or another—too much confinement in the clerkship, too much movement as the gentleman's companion—nevertheless explaining, "but I am not particular."[29]

The great irony is that he is actually very particular, but his will is paralyzed because he has a power too great for him: the freedom to determine his own life. As the freedom to prefer is an integral part of John Locke's definition of liberty, Melville's story is indeed an exploration of post-Reformation and Enlightenment-infused ideologies and their effects on American life.[30] Through this story, Melville shows that "the sea of infinite choices" is indeed a kind of enslavement. As Allan Moore Emery argues, though Bartleby is free, "that 'freedom' makes him finally incapable of action."[31] Expounding on the narrator's reference to his reading of Jonathan Edwards's treatise on free will, Emery explains that in order for an individual to be free, he must extricate himself from any forces that may influence his will, which results in the "mental paralysis" that leads to Bartleby's death.[32]

Although Emery goes on to demonstrate that Bartleby's alternative, the comfortable and somewhat brutal Calvinism of the lawyer, is portrayed without sympathy, what I want to highlight through my discussion of "Bartleby" is Melville's awareness of how closely one's assumptions regarding freedom are tied to the way one understands vocation. Although Melville is no advocate of Calvinism, he nevertheless gives his readers a devastating picture of what a post-Reformation, and by extension, Enlightenment, understanding of freedom does to a concept of vocation in the midst of modern life. Modern life gives individuals many choices regarding the direction of their lives, and when the power to determine one's own future lies solely in the hands of the individual, in his relentless ability to prefer, a person becomes a slave to her random preferences, leading to a state of paralysis. He shows that the absence of any force to direct or to determine one's choices means death to the American people. Without external forces to, as Emery notes, "energize" the will, people wither and die.[33] Melville's answer to this problem may not be God, but he shows that the absence of God when considering the direction of one's life has devastating results, specifically that the person who is guided by no external force is lifeless.

Sedgwick and Melville represent two opposing reactions to Protestant-American understandings of freedom, with Sedgwick celebrating the Declaration of Independence and hoping for greater fulfillment of its values while Melville's distrust of humanity leads him to a realistic pessimism that conveys little hope for Americans to be free in any sense of the word. One more example from literature will illustrate a view of freedom and vocation that, similar to Sedgwick's and Melville's works, responds to American values, but with a greater sense of how an individual's vocation is determined by her nature: Willa Cather's early novel, *O Pioneers!* (1913). *O Pioneers!* predates the author's commitment to organized religion, but it is evident in this novel that she was already interested in exploring forces beyond the human will, as she gives primacy to the role of nature and family in determining an individual's life, and not his or her whims or desires.[34]

In *O Pioneers!* Alexandra Bergson's dying father appoints her to lead and provide for the family he leaves behind, which includes her mother and three brothers. Alexandra's brothers are instructed to yield to their sister's leadership in all matters, particularly concerning their agricultural enterprises. Though at the beginning of the novel, the family is poor and in debt, sixteen years later, through Alexandra's leadership, they become the richest family on the Nebraskan Divide. Courtesy of their wealth, Alexandra takes delight in sending her youngest brother Emil to college, to be whatever he wants to be. Enamored by the American dream, in which college is the pathway to freedom and happiness, Alexandra says, "He shall do whatever he wants to [...] He is going to have a chance, a whole chance; that's what I've worked for."[35] She then explains, "Sometimes he talks about studying law, and sometimes, just lately, he's been talking about going out into the sand hills and taking up more land."[36] This explanation, which illuminates the diverse careers open to Emil, foreshadows the very difficulties that will eventually lead to his undoing, though his destiny remains hidden from Alexandra. She genuinely believes that giving her favorite brother "a whole chance" to "do whatever he wants to" is better than her own fate.

Emil, consequently, loafs restlessly through the novel. While it is clear that Alexandra was appointed by her family and by nature to interpret the land and eventually to work it into prosperity, a calling in which she had no choice, Emil, who should actually be working the land alongside Alexandra, believes he has no such calling on his life. He is cursed with a lack of calling, with having to determine his own future. This so-called freedom to choose from a seeming multitude of endeavors and professions ends up feeling more like slavery than freedom, for Emil's choices only remind him that there are "many, many things" he cannot do, namely, marry his childhood friend who has married another man.[37] When Emil dies pursuing the one thing he cannot have—another man's wife—the novel makes painfully clear that having the freedom to determine one's own life is at best a burden, and at worst, a form of mental slavery. While Alexandra had erroneously thought that Emil's freedom to determine his own future was infinitely better than being told what to do, at the end of the novel, after Emil's death, it is clear that Alexandra's calling, both by family and nature, is the true form of freedom while Emil is tragically stuck in the American ideology that presupposes the sovereignty of human will. At one point, Alexandra tells her brothers that she "didn't choose to be the kind of girl [she] was."[38] Although the calling to be who she is, to be the kind of girl she was born to be, is not an easy task, she experiences great freedom in embracing who she is by nature and in doing what her father called her to do with her life.

While Cather offers a perspective on freedom that is more aligned with the Christian tradition than the others, Sedgwick champions the American definition of freedom as "having our own way," and Melville shows that there are serious moral problems with Sedgwick's view without offering any hopeful alternatives. Reading these three texts together, therefore, reinforces the complexity of these issues in American thought. Consequently, through assigned readings, class lectures, and discussions, I have helped my own students glean a multifaceted picture of the ways in which American writers have questioned, championed, and critiqued freedom and its relationship to vocation in order to stimulate their own thinking about the tension between Christian and American ideals. Additionally, it is my hope that such readings and discussions will ultimately lead students to internalize Christian definitions of freedom and vocation so that they too will find ways to contest the melancholy of the world.

Freedom and Vocation in a Christian Education

While helping students to internalize a Christian view of freedom will potentially enrich their understanding of God's sovereignty and grace, and subsequently help them to make decisions with less fear of making the right or wrong choice, we have yet to address how these revolutionized definitions of freedom and vocation will help students forgo a consumerist view of college for a more holistic one. Ashley Woodiwiss calls this endeavor transforming students from tourists, whose main objective is to "consume" experiences and knowledge to feed their self-interest, into pilgrims, who undertake study for the purpose of "character formation."[39] Articulated using a different vocabulary, in his aptly titled book *Intellectual Appetite* (2009), Paul J. Griffiths writes about the same issue as Woodiwiss using the words "curiosity" and "studiousness," inspired by his reading of Augustine and other thinkers who predate the Enlightenment.[40] While curiosity is something like Woodiwiss's "tourist gaze," Griffiths' explanation of studiousness is not the equivalent of pilgrimage but a particular appetite for knowledge that stands in contrast to curiosity: "the studious," he writes, "do not seek to sequester, own, possess, or dominate what they hope to know; they want, instead, to participate lovingly in it, to respond to it knowingly as a gift rather than as potential possession."[41] One's penchant for "tourism" or "curiosity" is certainly heightened in college, particularly when having one's own way in life is the underlying reason to study for a Bachelor's degree.

However, when we understand learning as a pilgrimage and a right appetite for knowledge as studiousness, Conyers' definition of vocation as being "called forth to a divine purpose" complements the goals of Woodiwiss and Griffiths. If vocation is not about making a decision regarding a profession, and eventually practicing that profession, but living according to divine purpose, students' view of coursework and other aspects of college is likely to change. If they view their lives and their four years of college as a journey in discovering and growing into their vocations, a journey which is directed by a sovereign God, the shift in purpose, from a pragmatic cash return to a formative process in which every step matters, will challenge students not to be consumers but studious respecters of knowledge. They will be free to journey through college as if it were a pilgrimage or a quest rather than being bound by whatever studies or activities yield the highest measurable return. Moreover, embarking on a pilgrimage, a holy quest, is not ultimately about the individual who travels. While the individual expects to undergo character formation, to be transformed spiritually by the journey, the trek to the Holy Land, to the shrine of the revered saint, or to the edge of Mount Doom is guided by a good, external force whose vision both for the individual and the world is beyond human understanding.

As students are summoned to their vocations throughout college, and as they learn and internalize a right definition of freedom, they will be pulled out of their self-interest, or the "self-love" that Calvin considers a form of sin that derides God's sovereignty.[42] They will learn to fix their eyes on Jesus and to run the race that has been marked out for them. They will not, as F. Scott Fitzgerald dramatizes in the final lines of his tale of college life, *This Side of Paradise* (1920), lament with Amory Blaine, "I know myself [...] but that is all."[43] Fitzgerald, who was slightly younger than Cather, also responds to the values of earlier generations of Americans, particularly the transcendentalists Ralph Waldo Emerson, who wrote "Trust thyself" in "Self-Reliance" and Henry David Thoreau, who wrote "Explore thyself" at the end of *Walden*.[44] Fitzgerald's protagonist is a slave to his own mind, for he has not taken seriously any thoughts and ideas but his own. He spent his college years doing nothing but feeding his self-interest, the results of which are expressed by the tragic last words of the novel. Unlike Bartleby, Emil Bergson, and Amory Blaine, the students who are rightly catechized regarding freedom and its relationship to vocation will neither accept nor internalize individualistic aphorisms like "Trust thyself" and "Explore thyself," no matter how American and charming, as legitimate guiding forces. Instead, such students will view the end of college much in the same way the Westminster Shorter Catechism instructs them to view the chief end of man: to glorify God, and to enjoy him forever.

Notes

1. In 1775, the British philosopher and politician Edmund Burke expressed the relationship between the Reformation and the birth of the United States by describing the Revolution as "the dissidence of dissent, and the protestantism of the Protestant religion": *Burke's Politics: Selected Writings and Speeches of Edmund Burke on Reform, Revolution, and War*, eds. Ross J.S. Hoffman and Paul Levack (New York: Alfred A. Knopf, 1949), 71. Accordingly, my claim in this chapter is built from the idea that Protestantism and American individualism together have influenced how college students understand freedom and its relationship to vocation. This view of the Protestant Reformation also follows from the work of religious historians, such as Brad S. Gregory, who trace the features of current-day Christianity, including its privatization and individualization, back to the Reformation era: *The Unintended Reformation: How a Religious Revolution Secularized Society* (Cambridge: Belknap Press, 2012), 21.
2. Andrew Delbanco, *The Real American Dream: A Meditation on Hope* (Cambridge: Harvard University Press, 1999), 61.
3. Ibid., 103.

4. Although recent studies of Christian college students, such as Tim Clydesdale's *The Purposeful Graduate* (Chicago: The University of Chicago Press, 2015), argue that such students are generally optimistic about their futures, my argument seeks to address the fundamental melancholy of a culture that fixates on the self and from which Christian students are not exempt. Popular writer and journalist David Brooks provides an illustration of this self-centeredness in his gloss of cultural messages in *The Road to Character* (London: Penguin Books, 2016). "You are special," he writes, "Trust yourself. Be true to yourself. Movies from Pixar and Disney are constantly telling children how wonderful they are. Commencement speeches are larded with the same clichés: Follow your passion. Don't accept limits. Chart your own course" (ibid., 7). In contrast, Brooks' thesis suggests that people who have rejected such messages and subsequently focus less on their own strengths are the people who possess deep character. My argument aligns with Brooks' in my recommendation that teachers combat this cultural melancholy rooted in the self by directing their students away from the assumption that an individual's ability to be self-determining is the highest expression of freedom and happiness.
5. Andrew Delbanco, *College: What It Was, Is, and Should Be* (Princeton: Princeton University Press, 2012), 65.
6. Ibid., xv–xvi.
7. Katrina Trinko, "Choose Your College, Major and Loans Wisely," *USA Today*, April 22, 2012, http://usatoday30.usatoday.com/news/opinion/forum/story/2012-04-22/college-majors-student-loans/54474222/1.
8. Terri Williams, "Report Reveals Big Gaps Between the Degrees Students are Earning and In-Demand Jobs," Education News, May 2, 2016, https://www.goodcall.com/news/report-reveals-big-gaps-degrees-students-earning-demand-jobs-06415.
9. Basit Zafar, "Double Majors, One for Me, One for the Parents?" *Economic Inquiry* 50, no. 2 (2012): 287.
10. William C. Placher states that the Second Vatican Council promoted the idea among Catholics "that any job can be a vocation": *Callings: Twenty Centuries of Christian Wisdom on Vocation* (Grand Rapids: Eerdmans, 2005), 8.
11. Ibid., 10.
12. Delbanco, *The Real American Dream*, 61.
13. Paul J. Wadell, *Happiness and the Christian Moral Life: An Introduction to Christian Ethics* (Lanham, MD: Rowman & Littlefield Publishers, 2008), 94–95.

14. A.J. Conyers, "The Meaning of Vocation," *The Center for Christian Ethics at Baylor University*, 2004, 17.
15. Ibid., 18.
16. Ibid., 12–13.
17. Conyers, "The Meaning of Vocation," 17; Margery Williams, *The Velveteen Rabbit, or How Toys Become Real* (New York: Doubleday, 1922), 17.
18. Williams, *The Velveteen Rabbit*, 17.
19. Mark Edmundson's *Why Read?* (New York: Bloomsbury, 2004) is a particularly pertinent example of the countercultural nature of Conyers' understanding of vocation and its implications regarding a Christian view of freedom. In his book, Edmundson articulates a "vision of education in which we pursue our own visions, our own truths" (ibid., 140). He subsequently calls this vision "genuine democracy," an assertion that points to the challenges Americans in particular face regarding Conyers' ideas and my expansion of them (ibid., 141).
20. Placher expresses particular concern with the prospect that if any choice is the right one, and if there is no wrong answer, "then my choices cease to have any larger meaning": "Introduction" in *Callings: Twenty Centuries of Christian Wisdom on Vocation*, ed. William C. Placher (Grand Rapids: Eerdmans, 2005), 10.
21. John Calvin, *The Bondage and Liberation of the Will* (Philadelphia: Westminster, 1960), 114; Conyers, "The Meaning of Vocation," 12.
22. What shape this conversation takes for various professors and administrators at different schools will obviously vary, but it is worth noting that, as professor Ronald A. Berk writes in his "A Tribute to Teaching," which was published following his retirement after thirty seven years of teaching, "It's possible that *how* we teach has a more profound effect on our students than *what* we teach" (*College Teaching* 57.2 [2009], 127). For those of us teaching introductory-level classes that are designed to address "big questions" about college education as well as career orientation classes, the way we speak and the assumptions we convey regarding decisions will have an impact on students, providing us with opportunities to model a Christian perspective on human choice and freedom.
23. This chapter is not the place to debate the extent to which the Declaration of Independence is a Christian document; however, I do think that John Winthrop's understanding of freedom is more congruent with the Bible and the Christian tradition than that of the nation's Revolutionary Founding Fathers and the writers of the Declaration of Independence. For Winthrop, freedom was bound up with submission to God, as he states regarding his, and the community's, reasons for their departure to the New World: "The end is to improve our lives to do more service to the Lord": "A Model of Christian Charity." *The Norton Anthology of American*

Literature, Shorter Eighth Ed. Eds. Nina Baym and Robert S. Levine (New York: Norton, 2013), 100. Consequently, I am more in line with Mark A. Noll, George M. Marsden, and Nathan O. Hatch, authors of *The Search for Christian America* (Westchester, IL: Crossway Books, 1983), than Gary T. Amos's credulous book, *Defending the Declaration* (Brentwood, TN: Wolgemuth & Hyatt, 1989). For further reading, two recent studies that address this topic include D.G. Hart's *From Billy Graham to Sarah Palin* (Grand Rapids: Eerdmans, 2011) and John Fea's *Was America Founded as a Christian Nation?* (Louisville: Westminster, 2011). Hart and Fea both offer more nuanced, and perhaps more helpful, approaches to this issue than the earlier works by Noll, Marsden, Hatch, and Amos (Hart, *From Billy Graham*, 80–83; Fea, *Was America Founded*, 127–33).

24. Catharine Maria Sedgwick, *Clarence* (New York: Broadview, 2012), 307, 355.
25. Ibid., 241.
26. Catharine Maria Sedgwick, *Hope Leslie or, Early Times in Massachusetts* (New York: Penguin, 1998), 235.
27. Many stories about young people, particularly in television and film, follow a narrative that champions the individual who insists on making his own choice regarding his future, despite the disapproval of his parents, friends, or mentors. The film *October Sky* (1999) is a classic example of this narrative, as it tells the story of a high school student who wants to build rockets and succeeds even when much of his community, including his father, thinks his endeavors are foolish and pointless. While this chapter was composed, the popular British miniseries *Downton Abbey* featured a subplot in which the youngest daughter, Sybil, against the wishes of her parents and family, marries the chauffer, her social inferior. What interests me about these narratives, also present in *Clarence*, is that the stories are presented in such a way as to direct the sympathy of readers and viewers towards the person who resists the authority of her elders. We are made to feel that it is Sybil's right to determine her own future and disobey her parents.
28. Louise K. Barnett's "Bartleby as Alienated Worker," which appeared in *Studies in Short Fiction* in 1974, started this vein of criticism.
29. Herman Melville, *Melville's Short Novels* (New York: Norton, 2002), 30.
30. John Locke, *An Essay Concerning Human Understanding*, Vol. 1 (New York: Clarendon Press, 1894), 325.
31. Allan Moore Emery, "The Alternatives of Melville's 'Bartleby,'" *Nineteenth-Century Fiction* 31, no. 2 (1976): 173.
32. Ibid., 178.
33. Ibid., 178.
34. Willa Cather joined the Episcopal Church in the 1920s.
35. Willa Cather, *O Pioneers!* (New York: Norton, 2008), 54.

36. Ibid., 54.
37. Ibid., 68.
38. Ibid., 74.
39. Ashley Woodiwiss, "From Tourists to Pilgrims: Christian Practices and the First-Year Experience," in *Teaching and Christian Practices: Reshaping Faith and Learning* (Grand Rapids: Eerdmans, 2011), 125–27.
40. In *Confessions*, Augustine explains curiosity alongside lust: "there can also be in the mind itself, through those same bodily senses, a certain vain desire and curiosity [...] cloaked under the name of learning and knowledge. Because this is in the appetite to know, and the eyes are the chief of the senses we use for attaining knowledge, it is called in Scripture *the lust of the eyes*" (2nd ed., trans. F.J. Sheed, ed. Michael P. Foley [Indianapolis: Hackett Publishing Co., 2006], 219).
41. Paul J. Griffiths, *Intellectual Appetite: A Theological Grammar* (Washington, DC: Catholic University of America Press, 2009), 21.
42. John Calvin, *The Institutes of the Christian Religion*, Vol. XX (Philadelphia: Westminster, 1960), 243.
43. F. Scott Fitzgerald, *This Side of Paradise* (New York: Everyman's Library, 1996), 264.
44. Ralph Waldo Emerson, *Essays: First and Second Series* (New York: Library of America, 1991), 30; Henry David Thoreau, *Walden, Civil Disobedience, and Other Writings* (New York: Norton, 2008), 216.

CHAPTER 4

Putting Down Roots: Why Universities Need Gardens

Jeffrey Bilbro and Jack R. Baker

In "The Loss of the University," Wendell Berry proposes that contemporary universities should return to a model of learning that envisions knowledge as a tree.[1] Practicing such a rooted, interconnected form of education, however, is difficult in a culture of "boomers" (Berry's term for people who are always looking for a better place somewhere else) who value specialized, commodifiable knowledge rather than wisdom that leads to health and flourishing. These models of learning stem from different underlying desires: if we want to maximize profit, we will isolate and divide and specialize knowledge, but if we want to cultivate health, we will seek to draw together and integrate our knowledge. Thus our attempts to educate students in rooted wisdom begin with our own commitment to our place. Rather than trying to build an impressive CV so that we can move to "better" jobs elsewhere, we want to do good work where we are, even if such work does not bring professional

J. Bilbro (✉) · J.R. Baker
Spring Arbor University, Spring Arbor, MI, USA

T.L. Scales and J.L. Howell (eds.), *Christian Faith and University Life*,
DOI 10.1007/978-3-319-61744-2_4

prestige, even if the place is not exactly what we expected. In the following essay, then, we turn to Wendell Berry to work out reasons to hope for higher education even in our industrial, boomer culture. While he does not lay out his argument in quite the following way, we think it is helpful to understand Berry's hope for the recovery of the university as resting upon three requirements: an imagination guided by a unified organization of knowledge, a common, communal language, and responsible work. A university that embodies and unites these three principles might provide students with a rooted education, one that would form fully developed humans capable of serving their places. After offering a diagnosis of how universities came to embrace disintegrated and deracinated knowledge, we will sketch how a healthy imagination and precise language could restore unity. Then we will suggest one practice—gardening—that can foster more responsible connections to our place.

Boomers and Stickers

Currently, our universities tell stories about the need for "upward (and lateral) mobility" that come from the broader culture's stories about progress and success.[2] A recent story in the satirical newspaper *The Onion* captures our culture's dominant belief that mobility is an indicator of success.[3] Titled, "Unambitious Loser With Happy, Fulfilling Life Still Lives In Hometown," the article recounts a sad story: "Longtime acquaintances confirmed to reporters this week that local man Michael Husmer, an unambitious 29-year-old loser who leads an enjoyable and fulfilling life, still lives in his hometown and has no desire to leave." As the reporter talks with Husmer's more successful high school classmates, the dreary life he leads comes into focus:

> Former high school classmates confirmed that Husmer has seemingly few aspirations in life, citing occasional depressing run-ins with the personally content townie during visits back home, as well as embarrassing Facebook photos in which the smiling dud appears alongside family members whom he sees regularly and appreciates and enjoys close, long-lasting relationships with. Additionally, pointing to the intimate, enduring connections he's developed with his wife, parents, siblings, and neighbors, sources reported that Husmer's life is "pretty humiliating" on multiple levels.
>
> In particular, those familiar with the pitiful man, who is able to afford a comfortable lifestyle without going into debt, confirmed that he resides just two blocks from the home he grew up in, miles away from anything

> worthwhile, like high-priced bars and clubs. In fact, sources stated that the pathetic loafer has never had any interest in moving to even a nearby major city, despite the fact that he has nothing better to do than "sit around all day" being an involved member of his community and using his ample free time to follow pursuits that give him genuine pleasure.

Our laughter at this portrayal of a "loser" reveals our awareness that we do associate leaving home with having "made it," even though the stress and anxiety of Husmer's "successful" acquaintances call into question the desirability of such a mobile life.

Berry has been describing this cultural obsession with restless mobility for decades now, arguing that it causes extensive damage to our land and our character. For as he explains, "Upward mobility, as we now are seeing, implies downward mobility, just as it has always implied lateral mobility. It implies, in fact, social instability, ecological oblivion, and economic insecurity."[4] Elsewhere, Berry uses the term "boomers" to describe those who are always on the lookout for better career opportunities in better places. Berry derives this term, and its opposite, "sticker," from Wallace Stegner's description of the two contrasting types of pioneers who settled the West. Stegner, a twentieth-century author who writes about the Western landscape in which he was raised, identifies boomers as those who came to the West looking to get rich; they were willing to damage the land and its existing communities for a quick profit. Once they had extracted all they could easily get from a place, whether a mine, a forest, or a farm, they moved on to a more abundant place. But, as Berry explains, "Not all who came to American places came to plunder and run. Some came to stay, or came with the hope of staying. These Stegner called 'stickers' or 'nesters.'"[5] These stickers came West looking to transplant themselves into a new home. In another essay, Berry describes such people as "nurturers," those whose "goal is health," the health of the land, the community, and the country.[6]

The root difference between boomers and stickers is not simply that one group is mobile and one group is stationary; rather, they are defined by their contrasting narratives, motivations, and affections. As Berry explains in his recent Jefferson lecture, "It All Turns on Affection," "The boomer is motivated by greed, the desire for money, property, and therefore power."[7] Berry's title indicates that his emphasis on this distinction is on one's affections, and this clarifies a common, but misguided, criticism of his thought. Berry does not say "everyone who leaves" home is "a greedy, selfish 'boomer.'" Rather, he simply reiterates that our affections are never without consequences. Thus, the individual motivated by "greed, the desire for money, property, and therefore power," is not necessarily the individual who moves to the only state where she can find gainful employment, leaving loved ones half a nation away. Nor is the boomer the individual who leaves his small town where his entire family lives because he has suffered abuse at their hands. Instead, the boomer is the individual who is guided by wrongheaded affections—affections for power, for wealth at whatever cost, for personal success. We must be clear that "boomer" names a story—a way of imagining success that leads to a way of living characterized by disinterest in place, limits, and externalized consequences—not a person who leaves a place. So perhaps an important distinction is that a sticker may be forced to leave a place but will nest in a new place; a boomer wants to leave a place and is willing to leave again should a better opportunity arise elsewhere.[8]

Currently, "boomerism" pervades our educational culture to such an extent that nearly all departments in nearly all universities are infected by it. As Wes Jackson claims, "upward mobility" is now the only major that universities offer: "Little attention is paid to educating the young to return home, or to go some other place, and dig in. There is no such thing as a 'homecoming' major."[9] Steven Bouma-Prediger and Brian Walsh extend Jackson's argument in their essay, "Education for Homelessness or Homemaking? The Christian College in a Postmodern Culture," claiming, "Colleges and universities—small or large, public or private, Christian or secular—tend to educate for upward mobility, to alienate people from their local habitation, and to encourage the vandalization of the earth."[10] What such an education forgets is the need for a vocation that subsumes these techniques under a higher purpose: the restoration of health and the flourishing of one's community. As Berry trenchantly observes in "Higher Education and Home Defense,"

> Education in the true sense, of course, is an enablement to *serve*—both the living human community in its natural household or neighborhood and the precious cultural possessions that the living community inherits or should inherit. To educate is, literally, to 'bring up,' to bring young people to a responsible maturity, to help them to be good caretakers of what they have been given, to help them to be charitable toward fellow creatures.... And if this education is to be used well, it is obvious that it must be used some *where*; it must be used where one lives, where one intends to continue to live; it must be brought home.[11]

Graduates cannot serve their communities, they cannot take care of them, if they do not settle somewhere and bring their education home.

An education for health, one that forms students to serve their homes, will have to begin by reforming students' imaginations so that they begin to ask better questions. For, as Berry explains, their differently oriented affections lead boomers and stickers to ask different kinds of questions and to operate in different economies. The boomer or "exploiter asks of a piece of land only how much and how quickly it can be made to produce, the nurturer [or sticker] asks a question that is much more complex and difficult: What is its carrying capacity? (That is: How much can be taken from it without diminishing it?)."[12] Berry expresses this contrast even more simply in his 2013 interview with Bill Moyers: "The answers will come not from walking up to your farm and saying this is what I want and this is what I expect from you. You walk up and you say 'What do you need?'"[13] These different questions stem from differently orientated desires—one desires quick profit and the other health—and the different complexities of their accounting—one values only profit and externalizes costs and damages, and the other seeks to give an account for all things. These distinctions mark the contrast that Berry draws in "Two Economies" between our industrial economy, which "tends to destroy what it does not comprehend," and the "Great Economy" or the "Kingdom of God," which "includes everything" in its comprehensive "pattern or order."[14]

This fundamental difference between teaching students to get what they want from their places and teaching them to ask "what do you need?" marks not only the difference between boomers and stickers, but also the difference between a more medieval way of organizing knowledge like a tree and the organization (or lack thereof) in modern universities. Asking "what do I want?" simply leads to education in techniques of extraction for personal appetite, but the question "what do you need?" leads to an education in charity and health. C.S. Lewis describes this difference in terms of the contrast between medieval learning and the mere technical training increasingly offered today: "For the wise men of old the cardinal problem had been how to conform the soul to reality, and the solution had been knowledge, self-discipline, and virtue. For … applied science … the problem is how to subdue reality to the wishes of men: the solution is a technique."[15] The work of conforming our souls to reality via knowledge, self-discipline, and virtue is long and arduous, but if we desire to be responsible members of our places, this is the work we will have to take up.

The contrast between boomers and stickers—the different desires they have, the different stories they tell, the different questions they ask, the different economies they participate in, and the contrasting models of the university that they propose—should now be clear: the boomer wants to isolate knowledge from its origins in order to maximize its utility and profitability, but the sticker values a medieval, rooted kind of learning whose branches connect as much as possible. Thus, the way we organize and order knowledge stems from the kinds of questions we ask, which in turn rise from the orientation of our desires.

Because such questions involve complex interconnections, they do not often lead to simple answers. As professors, we believe that we are called to model for our students ways of living with such questions and working them out slowly and patiently. In *Jayber Crow*, one of Berry's novels, Jayber is attending seminary with the view to becoming a preacher. But his studies lead him to ask many questions about the core of the Christian faith, how prayer works, and how it might be possible to love our enemies. So one day he goes to a professor's office and musters the courage to ask these questions. The professor listens patiently until Jayber gets through his list, and then simply says to the confused young man, "You have been given questions to which you cannot be given answers. You will have to live them out—perhaps a little at a time."[16] Jayber is shaken; he leaves seminary, eventually returns to his hometown, and does not pray again for many years. Yet by honestly sticking with his questions, he finally comes to a place where he is again able to pray, not with the vending machine mentality of his childhood faith, but with a sober, terrifying awareness that Jesus' own most fervent prayer in Gethsemane was not answered.

Rooting Ourselves

Professors who feel compelled to look for better jobs elsewhere, though, find it hard to model this patient process of living out answers to difficult questions. One of the reasons that students look for simple, actionable answers is likely that professors, as a whole, often fail to stick with difficult questions and situations. Instead, it often seems that our profession has largely acquiesced to the promiscuous temptations of boomerism: we look to pad our C.V.s with impressive accolades so that we can negotiate light teaching loads and high salaries and shop around for the best research fellowships. In other words, we are much like the opportunistic pioneers Stegner writes about or the exploitative strip-miners that Berry criticizes, always on the lookout for more profitable pastures.[17] And yet when we seek better opportunities elsewhere, we fail to stick it out where we are and live with our questions until we find ways to make the place in which we already abide healthier.

In our own lives, we have worked out such vocational challenges in different ways, and these differences may be instructive in that they indicate that seeking the health of one's place is a process that can take many different forms. I (Jeff) grew up in Washington State, near Seattle, and developed a deep affection for the mountains, forests, rivers, and people of my home. Most of my extended family still lives in the area, and my wife's family is also in the Northwest. When we left to go to graduate school in Texas, we told ourselves that this would be a five or six-year adventure and that then we would return home. But the academic job market being what it is, my interviews with schools in the Northwest did not result in job offers, and we had to choose between jobs in Tennessee and Michigan.

The economic reasons that led us to Michigan are well respected in our boomer culture. But my parents' story made me know that staying away from home for the sake of a job was not the only option. My parents moved to Connecticut for my dad to go to graduate school, and when he earned his master's degree, they turned down a job back east in order to return to Seattle, without a home, with no job prospects, and with an infant daughter. The economics of their situation were different, I know, and my dad was able to find a good job within a few weeks, but I am still impressed by the courage they demonstrated in moving home without the assurance of a job to support their young family.

Yet even though we did not return home, we are working to make a home in this place. We attend church, subscribe to the local paper, shop at the farmer's market, pick and preserve local fruit, and visit local cultural venues. We have bought a neglected house, worked hard to repair and restore it, and planted a garden. We built a shared mailbox with several neighbors and took Christmas cookies around the neighborhood. We have learned the history of the neighborhood over coffee in others' homes and exchange greetings as we work in our yard or take walks. This is not an intergenerational, economically interdependent community. This is not the rich membership that Berry describes in his fiction, but we are trying to deepen the forms of neighborliness and community that are available to us in our suburban place. We are trying to knit ourselves into the fabric of this place.

I (Jack) grew up in Shelby, a small town in West Michigan. With a population of just over 2000, it is easy to miss as tourists travel U.S. 31 on the shoreline toward golden beaches and crystal blue waters at Silver Lake or the Charles Mears State Park in Pentwater. Like many small towns in America, Shelby used to be a thriving community—surviving on tourism, robust fruit farms, and local processing and canning factories. I love my hometown. I miss it dearly. But most of all, I mourn for it. My parents still reside in my childhood home—a craftsman foursquare built in 1907 by the original owner of the Rankin Hardware store in town. The town is dying. Jobs have disappeared, homes have lost considerable value, and culture has quickly petrified.

Before I left home for college, I could already sense what was happening to my hometown, which only further encouraged my affections to leave home for good. I saw college as the opportunity to make something of myself, something living and not dying; and Shelby stood for everything stagnant—for lost health and wholeness. Of course, my affections in some ways were misguided. Was not it this same mindset—that leaving Shelby was good for me—that guided so many other young and old alike to turn away from their homes in hopes of finding a better life elsewhere? And how many found that life? How many began their journey as itinerants, never to settle down long enough in a place to really be a part of it? Well, I was one of those itinerants throughout my higher education, and it was not until we left Michigan for graduate studies in Indiana that I began to feel the deep connection I had to my home state and hometown.

When we would drive back to Shelby to visit my family during this period, I was struck by the deep longing I had to be a part of the geography with which I was so accustomed. On weekend visits with family, I waxed poetic about how much I desired to return to my home state. Until I lived elsewhere, I never knew how connected to Michigan I was in a very real spiritual way. It was what I knew, where I had lived all but a few years of my life, and I could not shake the overwhelming sense of loss I had at the prospect of not returning there for a job at a university. Of course, in humility we rejoice that we were able to return to work in Michigan; and while we now live in the South-Central region of the state, we are directly between both sets of parents, working to make Spring Arbor, MI our home. And it is here that I am continuing the process of reshaping my affections for a different place, thinking often about how I ought to live in order to care for the health of Spring Arbor, as well as the health of my students—to be committed to a sticker mentality in a boomer profession. To echo Jayber Crow once again, we simply cannot have any hope of this place being home if we have no prospect of staying here. And so in some ways, Spring Arbor has become my Shelby—my new hometown—and I will work to cultivate the right affections in my own heart, in the hearts of my children, in the hearts of my students.

We are not alone in our desire to articulate the stories of our places as significant toward encouraging the sticker mentality. In fact, our stories are part of a protean genre that is often featured on the Front Porch Republic, a website whose authors follow Wendell Berry in valuing place, limits, and liberty. One poster, Mark Signorelli recently argued for a more nuanced understanding of the "arch-typical narrative that has become quite popular here at FPR, and in some sense, emblematic of its defense of place and home. It is the "Going Home" story, the story of someone rejecting the allures of wealth and status in the big-city, and returning to the fixed traditions of his or her hometown."[18] Signorelli offered his own autobiography of growing up in a nowhere suburb as evidence that not everyone has a home to return to, and yet such people can still find a place to plant themselves. So while some Porchers, like Jeff Polet and Conor Dugan, have been able to find good jobs in their hometowns and thus enact the more typical going home narrative, others work to make a home in the place their vocation has taken them.[19]

The protagonists in these "Going Home" stories offer an alternative to the boomer narrative that undergirds much of our culture and is particularly prevalent in higher education. We live in a society that values the peripatetic ladder climber whose success is in large part attributable to his ability to cut and run as soon as the getting is better elsewhere. We have made leaving a place the great indicator of one's success in the world. If you seek an education, leave home, it is somewhere else. If you seek a good paying job, leave home, it is somewhere else. If you seek to make something meaningful of your life, leave home, it is somewhere else.

One of Wendell Berry's characters, Hannah Coulter, lives her life in opposition to such a narrative, and when she sends her children to college, she mourns the way their education shapes them to become boomers: "The big idea of education, from first to last, is the idea of a better place. Not a better place where you are, because you want it to be better and have been to school and learned to make it better, but a better place somewhere else. In order to move up, you have got to move on."[20]

This "big idea" is what we must change if we hope to form our students to be caring stickers. For while we may not all be able to return to the street on which we grew up or the town in which we were raised, and some of us may not even be able to return to our natal state, all of us can and should set about deliberately rooting ourselves in our place and finding ways to make it a better place. Such roots teach us about the complex interdependencies on which health depends, they teach us how to desire this health more fully, and they teach us what kinds of questions might lead to a greater understanding of how we can serve this health.

Affections and the Organization of Knowledge

If we want an education that forms students to serve their places and local communities, universities will have to stop genuflecting before the industrial economy and the motives of personal success and affluence that it rewards. It may seem trivial to state this, but we seem to forget that the only value the money economy recognizes is money; it justifies any technique that brings in more money. Techniques of division and specialization have been the most lucrative methods employed by modernity, and universities have adopted them in their quest for economic profit. Yet if we commodify education, dividing it from other sources of value, Berry argues that we will turn it into a weapon that will be wielded to consolidate power:

> When educational institutions educate people to *leave* home, then they have redefined education as "career preparation." In doing so, they have made it a commodity—something to be *bought* in order to make money. The great wrong in this is that it obscures the fact that education—real education—is free. I am necessarily well aware that schools and books have a cost that must be paid, but I am sure nevertheless that what is taught and learned is free.... To make a commodity of it is to work its ruin, for, when we put a price on it, we both reduce its value and blind the recipient to the obligations that always accompany good gifts: namely, to use them well and to hand them on unimpaired. To make a commodity of education, then, is inevitably to make a kind of weapon of it because, when it is disassociated from the sense of obligation, it can be put directly at the service of greed.[21]

Berry's claim about the ultimate freedom of education implies that whenever education is made to serve the industrial economy, it will become an education in the service of greed rather than of the health of our homes.

The connection between greed and the modern fragmentation of knowledge in the multiversity may not be immediately apparent, but the two are directly related. The desire to use knowledge for power and money contributes to the fragmentation of the disciplines. To shift metaphors, if we want to control and manipulate reality, we will organize knowledge into a map, but if we want to conform our souls to reality, we will understand knowledge as taking us on a pilgrimage. As Paul Griffiths argues in *Intellectual Appetite*, "There is a direct genealogical link between the seventeenth-century aspiration toward a *mathesis universalis*—of, that is, mapping all knowledge onto a manipulable grid and providing clear principles of method that would permit the attainment of certainty about any topic—and the late-nineteenth and early-twentieth century hope for institutions of higher education free of commitments to value."[22] This "*mathesis universalis*," or universal knowledge, causes the strict departmental divisions within modern universities, divisions that Berry decries as arbitrary and opposed to our understanding of the true interconnections between all knowledge. But knowledge that has been divided into discrete bits and arranged in a scheme is much easier to use, so if all we care about is knowledge that we can use, knowledge that gives us power, then we tend to organize our universities in such fragmented ways.[23]

Indeed, the same desires that contribute to the fragmentation and specialization of knowledge in universities have a similar effect in other areas of modern life: diverse, healthy neighborhoods with residences, businesses, and stores are replaced by segregated zones that isolate each function[24]; complex farming patterns with polycrops and integrated animals are replaced by monocultures and factory farming; family doctors who know their patients are replaced by specialists who each treat only one particular disease; jobs requiring diverse skills are replaced by assembly-line jobs where each person fulfills only one function. Division enables control, and so we divide madly: "The first principle of the exploitive mind is to divide and conquer."[25] With the mounting ecological and social costs, however, it seems more and more clear that the "divide and conquer" mantra leads only to pyrrhic victories. As we have already seen, this greedy desire for control characterizes, as Lewis argues, applied science, not those who want to conform their souls to a reality that is, in fact, interconnected in endlessly complicated and interesting ways. Yet if we demand that our places provide what we want, then we will organize and divide knowledge as we have done in our modern research universities. If, on the other hand, we are to learn how to ask of our places, "What do you need?" we will seek to organize knowledge differently.

The Tree of Wisdom

In his essay "The Loss of the University," Berry proposes that we might recover a true university by remembering that the task of the university should be to form good human beings: "Underlying the idea of a university—the bringing together, the combining into one, of all the disciplines—is the idea that good work and good citizenship are the inevitable by-products of the making of a good—that is, a fully developed—human being."[26] Berry explores some of his ideas regarding what such a unified education would look like in the rest of this essay. In essence, his ideas rest upon cultivating healthy imaginations—which as we have seen begins with fostering affection for our places rather than seeking to extract what we can from them—and a common language, and then keeping both of these responsible to their place through local work.

If we desire to serve the health of our places, Berry argues, we should return to the ancient understanding of knowledge as a tree. Re-imagining knowledge through this metaphor reminds us to pay attention to the ways that knowledge coheres, a particularly important reminder in our highly specialized age:

> This Tree, for many hundreds of years, seems to have come almost naturally to mind when we have sought to describe the form of knowledge. In Western tradition, it is at least as old as Genesis, and the form it gives us for all that we know is organic, unified, comprehensive, connective—and moral… If we represent knowledge as a tree, we know that things that are divided are yet connected. We know that to observe the divisions and ignore the connections is to destroy the tree. The history of modern education may be the history of the loss of this image, and of its replacement by the pattern of the industrial machine, which subsists upon division—and by industrial economics ("publish or perish"), which is meaningless apart from division.[27]

If the history of modern education, and the loss of the university, is a story of the loss of this image, then the recovery of the university should begin with re-establishing this metaphor of knowledge as a tree.

The image of a tree cultivates in us a fidelity to both people and the earth, calling us to consider how such an image might shape the form and content of the work universities do. If knowledge is like a tree, each discipline needs to work out its relationship both to the trunk of truth and to the land in which the truth is rooted. Universities must, first of all, provide their students with a coherent trunk of knowledge, a clear sense of the way that various disciplines cohere. Hence Berry maintains that the "need for broadly informed human judgment... requires inescapably an education that is broad and basic." Such an education would begin by leading students up the trunk of this tree, and only once they have grasped the trunk would it guide them into more specialized knowledge. As Berry explains, "The work that should, and that can, unify a university is that of deciding what a student should be required to learn—what studies, that is, constitute the trunk of the tree of a person's education." Berry acknowledges that determining what constitutes this trunk, or core curriculum, is a difficult matter, but our current practice of leaving it up to the student is an avoidance of responsibility. How can we expect an eighteen-year-old freshman to know what they need to know if their professors cannot even agree on the necessary common knowledge?

Berry suggests that our conversations about what should form this trunk begin with the classic understanding of the liberal arts:

> It cannot be denied, to begin with, that all the disciplines rest on the knowledge of letters and the knowledge of numbers.... From there, one can proceed confidently to say that history, literature, philosophy, and foreign languages rest principally on the knowledge of letters and carry it forward, and that biology, chemistry, and physics rest on the knowledge of numbers and carry it forward.[28]

He thinks that further definition of this foundational knowledge should be provided by the local faculty, but what he particularly decries is our current refusal to define a trunk at all. For "although it may be possible to begin with a branch and develop a trunk, that is neither so probable nor so promising."[29] Thus universities have a responsibility to define for their students a common curriculum that anchors their further studies. If a university community is not rooted in a common narrative and common understanding of its community, then it will wither. And if a university is not unified in its reaching toward a shared vision of the good, of the light of the sun, then it will sprawl in confusion.

Learning how language ought to make meaning within a community is essential for practicing this rooted learning, and it is for this reason that a liberal arts education begins with the *Trivium*, or the study of language. The Trivium, or the "Three Ways," consists of *grammar*, the art of order, or questions about the structure of language; *logic or dialectic*, the art of thinking with language, or questions about truth; and *rhetoric*, the art of soul leading, or questions about how to use language to persuade others of truth.[30] The classical liberal arts also included the Quadrivium, and while these mathematical arts of order are also important, the Trivium is particularly foundational for any institution of higher education because it investigates the connective human faculties of order, sound thought, and wisdom through persuasion. The fruit of these arts is a liberated thinker and doer who wields a precise language with which to assign value to people, places, and problems.

An education founded in the liberal arts necessarily and somewhat paradoxically frees humans to be accountable. While our culture tends to think of freedom in negative terms—we want to be free *from* all restraints—the liberty offered by the liberal arts is a positive freedom—we are free *for* generous service. Indeed, the etymological link between liberty and liberality points to the traditional belief that generosity and concern for others were the proper posture of a free person.[31] In other words, a liberally educated person is responsible to exercise her freedom in a way that serves the health of her place and community.[32] Learning how language ought to make meaning within a community is essential for practicing this responsibility.

The liberal arts, then, teach students how language orders our thoughts and lives, thereby freeing them from the oppression of the unimportant things that so often preoccupy their time. This is why Berry argues that the proper task of contemporary education is to teach students how to responsibly order their lives:

> The complexity of our present trouble suggests as never before that we need to change our present concept of education. Education is not properly an industry, and its proper use is not to serve industries, either by job-training or by industry-subsidized research. Its proper use is to enable citizens to live lives that are economically, politically, socially, and culturally responsible. This cannot be done by gathering or "accessing" what we now call "information"—which is to say facts without context and therefore without priority. A proper education enables young people to put

> their lives in order, which means knowing what things are more important than other things; it means putting first things first.[33]

In order to learn "what things are more important than other things," we must cultivate a responsible, common language—a particularly necessary task at a time when the role of language in universities is understood as just one more piece in the puzzle of a student's education.

If we imagine a concerned student who has been trained in the Trivium present at a township meeting along with other citizens, all from various socioeconomic and educational backgrounds, we can begin to see the responsibility this student has to these people and their place. She feels a moral obligation to share her concerns for the sanitation policy and is unafraid to do so. She knows that if her thoughts are unordered, or she argues unsoundly or articulates herself poorly, she will likely fail to communicate adequately the truth in her concerns. In other words, she will struggle to imagine how to responsibly persuade the township board if she has not practiced the arts of the Trivium. We hope that her university community has not failed her and that it has instead prepared her—through the order of Grammar, the soundness of Logic, and the persuasive force of Rhetoric—to stand by her words and to foster a healthy language that responds clearly and wisely to the problem at hand.

Incorporating the Trivium more deeply into higher education could take different forms at different institutions. Revising the general education curriculum to require students to take a foreign language might be one way, and indeed Berry advocated for this requirement at the University of Kentucky.[34] But even without such curricular revisions, faculty and students can find more immediate ways to practice a caring, responsible language. For instance, when Berry taught at the University of Kentucky in the late 1980s, he posed a question from the day's reading at the beginning of each class. He then gave students twenty minutes to write their response to this question. The catch was that they had to do so in a single sentence. As one of Berry's students recount, this assignment was quite challenging:

> The first quiz was a disaster for most of the class, including me, mainly because we were not accustomed to writing, much less thinking, so directly and precisely. His quizzes demanded archer like strength and accuracy, and we had to get in shape and practice. Focusing our minds to make every sentence and every word matter, we tried our best to rise to our

> teacher's challenge. Some of our sentences even came close to the mark. Of all of the skills I practiced as a graduate student, this skill of achieving directness and accuracy—this astonishingly practical but difficult skill—is the single most valuable one to me as a writer and a teacher.[35]

This sort of simple assignment may not seem very significant, but it clearly made a difference in the life of one student, and it represents the kind of small steps that faculty and students can take toward cultivating responsible language.

Thus an education unified by a common trunk of knowledge and a responsible language forms students' imaginations to perceive the connections between seemingly disparate fields; in this way they can keep their specialized knowledge faithful to the whole tree. Yet while such a liberal arts curriculum is undoubtedly important, it is not sufficient to form healthy imaginations, imaginations capable of judging whether or not our knowledge and work are serving the health of our places. For the standard by which we need to judge all our learning and work is found outside of the university, in the ground in which the tree of knowledge is rooted. This rootedness is not only metaphorical but also literal; as Berry explains, the standard to which we must ultimately remain faithful is "the life and health of the world."[36] Elsewhere, Berry calls this external standard against which we should judge all our work the "Great Economy" or the "Kingdom of God."[37] This Great Economy is much more comprehensive than the market economy—in fact, it "includes everything."[38] Of course the task of making our knowledge and work faithful and responsible to everything is a task that is never complete. It requires the ongoing work of judging and correcting our visions, and it ultimately requires a healthy imagination, one that sees the complex needs of its community. Difficult though this task may be, it is a necessary one, for if the learning that universities foster fails to stem from and contribute to the health of the "Kingdom of God," then the university and the communities it exists to serve will wither and die.

Growing a Garden

Imagining knowledge as a rooted tree, teaching the liberal arts, and being imperfect exemplars of rooted living are not sufficient to form our students to desire to be stickers who seek the health of their homes, particularly when the broader culture continues to foster boomer values.

So while we work to shape our curriculum in ways that will bring questions of place into the heart of our classroom conversations, such a curricular shift is not adequately formative. Thus, inspired by Wendell Berry and the philosopher James Smith, we have worked here at Spring Arbor University with other members of our community to start a campus garden. Is growing a garden sufficient to root students' learning? Probably not, but our hope is that the practice of gardening together will shape our students' imaginations, their affections, and their questions.

Smith, in his Cultural Liturgies series, draws on an Augustinian anthropology to argue that we humans are liturgical animals, by which he means desiring, imaginative creatures whose affections are shaped by our practices and shared stories. What this means for the university is that "the mission of the Christian university should be conceived not just in terms of dissemination of *in*formation but also, and more fundamentally, as an exercise in *form*ation."[39] Practices that form students in rooted living are difficult to imagine in institutions where students only live for four or five years and then set off to follow their careers wherever they may lead. It is even harder to implement such practices in a fifteen-week class, although the contributors to *Teaching and Christian Practices: Reshaping Faith and Learning* display remarkable creativity in adapting to this context practices that form students in other ways. Our hope, though, is that the practice of gardening as a community might shape students to care more deeply about their connections to their place, to desire a more vigorous health, and to adopt a posture of gratitude.

Gardening places us in our time and location; it reminds us of our limits as placed creatures and fosters a language accountable to such limits. Plants grow in particular places from the soil and nutrients and light available to them there. We cannot grow bananas or mangoes in Michigan. We have to learn which plants will thrive here, and which will thrive in our particular conditions. We learn to accommodate our appetites to these plants, and to the seasons in which they bear fruit. Such learning clarifies and roots our language. Now when we say the word "tomato," our associations include not merely the pale red slices on a McDonald's hamburger, but also the rich red globes hanging from the deep green foliage on a summer afternoon we spent weeding with our friends in the garden. Gardening also sharpens our language because it forces us to, as Berry says, stand by our words; we have to test the language we use against the reality of the things we are talking about, the seeds, soil, bugs, work, sun, and water that foster or inhibit life. With this more accountable language, we became able to respond to the conditions and needs of our place. We thus begin to live within the limits of what our place can allow and become more able to lead lives of reciprocity and responsibility.

This more accountable and rich language reflects the complex health and beauty that a garden can embody. Our culture's vision of a healthy life is about as simplistic as its vision of a healthy lawn: 1.5 children, a nice house in the suburbs with a three-car garage, and a good career indicate the monocultural, impoverished cultural imagination we have. It is this imagination that leads us to flatten the space around our houses and buildings and dump chemicals on it until it looks evenly green. But when we trade this relationship with our environment for one in which we cultivate different kinds of plants and carefully tend their growth, we begin to enrich our imaginations. As Berry writes in "Think Little" about the way that gardening can transform our thinking, when we apply our "minds directly and competently to the needs of the earth, then we will have begun to make fundamental and necessary changes in our minds."[40] These changes in our minds will expand our imaginations as we participate in the economy of the soil, where water and sun and organic nutrients, brought together with human care, grow good food. Faculty, staff, and students may then be better able to envision how this healthy pattern might be cultivated in our marriages, our churches, and our communities. This formation in an aesthetic of health can help us all to be better participants in the Kingdom of God rather than simply accommodating ourselves to the simplistic, boomer economy of consumerism.

Finally, gardening can cultivate the gratitude that should characterize our posture as placed creatures. When all of our food comes from the grocery store, we begin to treat food, as we already treat most everything else, as a commodity that we deserve. This sense of entitlement, as we have already argued, infects our attitude toward education as well. But gardening can remind us of the proper gratitude we should have for our food. When some vegetables actually survive the vicissitudes of weather, bugs, disease, and deer, we recognize more deeply the true miracle that life is, and our gratitude for this gift springs almost unbidden. Our affections and imaginations have begun to be oriented toward our place, and while this can seem insignificant, this orientation may have far-reaching consequences, changing the questions we ask, the life choices that we make, and the economy in which we participate.

Gardening is no panacea for the ills that infect our deracinated culture and universities. What we are urging is that particular communities in particular institutions begin imagining ways that they can actively root themselves in their places. Gardening is one way to do this, but such formation will look different in different places. One of our friends at University of Mobile has begun a regular "Foxfire Evening" where students and professors gather to learn handicrafts. Other schools, like St. Catherine's College and Berea, incorporate the physical work of caring for their place much more comprehensively. Our hope is that local curricula, committed faculty, small reading groups, long-term involvement with the surrounding community, and a shared sense of institutional purpose can all contribute to offering students an education that will root them and prepare them for the work of restoration. Such an education can perhaps form us and our graduates not to desire a better place somewhere else, but, as Hannah Coulter longs for, "a better place where [we] are, because [we] want it to be better and have been to school and learned to make it better."[41]

Notes

1. This essay was first published in *Christian Scholars Review* 45.2 (2016): 125–42 and is reprinted by permission. We explore these themes at greater length in *Wendell Berry and Higher Education: Cultivating Virtues of Place*. Lexington: University Press of Kentucky, 2017.
2. Berry, Wendell. "Bellarmine Commencement Address," 2007. http://christianstudycenter.org/wp-content/uploads/2009/10/WendellBerry-BellarmineCommencement.pdf.
3. "Unambitious Loser With Happy, Fulfilling Life Still Lives In Hometown," *The Onion*, July 24, 2013, http://www.theonion.com/articles/unambitious-loser-with-happy-fulfilling-life-still,33233/.
4. "Major in Homecoming." In *What Matters?: Economics for a Renewed Commonwealth* (Berkeley, CA: Counterpoint, 2010), 33.
5. "The Conservation of Nature and the Preservation of Humanity." In *Another Turn of the Crank: Essays* (Washington, DC: Counterpoint, 1995), 68–69.
6. *The Unsettling of America: Culture and Agriculture* (Revised. San Francisco: Sierra Club Books, 1996), 7.

7. *It All Turns on Affection: The Jefferson Lecture and Other Essays* (Berkeley: Counterpoint, 2012), 11.
8. Our argument here has been clarified by conversation with some of Berry's sympathetic critics. For the context of this online discussion, see Jeffrey Bilbro, "Place Isn't Just Geographical," *Front Porch Republic*, May 2013, http://www.frontporchrepublic.com/2013/05/place-isnt-just-geographical/.
9. *Becoming Native to This Place* (Washington, DC: Counterpoint, 1996), 3.
10. "Education for Homelessness or Homemaking? The Christian College in a Postmodern Culture," *Christian Scholars Review* 32, no. 3 (2003): 281–82. Mark Mitchell describes the problem in similar terms: "liberal education too often amounts to little more than an overpriced means of creating cosmopolitans of the worst sort: people who have little interest in or concern for local communities, customs, stories, or places," *The Politics of Gratitude: Scale, Place & Community in a Global Age* (Dulles, VA: Potomac Books, 2012), 173.
11. Berry, "Higher Education and Home Defense," in *Home Economics: Fourteen Essays* (Berkeley, CA: Counterpoint, 1987), 52.
12. Berry, *The Unsettling of America: Culture and Agriculture*, 7. Berry also expands on this line of questioning in his two recent commencement addresses, urging graduates to ask questions about where they are and how they can serve these places. "Bellarmine"; "Major in Homecoming," 34–35.
13. Wendell Berry on His Hopes for Humanity, interview by Bill Moyers, Television, November 29, 2013, http://billmoyers.com/segment/wendell-berry-on-his-hopes-for-humanity/.
14. "Two Economies," in *Home Economics* (New York: North Point, 1987), 54–55.
15. *The Abolition of Man, Or, Reflections on Education with Special Reference to the Teaching of English in the Upper Forms of Schools* (San Francisco: Harper, 2001), 83.
16. Berry, *Jayber Crow: A Novel* (Washington, DC: Counterpoint, 2000), 54.
17. Eric Zencey describes this academic culture well in his essay "Rootless Professers," in *Rooted in the Land: Essays on Community and Place*, ed. William Vitek and Wes Jackson (New Haven, Conn: Yale University Press, 1996), 15–19. While professors may be more stationary now than when this essay was first published in 1986, much of this can be attributed to the terrible academic job market that makes it harder to move up the professional ladder.
18. Mark A Signorelli, "Going Home Again? Not Likely," *Front Porch Republic*, accessed June 1, 2013, http://www.frontporchrepublic.com/2013/03/going-home-again-not-likely/.

19. Jeffrey Polet, "Education and the Way Home," *Front Porch Republic*, accessed June 1, 2013, http://www.frontporchrepublic.com/2012/01/21097/; Conor Dugan, "The Journey Home," *Front Porch Republic*, accessed June 1, 2013, http://www.frontporchrepublic.com/2013/03/the-journey-home/.
20. *Hannah Coulter* (Berkeley: Counterpoint, 2005), 112.
21. "Higher Education and Home Defense," 52.
22. *Intellectual Appetite: A Theological Grammar* (Washington, DC: Catholic University of America Press, 2009), 16.
23. Schreck also notes the broader cultural divisions that Berry sees contributing to the divisions within universities: "[Berry] argues that higher education represents disconnection itself: institutions disconnected from their communities, disciplines disconnected from each other, research disconnected from its consequences, teaching disconnected from emotions or values, and curricula disconnected from possibility. Often the result is that higher education works to disconnect students from home," Jane Margaret Hedahl Schreck, "Wendell Berry's Philosophy of Education: Lessons from Port William" (The University of North Dakota, 2013), http://gradworks.umi.com/35/87/3587458.html, 350.
24. Eric O Jacobsen, *The Space Between: A Christian Engagement with the Built Environment* (Grand Rapids: Baker Academic, 2012), 33–54.
25. Berry, *Unsettling*, 11. Berry expands on his diagnosis throughout *The Unsettling if America*, and his critique centers on these divisions and the unhealthy level of specialization they lead to. As he states, "The disease of the modern character is specialization," 19. See also Alasdair MacIntyre's essay "Politics, Philosophy, and the Common Good" where he claims that "the forms of compartmentalization characteristic of advanced modernity are inimical to the flourishing of local community," *The MacIntyre Reader*, ed. Kelvin Knight (Notre Dame: U of Notre Dame P, 1998), 248.
26. "The Loss of the University," in *Home Economics: Fourteen Essays* (Berkeley, CA: Counterpoint, 1987), 77.
27. Ibid., 82–83.
28. Ibid., 86.
29. Ibid., 82.
30. For a thorough introduction to the Trivium, see Sister Miriam Joseph, *The Trivium: The Liberal Arts of Logic, Grammar, and Rhetoric*, ed. Marguerite McGlinn (Philadelphia: Paul Dry Books, 2002). We have also been influenced by Stratford Caldecott's efforts to "translate" the Trivium in *Beauty in the Word: Rethinking the Foundations of Education* (Angelico Press, 2012).
31. C.S. Lewis traces this development in the meaning of the words "free" and "liberty," *Studies in Words* (Cambridge: Cambridge UP, 1960).

32. William Cronon makes a similar argument in his excellent essay on liberal arts educatio, "'Only Connect...': The Goals of a Liberal Education," *The American Scholar* 67, no. 4 (1998): 79. See also Joseph A. Henderson and David W. Hursh, "Economics and Education for Human Flourishing: Wendell Berry and the Oikonomic Alternative to Neoliberalism," *Educational Studies* 50, no. 2 (March 1, 2014): 167–86, doi:10.1080/00131946.2014.880927.
33. "Thoughts in the Presence of Fear," in *Citizenship Papers* (Washington, DC: Shoemaker & Hoard, 2003), 21.
34. *Conversations with Wendell Berry*, ed. Morris Allen Grubbs, Literary Conversations Series (Jackson: UP of Mississippi, 2007), 11.
35. Morris Allen Grubbs, "A Practical Education: Wendell Berry the Professor," in *Wendell Berry Life and Work*, ed. Jason Peters (Lexington: UP of Kentucky, 2010), 140.
36. "Discipline and Hope," in *A Continuous Harmony: Essays Cultural and Agricultural* (San Diego: Harcourt Brace & Co, 1972), 164.
37. "Two Economies," in *Home Economics* (New York: North Point P, 1987), 54–56.
38. Herman Daly compares these two contrasting economies to Aristotle's *oikonomia* and *chrematistics*, "Forward," in *What Matters?: Economics for a Renewed Commonwealth*, by Wendell Berry (Berkeley, CA: Counterpoint, 2010), x. See also Henderson and Hursh, 180–82.
39. *Imagining the Kingdom: How Worship Works*, Cultural Liturgies (Grand Rapids: Baker Books, 2013), 4.
40. "Think Little," in *A Continuous Harmony: Essays Cultural and Agricultural* (San Diego: Harcourt Brace & Co, 1972), 84. See also his essay "The Reactor and the Garden," in *The Gift of Good Land: Further Essays Cultural and Agricultural* (Berkeley: Counterpoint, 2009), 161–70.
41. See Berry, *Hannah Coulter*, 112.

CHAPTER 5

Liberal Learning and Christian Practical Wisdom

Mark Schwehn

For my morning devotions, I use the Benedictine prayer book called *The Work of God*.[1] The order for Monday morning prayer (Week II) includes the following reading from the Book of Sirach, a piece of Wisdom literature decreed by both the Orthodox and the Roman Catholic churches to be canonical and included by most Protestant churches as part of the Apocrypha. The reading is as follows:

> My child, from your youth choose discipline,
>
> and when you have gray hair, you will still find
>
> wisdom.
>
> Come to her like one who plows and sows,

Some of the ideas in this essay are adapted from Mark R. Schwehn, "Embracing Wisdom," in John Steven Paul and James Old, eds., *For the Whole of Creation: Christianity and Scholarship in the Public Square, the Guild, and the Church* (Valparaiso, IN: Valparaiso University Press, 2010), 117–28.

M. Schwehn (✉)
Valparaiso University, Valparaiso, IN, USA

T.L. Scales and J.L. Howell (eds.), *Christian Faith and University Life*,
DOI 10.1007/978-3-319-61744-2_5

and wait for her good harvest.
For when you cultivate her you will toil but little,
and soon you will eat of her produce.
She seems very harsh to the undisciplined;
Fools cannot remain with her.
Come to her with all your soul,
and keep her ways with all your might.
Search out and seek, and she will become known to you;
and when you get hold of her, do not let her go.
For at last you will find the rest she gives,
and she will be changed into joy for you. (*Sirach* 6:25–8)

Many, probably most, academicians today, even if they were to agree with the representation of wisdom in this passage, would object to the idea that the quest for wisdom is the proper business, much less the primary business, of a college or a university. In the declining number of universities where there remains a robust sense of common purpose, faculties would be more likely to describe their collective project as the pursuit of specialized knowledge, or the advancement of science, or service to society through scholarship, teaching, and professional formation. Wisdom would seem to most of them an ambition that is too exalted and vague at best and too archaic at worst, an old-fashioned piety that smacks too much of morality or religion or both.

This supposed linkage between religion and the quest for wisdom led David Ford, the Regius Professor of Divinity at Cambridge University, to worry in a 2003 lecture over the future of his university. Ford was speaking from the vantage point provided by his three-year term of service on Cambridge University's Personal Promotions Committee, which required him to read all of the papers submitted about every candidate put forward for a personal professorship or readership by every faculty and department of Cambridge. The worries that arose from his experience and his reflections upon it were neither borne of nostalgic longing for a lost age of Christian orthodoxy nor of a hankering for the return of the earlier restriction of admission to Cambridge to those of the Anglican faith. On the contrary, Ford noted with approval the fact that Cambridge had needed to reinvent itself at least five times during its eight hundred years, and he insisted that it surely would and should do so again in the near future.

Ford's worries instead stemmed from his own conclusion that Cambridge's challenges involved the sustenance and reinvention of the collegiate system, the improvement of teaching, interdisciplinarity, transgenerational responsibility, and the inseparability of questions of knowledge from questions of meaning and value, a series of challenges best summed up, or so he thought, as a renewed quest for wisdom, a quest that had to be guided, in his judgment, by the great traditions of wisdom, both secular and religious. Just three years before Ford spoke, however, the Regents of Cambridge had adopted a statement of core values that made one striking and unfortunate omission. Though the statement mentioned the importance of "sport, music, drama, the visual arts, and other cultural activities," it failed to mention religion. And so it seemed to Ford that, just at the moment that the university most needed the wisdom of *multiple* traditions of thought and practice, it had mysteriously and arbitrarily cut itself off from several of the oldest and richest of them.

In closing his address, Ford drew from another Biblical image of wisdom that shares with the image in the book of *Sirach* its feminine character, though the figure in the *Song of Songs* is much more elaborately and sensually drawn. In the midst of this description the poet exclaims, addressing wisdom, "Your neck is like an ivory tower" (7:4). Ford wondered what the university would be like if it were to seriously and purposefully anchor its aspirations in such imagery, if today's ivory tower really were a vital part of wisdom.[2]

Ford was, in my judgment, largely correct both in his assessments of the major challenges faced by Cambridge University at the beginning of the twenty-first century and in his suggestion that the best route to meeting some of them, such as the improvement of teaching and the reconnection of knowledge to both value and meaning, was a recovery of the search for wisdom. He was correct as well in arguing that any such search would necessarily require renewed attention to religion. Had Ford been addressing Christian academics primarily, as I will be in this essay, he might also have written that a certain kind of wisdom rooted within a particular religious tradition, Christian *practical* wisdom, may hold out the prospect of reintegrating curricula that have splintered into disconnected fragments, at least on a conceptual level, and of reinvigorating teaching across all of the disciplines. In sum, *all* academics need renewed attention to the wisdom within various religious traditions; Christian academics need renewed attention to the cultivation of Christian practical wisdom as an educational ideal.

The Search for Wisdom

What warrants might Christians in the ivory tower have for construing their enterprises as quests for wisdom? There are at least three: our titles and degrees; our spiritual/geographical location; and our vocations. Most academicians bear the degree Ph.D., with all the rights privileges, and honors thereunto appertaining—and the duties and responsibilities as well. Doctor of philosophy means literally that we are, or should be, lovers of wisdom, for this degree long antedated the period when philosophy became just another one among many academic specialties. Instead, philosophy then meant the passionate pursuit of the truth of matters high and low, human and divine, natural and cultural, and it surely entailed a search into the nature of things, into the meaning of the whole. Unless and until we are prepared to regard the titles we bear and the gowns we wear as merely the quaint reminders of a time far away and long ago, we should strive to live as best we can in vital communion with the tradition that gave rise to those titles and vestments. We should strive, even in the midst of our specialties, as well as within the larger community of which those specialties are a part, for wisdom.

Our second warrant comes to us by virtue of our spiritual/geographical location at the intersection of the ways to and from Athens and Jerusalem. If Socrates were here, of course, he would long since have invited us to wonder whether wisdom *can* be taught before we inquired into whether it *should* be. And he would, as well, have insisted that we cannot know whether wisdom can be taught unless and until we know what wisdom is. Rather than seeking to define it, we should for now simply note that most Christian academics inhabit at least two wisdom traditions, the one that began with the ancient Greeks and the other that began with the ancient Hebrews. These two are distinct, they sometimes conflict, and at best they stand in creative tension with one another. In our present-day academy, we all of course encounter many other living traditions, not only Athens and Jerusalem but also Benares, Shanghai, Tehran, and Istanbul, to name a few.

In the introductory chapter of his book *The Beginning of Wisdom*, Leon Kass draws the distinction between Athens and Jerusalem very sharply.[3] According to Kass, Athens grounds wisdom in the powers of human reason, whereas Jerusalem grounds wisdom in the fear of God and in awe and reverence in God's presence. For Athens, the eye is the primary sense organ of wisdom; for Jerusalem, the ear is primary—first, to hearken to God's commands, later to hear the good news of the Gospel. "For faith cometh by hearing, and hearing by the Word of God," Luther once said. And what Luther said of faith would also apply to wisdom, especially if we think of the inner ear that hearkens to the words on a page.

We could, of course, multiply and refine these distinctions. Instead of doing so at present, however, I should like to make only two brief observations about the place of wisdom within the various discourses of the academy today. First, over the course of the last quarter century, wisdom has become a subject of research among several of our colleagues in the social sciences, especially among psychologists and educationalists. Though this research is far from conclusive, marked, as you would expect, by fierce debate among scholars in the USA and Europe, some degree of broad agreement has emerged. Wisdom, most contemporary social scientists think, involves not only cognitive but also affective and moral dimensions of human life. Though this will not come as news to those who have studied wisdom through engagement with classic texts, we should, I think, resist the temptation to be condescending or dismissive toward colleagues here and abroad who are now seeking to measure wisdom, and even to test for it. After all, this kind of research, dressed up in footnotes, mired in controversy over research methods, and featuring the development of intricate machinery for empirical testing, is that sort of thing that is more likely to put wisdom on the explicit agenda of the academy at large than invocations of Aristotle or Aquinas. We should welcome allies wherever we can find them.

And second, however conflicting the Athens and Jerusalem traditions of wisdom might be, they are both equally opposed, though for different reasons, to the comparatively narrow tradition of instrumental rationality that governs and informs so much of higher learning today. This latter and relatively new tradition of human thought is often indifferent, if not hostile, to the quest for wisdom, being suspicious of inquiry into the nature of things. Worse still, and this is a development that is peculiar to our own time, many professionals who are guided exclusively by this tradition of modern instrumental rationality threaten to make human beings over into the very flat and soulless creatures that their sciences imagine them to be. Here is how a seasoned observer puts the matter:

> Today, our view of genuine reality is increasingly clouded by professionals whose technical expertise often introduces a superficial and soulless model of the person that denies moral significance. Perhaps the most devastating example for human values is the process of medicalization through which ordinary unhappiness and normal bereavement have been transformed into clinical depression, existential angst turned into anxiety disorders, and the moral consequences of political violence recast as post-traumatic stress disorder. That is, suffering is redefined as mental illness and treated by professional experts, typically with medication. I believe that this diminishes the person, thins out and homogenizes the deeply rich diversity of human experience, and puts us in danger of being made over into something new and frightening: individuals who can channel all of our desires into products available for our consumption, such as pharmaceuticals, but who no longer live with a soul: a deep mixture of often contradictory emotions and values whose untidy uniqueness defines the existential core of the individual as a human being. When this happens, the furnishings of our interior are no longer the same, we are not the same people our grandparents were, and our children will not be the kind of people we are. [4]

In brief, the search for wisdom today is by no means merely academic, so to speak, if it ever was. The stakes of inquiry are very high, and participants in that inquiry should be very broadly inclusive.

We come finally to the third possible warrant for Christian academics to seek wisdom in our common work, namely, our sense of vocation. Though the Christian tradition includes a variety of accounts of a vocation or a calling, one of the richest and most pertinent for our purposes here comes from Dietrich Bonhoeffer's *Ethics*.[5] Writing in the midst of a threat to humanity even graver and more urgent than those we face today, Bonhoeffer insisted that we Christians have but one call, the call to follow Jesus unconditionally. From our vantage point, this call becomes our responsibility exercised through, and limited to some extent by, our socially defined work, but extending always to a care for the whole of creation. Bonhoeffer dwells for some time on those comparatively rare cases where we must, in order to heed the call of Christ, go beyond or break through the narrower specifications of our professions to exercise our responsibility for the whole. He uses the example of the doctor who, he says, will carry out her vocation for the most part at the bedsides of patients in her care. But she and all Christian physicians must, Bonhoeffer insists, be ready at times to stand up for medicine itself, for the science behind it, and for public health, even if this means putting the narrower understanding of professional responsibility at risk.

Just so with us. We will and we should spend most of our time working within the narrower domains of our specialties and sub-specialties. But we must, especially in these times, be ready to stand up for the good of both our disciplines and of the larger field of higher learning of which those disciplines are parts in order to secure a collective search for wisdom. In doing so, we must be ready, even eager, to join hearts, hands, and minds with others who may not share our religious convictions, but who do share our longing for wisdom and truth and our love for fundamental and enduring questions about the shape and meaning of our lives and destinies. The man whom I quoted above about the perilous condition of our times happens to be a secularized Jew who was serving, at the time he wrote his book *What Really Matters*, as the Chair of Anthropology at Harvard. The book explores, through a series of marvelous biographical sketches, what it means to live a moral life among uncertainty and danger.

Too often, those of us who, like me, are prone to despair over the present condition of the academy in general, or over the condition of a particular academic discipline, ignore the self-corrective powers of the academy at its best. The great questions are irrepressible, as is the longing for wisdom. When one department or guild or discipline abandons altogether concern for fundamental questions in favor of merely technical or fashionable or lucrative and trivial pursuits, some other departments, or groups of scholars, or individuals like Arthur Kleinman take up these questions with renewed vigor and fresh formulations. As I have written elsewhere, the great divide within higher education today is not between the secular academy and the church-related academy. It is instead between those who remember and cherish those traditions of wisdom that justify the university at its best and those who have forgotten or who willfully ignore them.

Practical Wisdom

Examining, through the lens of Christian vocation, the attainment of wisdom as the primary aim of education should direct our attention to *practical* wisdom or *phronesis*, which is concerned with action, more than *sophia*, which is concerned with understanding the nature of things, especially the highest eternal truths, and their relation to the whole. Vocation on one side is concerned with self-knowledge and identity to be sure, especially with baptismal identity and our being received into Christian community as children of God. But vocation is also concerned with action, with what we do in the world. Practical wisdom includes good deliberation leading to good judgment, the ability to choose to do the right thing at the right time in the right way for the right reason. And practical wisdom is formed in our bodies and our feelings as much as it is in our minds. The authors of a recent book on Christian practical wisdom define *phronesis* this way:

> *Phronesis* ... denotes a kind of knowing that is morally attuned, rooted in a tradition that affirms the good, and driven toward aims that seek the good. It is not a package of pre-planned rules but stays open and adaptive to new situations. It is nimble and at times even self-critical. Most of all, this knowledge is practical, grounded in ordinary experience, and learned over time in the company of others and for the sake of others.[6]

If we think that the cultivation of such practical wisdom ought to be the primary aim of a college of university education, what is to be done? Some Christian colleges and universities have organized an entire course of study around the virtue of practical wisdom. Gordon College's honors program, "The Jerusalem and Athens Forum," was founded in 2003 with a curriculum designed in part to cultivate within students the virtue of practical wisdom. One of its founders, Professor Thomas Albert (Tal) Howard, used St. Thomas Aquinas's definitions of the various parts of the virtue of practical wisdom to think about the functions of various courses. Aquinas had defined eight constituent parts of prudence, which Howard and his colleagues in turn related to the content and purposes of various courses. Aquinas had defined the eight elements of prudence, summarized by Professor Howard, as follows:

- Intelligence (*intelligentia)*, a correct understanding of first principles;
- Shrewdness and quick-wittedness (*solertia*), the ability to size up a matter quickly;
- Discursive reasoning (*ratio*), the ability to consider and compare alternative possibilities;
- Foresight (*providential*), the capacity to estimate whether a particular action will lead to the realization of a goal;
- Circumspection (*circumspection*), the ability to take relevant circumstances into account;
- Precaution (*caution*), the ability to mitigate risks and avoid foolish outcomes;
- Teachableness (*docilitas*), a disposition of mind that seeks out and recognizes reliable authorities;
- Accurate memory (*memoria*), the ability to remember what is true to the reality of the past.[7]

Even a cursory examination of this list will show both the capaciousness of the virtue of prudence or practical wisdom and the obvious relationships between its constituent elements and the primary purposes of various college and university courses. History courses, for example, would surely have as one of their primary aims the cultivation of *memoria*. Construing many parts of liberal arts curricula as contributing together to form prudent students can provide renewed meaning and overall purpose to courses of study that have lost a sense of common mission. Such renewal would, of course, include the reconsideration and reform of course syllabi so as to bring them into an explicitly articulated integral relationship with one another.

Although curricular innovations such as those at Gordon College are very important, such large-scale reformations are very difficult to achieve, and grand schemes are meaningless unless the kind of teaching and learning that goes on arises from a collective sense that practical wisdom is all important. If we are serious about seeking to cultivate practical wisdom in our students as a primary aim of a college education, we must above all else reform our pedagogy. The cultivation of practical wisdom should be undertaken classroom by classroom through the kind of assignments that are given, the kind of assessments that are done, and the kind of questions that are explored. The syllabus and its life in the classroom should be the primary locations for renewal.

In other words, the cultivation of practical wisdom will be contextual and circumstantial, dependent upon what is being taught to whom at what stage of a college education. Only specific examples, not general pronouncements or exhortations, might prove instructive here. Consider the following excerpts, the first and last paragraphs, from a student paper that I received last term:

> Families are nowhere near perfect. Arguments arise between siblings over whose turn it is to unload the dishwasher. Parents fight about unpaid bills and forgetting to put the wet clothes in the dryer. Children yell at parents for being unfairly punished. The routine goes on and on, these scenarios never avoided no matter how hard one may try. Forgiveness is the one thing that families can rely on to overcome disagreements in most cases. Yet many individuals struggle with forgiveness, because although it may be easy to forgive, it is quite hard to forget. It's hard to forget the unkind, dehumanizing, cold words often said, as they pierce the heart and rip all self-confidence away. It's hard to forget the abandonment felt from a father when the answer to his question was not what he wanted to hear. It's hard to forget the sinking lonesome feeling of being distant with a father when there is really no good reason as to why there is something holding him back. Both Cordelia and Edgar were wronged by their fathers in Shakespeare's *King Lear*, just like I was wronged by my mother growing up. Looking back at my reaction to these transgressions, I wish I had handled things the way Cordelia did, graciously, rather than how Edgar did. By studying and examining these two characters, the proper way to forgive and forget an injustice committed by a parent can be determined, and changes can be made within oneself to truly make amends for past repressions.

> Examining both of these characters gives me hope for the future with my mother. Despite Edgar's disguise being an unhealthy way to cope with injustice, he does incorporate gentleness, kindness, and grace in order to make things right with his father. Because I did change myself to please my mother, as Edgar did, I can only hope that there will be an opportunity to sit down and find the same grace, kindness, and gentleness with her. However, reaching this forgiveness should not be based on disguises. Instead, I hope to remove resentment and anger that occasionally occupy my thoughts, and fill my thoughts with forgiveness and grace. This way, I no longer have to live with self-confidence issues, fear, and emotions. I wish to adopt the characteristics of Cordelia, relentlessly loving my mom even though she may hurt me again, and trusting that everything will be

> okay as long as I remain kind. Nothing can stop me. For future scenarios I plan to remove my disguise and do just as Cordelia did. For now, I need to let forgiveness and grace take over. One day I will see that adopting characteristics of Cordelia was all worth it.

The paper was written by a junior in a class I taught in Christ College, the honors college of Valparaiso University. Notice that the student was able to review and reevaluate an important broken relationship in her life in conversation with a great text, Shakespeare's *King Lear*, at the same time that she was able to interpret aspects of *King Lear*, especially the use of disguise in an effort to please those from whom we are estranged, in view of her real-life experiences. Reading enriched life as life enriched reading. And all of this dialectical inquiry led to a deliberation over what to do in the future to mend the relationship that had been broken.

Inviting students to think and write in a manner similar to the way this student managed to do in the paper she wrote, required me to amend slightly my own assignments, my own discussion questions for class consideration, and my own statement of overall objectives for the course. Instead of restricting inquiry to textual analysis and interpretation and the thematic connections among the several assigned texts, I broadened the inquiry to consider how the imaginative strategies used by the writers of the texts might be deployed in the lives of the students themselves to comprehend or to remedy broken situations. I had always asked questions like, "How does Norman Maclean order the complicated story of *Young Men and Fire* so as to provide consolation for himself and his readers?" Or, "Why is it so important to Maclean that he be able actually to *find* a story in Mann Gulch instead of simply *inventing* one or *imposing* one upon the materials he has discovered?" But I now added discussion or examination questions like the following: "How do Maclean's intricate and extended imaginative efforts to come to terms with a 'natural catastrophe' strengthen your resourcefulness in coming to terms with natural catastrophes in your own life, including disease and death?"

These amendments were not revolutionary. On the contrary, they simply invited students to discover how critical reflection upon their lives could make them better readers and how becoming better readers could in turn enable them to make better choices. These invitations were *not* an effort to make texts "relevant" in some kind of simple and straightforward way. Rather, course materials and assignments were designed to enlarge and strengthen the students' imaginations so that they could in turn be more imaginative in their efforts to remedy wrongs, mend broken relationships, or otherwise advance human flourishing. My reforms, in other words, were more like adjusting the course of the Queen Mary ocean liner by one degree at the beginning of a journey of 2000 miles. Small course alterations (pun intended) at the beginning can yield very different destinations at the conclusion of a journey.

I had been, over the course of my teaching career, influenced by two very different but overlapping accounts of the purpose of liberal arts study as follows:

> The liberal arts cultivate those skills and arts of interpretation, analysis, and criticism that enable students to understand a variety of texts, including the book of nature and social actions.

> The liberal arts initiate students into great conversations about fundamental matters of human concern. Such initiation includes the reading of great books that contain "the best that human beings have thought and said," the practice of productive conversation, and the cultivation of habits of attention both to the texts and to others collectively engaged in an effort to comprehend them.

Since I myself have been trained in history and literature, my working understanding of the purpose of liberal education has been and still remains very "text centered." The first account of liberal education above informed the Humanities Division Common Core course at the University of Chicago. The pedagogy involved very "close reading" of a very few texts with no attention either to context or to the life situations of the readers. The course, in my experience, accomplished very well what it set out to do precisely because its objectives were clear, reasonable, and appropriate for *beginning* students.

The second account of the purpose of a liberal education informs or once informed the common core courses at places like Columbia and Harvard. By contrast to Chicago's core, the pedagogy in these courses featured many texts in conversation with one another, not considered in isolation as self-contained objects of analysis and interpretation. But like the first account, the second one makes no effort to connect what is being read to the lived experience of the readers. Also, like the first account, the second one requires that classroom discussion is to be preferred to lectures as the primary mode of learning.

I have at long last, largely because I have come increasingly to see the importance of practical wisdom as an educational objective, come to yet a third working account of the purposes of a liberal education, one that incorporates aspects of the first two as follows:

> The liberal arts, through their various practices, cultivate within students the virtue of practical wisdom first by enlarging the variety of their experiences, second by inviting appropriation of those experiences through multiple forms of disciplined reflection upon them, and third by enlarging and strengthening the imagination so as to instill habits of flexible and creative responsiveness to the world in order to advance human flourishing within it.

This account of the purpose of the liberal arts did not require me radically to change my classroom teaching at all. Instead, it impelled me to reframe much of what I had been doing and to amend slightly but significantly what I hoped to accomplish through the kind of disciplined reflection I had for years been fostering. In other words, the sample paper I have shared above could not and would not have been written in my own classes that included a study of *King Lear* until this last semester.[8]

Practicing for Practical Wisdom

What other implications might there be for our thought and practice if we come to think that the proper understanding of our vocations as Christian teacher/scholars impels us to comprehend our work within the academy as seeking wisdom? I have already addressed our need to become more responsible academic citizens, caring for the good of the whole, and our pedagogical challenge to formulate our study questions, our writing assignments, and our examinations in a way that invites our students to move back and forth between the materials they are studying and the experiences in their own lives that they are struggling to understand and sometimes to resolve. Let me now mention three more practices that I think are essential if we seek wisdom for ourselves and seek to cultivate it in others.

First and last, worship—both private, daily devotions and regular attendance at a local parish or the college's or university's chapel. Though we may stand at the intersection of Athens and Jerusalem—and Benares and Beijing and Rio and Nairobi and Tehran—we must incline finally toward Jerusalem and the heavenly city, a place not of this earth.

And if we think that wisdom begins in the fear, love, and trust of God, we should know that those spiritual virtues have their home and their sustenance in the church through liturgy and the practice of corporate worship.

A second practice that we must undertake is to maintain breadth of vision, even at the same time as we narrow the focus of our scholarship. Individual Christian scholars will each have favorite ways of doing this, of keeping up with the larger conversation of the academy with itself and its publics. I myself try to read both *Books and Culture* and the *New York Review of Books* from covers to covers. I regard this exercise less and less as a matter of achieving breadth of vision and more and more as a way of finding friends on the way to wisdom, people like Arthur Kleinman, for example. And of course the quest for wisdom must be a communal undertaking before it can become an individual aspiration.

Third and finally, I think we must learn first to discern and then to encourage and strengthen those students who already show signs of wisdom. It should come as no surprise, though it did come as something of a surprise to some of the aforementioned social scientists, that wisdom is not directly correlated with intelligence of the sort that can be measured on IQ tests and that often shows itself in the preparation of clever, sometimes even brilliant, papers within a given specialty. Many of us tend, I think, to gravitate more to the bright students than to the wise ones. And I think we must learn to correct this tendency to some extent. I suggest we do so by broadening the range of students who habitually engage our extra attention and care and by resisting the temptation to lavish excessive attention upon those who show the greatest promise as future practitioners of our own favored disciplines.

These recommendations of attention to academic citizenship, pedagogical innovation, worship, intellectual friendship, and formation are sometimes bundled together at both secular and church-related colleges and universities today under the rubric of "educating the whole person." Though this formulation arose initially under Jesuit provenance, it has since been adopted by student service people and others all over the country, most of whom have no conception of the rich tradition of thought and practice that gave rise to it. The *point* of "educating the whole person" has been lost upon many, and its anchorage in the Christian tradition has been largely forgotten, leaving only a somewhat anemic, trendy, and vaguely therapeutic vocabulary where there was once spiritually robust understanding. Intercollegiate athletics, yoga, and wellness courses are, as a result, claimed by many to be equally important to a college education as the study of mathematics, history, or a foreign language. Are we not better advised to speak in the vocabulary of wisdom, thereby reminding ourselves always of the purpose of our common endeavors? And does not that vocabulary best capture what we and those communities of learning that we serve might be at our best?

Everlasting Joy

In bringing this inquiry to a close, let me admit that I chose this title, "Embracing Wisdom" to imply a partial critique of the book of *Sirach*'s meditation upon wisdom, one that has implications for how we might finally understand our own vocation as lovers of, and seekers after, wisdom. Whereas there are, as I have indicated, many virtues and advantages in representing wisdom by the figure of a woman, there are some disadvantages as well. These disadvantages are more obvious, perhaps, in the book of *Sirach* than they are in the *Song of Songs*. Notice that, in the passage I quoted at the outset of this essay, readers are exhorted to "search out and seek" wisdom, "and when you get hold of her do not let her go." This is the language of masculine conquest softened only by the final line, "For at last you will find the rest she gives, and she will be turned into joy for you."

The vocabulary of seizure and possession should apply to wisdom if and only if the movement between wisdom and those who seek her is reciprocal. I therefore chose a title for this essay that is a *double entendre*, which on the one hand describes wisdom as the one who does the embracing and on the other hand describes the activity of those who seek her. We must and do believe that the one who is wisdom seeks out and embraces us before we seek to embrace wisdom. As Kierkegaard put it in *Training in Christianity*, "For it is not as though we must hold fast to Christ; rather, it is Christ who holds us fast, now and even forevermore." This embrace is the very embrace that is both the beginning and the end of all of our seeking and finding, and it is the embrace that gives us the freedom to pursue our inquiries, our own various quests for truth, with a wild abandon—knowing that we are held fast, even as we strive to possess the truth that possesses us.

What happens, we might wonder, if and when we come into full possession of that wisdom we love and seek? Does our love of wisdom cease once our desire for it has been fully satisfied, once we live wholly and completely in the presence of God? Such a thing cannot happen in this world, of course. Even so, the book of *Sirach* teaches truly here when it says of wisdom, "For at last you will find the rest she gives, for she will be changed into joy for you." (*Sirach* 6:28). This is just right. You find what you have first been given. And when you find it at last, your longing for knowledge and truth will then be met by a good appropriate to that longing. Such a culmination can only give way to a delight in the perfect marriage between desire and its object, even as restlessness gives way to rest. And so it is, and so it must be, that at the last embrace, wisdom will indeed "be changed into joy for you."

When you are fully and completely at work in your callings as seekers of wisdom, you will sense intimations of this everlasting joy, foretastes of the feast to come, as it were. In the midst of those small transactions of everyday life, you really will, from time to time, figure something out, discover some part of the truth about the world, catch a fragment of the logos, and see the flicker of light in the darkness. And when this happens, you will have an evanescent sense of the deep joy that can be fully known only in eternity.

Notes

1. Judith Sutera, *The Work of God: Benedictine Prayer* (Collegeville, MN: Liturgical Press, 1997).
2. David Ford, "Knowledge, Meaning, and the World's Great Challenges: Reinventing Cambridge University in the Twenty-first Century," *Studies in Christian Ethics* Vol. 17, no. 1 (2004): 22–37.
3. Leon R. Kass, *The Beginning of Wisdom* (New York: Free Press/Simon & Shuster, 2003), 17.
4. Arthur Kleinman, *What Really Matters: Living a Moral Life Amidst Uncertainty and Danger* (New York: Oxford University Press, 2006), 9–10.
5. Dietrich Bonhoeffer, "The Place of Responsibility," in Mark R. Schwehn and Dorothy C. Bass, eds., *Leading Lives that Matter: What We Should Do and Who We Should Be* (Grand Rapids: Eerdmans, 2006), 107–11. Also see *Ethics* in *Dietrich Bonhoeffer Works,* Vol. 6 (Minneapolis, MN: Augsburg Fortress Publishers, 2004), 289–97.

6. Dorothy C. Bass, et al, *Christian Practical Wisdom: What It Is, Why It Matters* (Grand Rapids, MI: Eerdmans, 2016), 5. This book was written in a deeply collaborative way by five Catholic and Protestant scholars working together for several years. The introduction and conclusion are excellent resources for college and university teachers who think of the cultivation of practical wisdom as among their primary pedagogical objectives. The book does not itself consider, as I do in this present essay, the implications for university teaching of what they describe and commend; however, my own discussion of this matter is indebted to their work.
7. Thomas Albert Howard, "Seeing with All Three Eyes: The Virtue of Prudence and Undergraduate Education," in David S. Cunningham, ed., *At This Time and In This Place: Vocation and Higher Education* (New York: Oxford University Press, 2016), 225. Howard Provides a detailed description of the "Jerusalem and Athens Forum" and some of his own courses on pp. 226ff.
8. For another recent and complementary account of the relationship between liberal education and practical wisdom, see William M. Sullivan, *Liberal Learning as a Quest for Purpose*, especially Chapter III, "The Examined Life: Reflection and Practical Wisdom" (New York: Oxford University Press, 2016), 67–90.

PART II

Faithful Teachers and Pedagogical Practices

CHAPTER 6

Ever Ancient, Ever New: Reading to Become Wise

Matthew A. Rothaus Moser

Educating for Wisdom

I teach a number of theology courses for my university's core curriculum, and I'm constantly under pressure to justify that curriculum to my students. As anyone who has taught core classes will know, many students see these courses as impediments or distractions from what should be the main focus of their attention: their selected major area of study leading to a (hopefully lucrative) career following graduation. But is this careerist focus really the purpose of the university, of education? Despite the necessity and the importance of such pragmatic goals for education, the reduction of learning to its professional utility misses out on the humane and sapiential vocation of education. We read, we study, we learn, not to become employable, but to become wise.

But wisdom often gets overlooked in the fast-paced, competitive, careerist educational market. An education concerned exclusively with pragmatics might be excellent at producing *workers*, but it is noticeably

M.A. Rothaus Moser (✉)
Loyola University Maryland, Baltimore, MD, USA

T.L. Scales and J.L. Howell (eds.), *Christian Faith and University Life*,
DOI 10.1007/978-3-319-61744-2_6

incompetent when it comes to producing free and wise human beings. When bound to the demands of the economy, the market, and the bottom-line, the liberal arts cease being truly liberal. The great temptation of the university today is to capitulate to a utilitarian culture that would commodify knowledge and market itself as an educational strip-mall offering the best deals to its customers, the students. It is a temptation to reduce education to the transmission of information for the sake of preparing future professionals for the job market. Any form of knowledge that is not immediately useful to that end we look at askance, as a distraction from more relevant pursuits. T.S. Eliot laments just this tendency in his poem "The Rock:"

> The endless cycle of idea and action,
> Endless invention, endless experiment,
> Brings knowledge of motion, but not of stillness;
> Knowledge of speech, but not of silence;
> Knowledge of words, and ignorance of the Word.
> All our knowledge brings us nearer to death,
> But nearness to death no nearer to God.
> Where is the Life we have lost in living?
> Where is the wisdom we have lost in knowledge?
> Where is the knowledge we have lost in information?
> The cycles of heaven in twenty centuries
> Brings us farther from God and nearer to the Dust.[1]

Eliot paints a bleak picture, to be sure. Education apart from wisdom leaves us morally and spiritually bankrupt, even if informationally and technologically advantaged. Hans Urs von Balthasar calls this *titanic* knowledge—a form of knowledge that strives to conquer all things, and to overcome all boundaries by means of a dominating form of knowledge. This is knowledge that refuses to recognize boundaries, that wants to know for the sake of one's own benefit, as intellectual self-aggrandizement. St. Augustine calls this form of knowledge *curiositas* or the "concupiscence of the eyes."[2] René Descartes, writing at the advent of modernity, claimed that through the exercise of technical knowledge (*technē*), humans might become the "masters and possessors of nature"—a claim dripping with the kind of technocratic ambitions (and spiritual bankruptcy) that Eliot fears.[3] In this kind of world, wisdom is displaced by utilitarian knowledge. Balthasar fears "[t]he result will be a world… in which everything is viewed solely in terms of power or profit-margin, in which everything that is disinterested and gratuitous and use-less is despised, persecuted, and wiped out, and even art is forced to wear the mask and features of technique."[4]

Though perhaps overstated, I think Balthasar identifies real danger to which the university is increasingly prone. Part of this problem lies in the rapid deformation of the university from a place of learning to a business driven by the consumerist preoccupation with the bottom-line. The corporate structure of the university often works *against* the art of teaching and learning for the sake of wisdom—an art that is notoriously inefficient and resistant to universally applied "best practices."[5] I think many of our students have been formed to think of their education in these strictly utilitarian ways. They have inherited a careerist mentality aimed at acquiring useful information that resists the slow, difficult work of becoming wise.

How do professors resist this impulse and reform our students' approach to learning? How can we be stewards, not just of information but also of wisdom? What follows in this essay might best be understood as a strategy of pedagogical resistance to the careerist and utilitarian encroachment on the classroom. It is a way of reclaiming the classroom as a workshop for wisdom.

Malformative Reading

I'd like to suggest that this moral and spiritual bankruptcy manifests itself in the way that we have been formed to read by our contempo-rary educational system. Academics seem especially prone to reading and teaching books with a concern for objective fidelity: are we accurately understanding and representing the text in itself, as an object of study? I have often found myself giving my students the impression that the proper way to read old theological books is by asking narrowly defined historical questions about them: who wrote this and why? What did the text mean when he or she wrote it? Once we address *those* questions in class, we move on to the next book. This way of reading can easily succumb to treating books like dead specimens. Like cadavers, we know and comprehend by dissecting books down to their component parts.

I've since come to realize I have unintentionally reinforced the idea that we exhaust the value of a book once we address its objective meaning. As I taught my students to dissect the text at hand, I had implicitly taught them to see the text as a dead specimen; only dead things are fit for dissection, after all. I had formed in my students the mindset that theological education consists in scratching title after title off our reading list until we are able to impress (or bore) our family and friends with a sea of knowledge about old, esoteric books that few people read and fewer care about. We read the text as something dead, as *closed* and *complete*, and then we stand in judgment over it, assessing it as either good or bad.[6] Reading in this way may yield knowledge *about* a text, but often leaves us without any knowledge of ourselves. Wendell Berry laments the way the contemporary university cultivates "teachers and students [who] read the great songs and stories to learn *about* them, not learn *from* them."[7] While learning about texts is an important aspect of critical reading and thinking, when we neglect learning from texts, that is, when we neglect the living subjectivity of a text, we run the risk of misunderstanding and misrepresenting the book in itself. We also miss an opportunity for personal encounter and transformation. We miss an opportunity to grow in wisdom. The more stringently we read a book as a closed object, the more utilitarian our reading and learning become.

Eugene Peterson identifies two chief, malformative characteristics in the way we read today.[8] Both of these characteristics are antithetical to education to wisdom. These two characteristics of bad reading are "hurry" and "consumption." The two go hand-in-hand; they feed off of each other, and few of us living today are immune to them.[9]

We are busy today. Students are busy; they have so much reading to do and so much homework. They also have many fruitful activities and social commitments that cannibalize their time. This constriction of their time means that students often lack the leisure that good reading requires.[10] And so they hurry: they rush through their reading trying desperately to read *just enough* to get the main point and then move on to their next task. This sense of hurry often results in a consumptive reading style. Our entire reading is driven by the question, what do I need to get out of this text? We all ask this question in different ways.

Students might ask what they need to get out of the text in order to pass a course. Professors might approach the text asking what is most essential in it for them to teach. Regardless of our motivation, these consumptive reading practices distort our relationship with the text in such a way that it becomes a commodity meant to be used as a resource rather than as an invitation to transformative personal encounter.

There are certainly some books that are made to be read consumptively. Textbooks, handbooks, worksheets…these are collections of words meant to be read and digested efficiently. There's nothing wrong with reading these kinds of texts in a consumptive way because that reading style corresponds with the style of writing. But as Peterson warns us, there are other kinds of books out there. Books that are "revelatory and intimate instead of informational and impersonal."[11]

The risk of practices of hurried, consumptive reading is the commodification of the text. This results in what Rowan Williams calls a "pre-mature closure" of both the text and the reader.[12] Commodifying a text signals that we think the text is finished, its meaning self-contained in its pages, and, thus, able to be owned or rejected with the ease of a simple transaction. Likewise, the commodified reader becomes closed-off and self-contained, a completed human specimen, no longer *in* via, no longer growing and developing and transforming, but self-realized and actualized. Williams sees this closed, commodified self as one of the chief temptations of the Christian life that manifests itself in the way that we read and situate ourselves—or fail to situate ourselves—in our reading.[13] Our reading becomes vampiric, sucking the life out of the text for our own sake. Once we have gleaned what we need from the text, we can discard the book. There's no need for it anymore.[14]

We slip into this temptation of pre-mature closure when we privilege books as relevant simply due to their temporal proximity to us as readers.[15] We close off the text as a discrete thing that can be known and thereby controlled as a completed object. We can interrogate the text without letting it interrogate us. We delimit the meaning of the text as a closed object of knowledge as a way of mastering it so that we can use it for our own purposes, whatever they may be. But we end up neutering the text and elevating ourselves as the "masters and possessors" of the text at the same time. This is toxic, not only to reading and learning but also, as Eliot saw, to living as well. The way we read forms—not just *informs*—the way we live.[16]

But then the question becomes even more pressing: how then should we read? Certain texts of the Christian tradition must be met with a different reading style than a consumptive one: not only a slower style but also one that elicits a profoundly different relationship between the reader and the text. Reading is an act of intellectual and spiritual stewardship. I want to suggest that the joint task of stewarding of the texts of the Christian tradition and educating for wisdom involves reconceiving the relationship between text and reader. Part of the task of the stewardship of the Christian tradition is expanding our ways of reading, expanding our understanding of what fidelity to the text means. Many of the classic texts of the Christian tradition are not meant *only* to be read and assessed; they are also meant to be performed. Performing these old tests revivifies them, allowing them to live and speak again. In their performance lies their ongoing relevance. The professor is duly charged with the difficult task of teaching students this peculiar, performative way of reading as an important way of relating to the texts they read. Performance carries us from knowledge about the text toward wisdom, learning from and with the text.

Performative Reading

What does it mean to say that a text should be "performed?" In his essay on hermeneutics, Nicholas Lash reminds us that different texts require different ways of being read. While there are a number of acceptable ways to read a text, some fit the text better than others. Lash gives the example of a map. One might read the map for a number of reasons: to get a sense of the topography of a region; to marvel at the interplay of highways and byways; and so on. But the way of reading the map that best corresponds to the nature and purpose of the map itself is reading it to make your way through the world: we perform the map. We must learn to read, Lash says, in a way that is as "competent and responsible" as we can manage.[17] Lash suggests that certain texts require a performative reading for their proper interpretation.[18]

Lash provides a very helpful framework for teaching the Christian tradition, especially the ancient texts that are so often misunderstood as irrelevant to contemporary students. He reminds us of the experience we undergo after seeing a particularly impressive performance. Lash uses the example of *King Lear*:

> But, at the end of an outstanding performance of King Lear, is it only the play that we feel ourselves newly to have understood? If we say, after the performance, "I'd never seen that before," are we referring only to something which we had never previously said in the text? Or are we also referring to an element of self-discovery which the performance had helped us to achieve? And what is the relationship between these two discoveries? Might it be that, in the performance of a great work of art, a 'classic,' self-discovery and the discovery of fresh meaning in the text converge? Might it be that the "greatness" of a text lies in its inexhaustible capacity to express, to dramatize, fundamental features of the human drama?[19]

The great texts open themselves up in such a way that they become more truly themselves as they are performed anew through the years. Each reader puts his or her new "spin" on the text through the particularity of their performance, but they tell the same story.[20]

The ancient texts of the Christian tradition invite this kind of participative reading. Let me offer three texts that often come up in my own teaching that invite this kind of participative reading. First, Augustine's *Confessions.* Few students in Christian universities will make it through their degrees without confronting this classic and challenging text. Though *Confessions* is often taught as the "first autobiography" and as an intellectual pilgrimage and narrative of conversion—all of which are true—students often miss some of the most provocative aspects of *Confessions* when their interest is primarily observational and factual. Professors who teach *Confessions* often neglect pointing out that Augustine intended *Confessions* to be read aloud.[21] What makes this so significant is that *Confessions* is written in the form of a prayer. When we read the text aloud, we find ourselves praying the text; Augustine's written words become our spoken prayer. Imagine the way the opening lines of *Confessions* transform when we go from reading silently to reading aloud:

> Great are You, O Lord, and greatly to be praised; great is Your power, and of Your wisdom there is no end. And man, being a part of Your creation, desires to praise You, man, who bears about with him his mortality, the witness of his sin, even the witness that You "resist the proud,"— yet man, this part of Your creation, desires to praise You. You move us to delight in praising You; for You have made us for Yourself, and our hearts are restless till they find rest in You. (*Confessions* I.1)

Confessions is the recollection of Augustine's life, communicated in the language and spirit of prayer. My students get this. But then I draw their attention to Augustine's use of "us" and "our" in this opening prayer. We are meant, I tell them, to read this passage aloud. Suddenly it becomes a corporate prayer—*our* prayer. A text that has been analyzed for centuries, whose conceptual richness is well-known and perhaps a bit tired of being subject to so many eyes, is again charged with an existential, personal energy that the student does not expect. Reading *Confessions* aloud becomes an act of confessing, a moment when this ancient text stands forward in all of its immediacy and importance right here, right now.

Another example in this vein is Julian of Norwich's famous collection of mystical visions, *Revelation of Divine Love*.[22] The notable difference between Julian's short text versus her long text is that the language evolves from a private mystical vision to a social and ecclesial one. She switches from "me" language to "our" language. Her vision does not belong to herself but is offered up as a space for us, the readers, to share.

What is especially significant, I tell my students, is that Julian concludes the long version by saying that the vision she has seen has "not yet been performed to my sight" (ch. 86). Commentators on Julian are divided on what exactly she means by this phrase, but I think Frederick Christian Bauerschmidt is right to say that Julian "seeks to *create* readers who will endeavor to perform the drama of divine love scripted from her *Revelation*."[23] *We* are those readers that Julian is striving to create: readers who will perform her text until "all becomes charity." Julian intends that her readers will not study her visions of Christ's face as unmoved spectators, but rather, by sharing her vision—by performing her text—will behold the face of Christ themselves in such a way that they are transformed into images of Christ.

Finally, let me consider one of the most frequently taught texts from the Christian tradition, Dante's *Divine Comedy*. One of the most celebrated poems in the Western canon, Dante's *Comedy* is taught in a variety of settings: high school literature classes, Italian classes, religion classes, and history classes. Rightly celebrated for its brilliant combination of poetry, classical mythology, contemporary politics, and Christian doctrine, the *Comedy* is quite the specimen for students to analyze, deconstruct, and interpret. While the Christian flavor of the *Comedy* is difficult to ignore, the participative dynamic of the poem is easily overlooked, though signaled from the very first line: "Midway through the journey of *our* life, I woke to find myself in a dark wood for the straight-way had been lost" (*Inferno* 1.1–2).

Dante refuses to leave his readers outside the world of the poem. He does this in two chief ways. Most obviously, Dante invokes his reader throughout the poem, never letting us forget that he is self-consciously narrating his journey for his readers. He labors to render his historical particularity transparent to the universal. Or to put it another way, Dante asks his readers to find universal truths *in* the particularities of his poem by *sharing in* his imaginative labor. Dante's Farinata, Francesca, and Beatrice may not mean anything to us today in their historical particularity, but their universal appeal means that we the readers end up particularizing the text in our own way. We supply our own Farinata, Francesca, and Beatrice. Dante's contemporary readers discover the universality of the *Comedy* by applying it to our particular context. This is one of the ways the poem invites its readers to perform the text. As an example of this, I often assign my students one of the realms of Dante's afterlife which they need to rewrite for a twenty-first-century audience. Who from *our* day would populate Dante's Inferno? Purgatory? Paradise? As the students populate their versions of Dante, they are performing the *Comedy* in their own context: they have to understand Dante's account of the nature of sin, of purgation, of divine joy *and* understand their own world and context in light of what they have studied in Dante. Understanding Dante's context yields knowledge, but understanding themselves and their own context yields wisdom.

The second way that Dante brings his readers into his text is by presenting himself as both the protagonist of the poem and a vicarious representation of his readers. His journey is our journey. Dante wrote the *Comedy*, he explains to his patron, so that his readers will share in the protagonist's journey "from misery to happiness." The poet signals this through his use of the word "our" ("*nostra*") in critical moments at both the beginning and the end of the poem. The opening of the poem, quoted above, draws readers into the journey of the pilgrim. At the end, when the pilgrim finally gazes into the face of divine love in the beatific vision, he beholds the mystery of the incarnation. Dante's way of articulating this central Christian teaching—the heart and soul of the Christian tradition—is in an explicitly participative way. He sees the light of the divine Son "stamped with *our* [*nostra*] image." The entire poem is bracketed by this one word, *our*.

Dante draws his readers into the journey from the beginning and does not release us until the very end of the poem, when the literary journey ends and our own journey toward God begins. I had this experience just recently in class. At the end of the poem, as Dante gazes upon the mystery of the incarnation, he endeavors to apprehend its mystery, but is unable. Then, suddenly, he is graced with the understanding that arises within his mystical union with God. But the poem ends abruptly without Dante explaining what he has come to understand. My students are inevitably frustrated by Dante's abrupt retreat into silence. Though I doubt that many of them would want the *Comedy* to be any longer than it already is, they feel unresolved by the ending. The poem's lack of resolution is precisely the point: I ask them, do you want to know what Dante saw? Do you want to understand what Dante understood? Then you need to set off on your *own* pilgrimage. If Dante had told his readers exactly what he had seen in the beatific vision, then he would have done our work for us. Both the text and the human journey to God would be prematurely closed. Like Julian, Dante's poem "is not yet performed as to my sight." Reading the text of the poem is only the first step. We haven't truly read the *Comedy* until we are living it.[24]

Now, I recognize that not every student is able or willing to read texts in this way. Their reluctance may be for a number of reasons. They may be of a different religion from the author or have no religion. They may have significant theological or personal disputes with the author. Professors should not force their students to read these texts, or perform these texts, in a way that violates a student's conscience. Instead of forcing, the professor should *invite* the student to read in such a way.

To avoid forcing performative reading on unwilling students, instructors can look for other motivations apart from grading. This kind of learning is best when it is not being assessed by grading rubrics. Performative reading needs to be taught, but the actual practice of it need not be scholastically assessed. The goal is simply to teach the texts of the Christian tradition in a way that is faithful to the way those texts were written.[25]

Lectio Divina and the Formation of Reading

Let me conclude this essay with a heuristic overture of strategies for inviting students into this kind of performative reading. I believe that any reading-heavy class must take seriously the fact that reading requires formation. Reading is not an intrinsic good, and it is not morally neutral. We can, after all, perform texts poorly. We can perform the wrong texts. Dante gives a great example of the dangers of performative reading through one of his most compelling characters, Francesca (*Inferno* 5). She is damned because of her performative reading. Francesca, so the story goes, was reading the story of a carnal affair between Lancelot and Guinevere in a garden with her husband's brother, Paolo. Charged by the eroticism of the text, Francesca and Paolo fell into each other's arms, kissed each other's forbidden lips, and "that day [they] read no more." Francesca performed the text of the queen's betrayal of Arthur, but as Dante clearly indicates that, despite being an *accurate* performance of the text, it was also a morally bad one. She performed the wrong text in the wrong way.

In contrast, in the garden of Augustine's conversion (*Confessions* VIII), we find an altogether different kind of performance. By this point in the *Confessions,* Augustine has stopped performing the texts of his classical education, he has retired from his profession as a teacher of mendacity, and he has undergone an intellectual conversion to Christianity. His will, however, has remained bound to his impulses and carnal desires. He has not yet performed his intellectual conversion. In this garden, he heard a child chanting *Tolle lege, tolle lege*: take up and read. Augustine picked up his Bible, opened it, and saw what God wanted to say to him: "put on the Lord Jesus Christ and make no provisions for the flesh and its lusts" (Romans 13:14). That day, Augustine also read no more. This act of reading broke Augustine's resistance to God. He found himself performing the very text he read. He put on Christ, rejected his lusts, and made no more provisions for his desires. A saint was born. But all of this came only after Augustine had learned to stop performing other texts; his desire, his affections, and his reading (especially his reading of Scripture) had been transformed. He found that he could suddenly perform the Scriptural story in his life, which is in fact exactly what *Confessions* is.

* * *

So how do we form students to read performatively, but in ways that are ordered to wisdom and holiness? One of the strategies I adopt is inspired by the Christian tradition of *lectio divina*, holy reading. *Lectio divina* is one of the central practices of classical Christian spirituality, developed by the monastics of the late ancient world. Its goal is to draw the entire person—the mind, imagination, emotions, senses, and desires—to a careful mediation on the (biblical) text at hand. By inhabiting the texts according to a fourfold pattern, we are drawn into prayer, contemplation, and praise of God. As Dom Marion famously expressed it, *lectio divina* looks like this:

> *We read*
>
> *Under the eye of God*
>
> *Until the heart is touched and leaps to flame*

Each of the lines of this poem corresponds to the stages of *lectio divina*. The first step is reading, *lectio*; the second is meditation, *meditatio*; the third prayer, *oratio*; the final is contemplation, *contemplatio*. While these practices were developed as forms of the "holy reading" of Scripture, they can also act as the structure of a broader approach to a distinctly Christian, performative form of reading. As we will see, each step in *lectio divina* draws the reader deeper and deeper into the text, learning to inhabit the text anew by performing it.

Lectio

Lectio means reading. It is of obvious importance to all forms of university learning. Yet students must be trained to read well in order to learn well. What we read is the raw material of all subsequent learning and formation. Reading gives us the information that in-forms us; it involves taking in data. This invites us into further thought, contemplation, and learning.

Lectio is principally concerned with the "literal" meaning of the text. Its concern is with the words and the flow of the narrative itself. This kind of concentrated study of the text itself is the foundation of all interpretation that follows. Hugh of St. Victor, one of the great teachers of the Christian tradition, warns that no student can rush beyond this level of study, nor ever leave it behind: "I know there are certain fellows who want to play the philosopher right away. They say that stories should be left to pseudo-apostles. The knowledge of these fellows is like that of an ass. Don't imitate persons of this kind."[26] All study requires a firm foundation in the literal, historical meaning of the text. Here we must learn to read slowly, with care and attention and generosity.

Lectio is the proper place for the discipline and analysis of what we commonly call "scholarship." Let's reconsider Lash's metaphor of the performance of Beethoven. The performance, he says, "is neither the same as, nor in competition with, the academic skills of the textual critics who make the score available through scholarly research and the critics and musicologists who have their own contribution to make to the continuing history of Beethoven interpretation."[27] Similarly, the scholarly criticism of Augustine, Julian, or Dante is "indispensable but subordinate" to the performative reading of the text. Scholarship and academic reading help us to understand and appreciate the text on the *text's* terms.

How can we put *lectio* into practice in class? In some ways, this is the easiest practice of *lectio divina* to adopt. I often assign my classes "exegetical exercises" where they reread in class a small selection of the reading they did the previous night. As they read, I give them a very specific reading question to answer. I then ask them to partner with one or two of their peers and compare answers. If they have different answers, they are instructed to revisit the passage and see which of their answers is most faithful to the text at hand. The point of this exercise is to get students to attend very carefully and very precisely to the text *as a text*. Before they ask "so what?"—what does this text *mean*?—they must first ask themselves what the text *says*. This teaches them attentive reading, yes, but it also teaches them charitable judgment and fidelity to the text. They learn how to say "yes" and "no" to different interpretations of the text; they experience the text's openness and ambiguities, *and* its clarities and certainties. They feel more confident doing that because they have done the hard work of reading with attention, generosity, and sensitivity.

But were we to stop at *lectio*, we would be left with a routinely academic approach to reading. Where do we go from here? Exegesis, criticism, and dissection are important and necessary components to the study of the literal meaning of the text. But Hugh challenges our academic tendency to reduce the meaning of the text to the literal. He insists that studying the text's literal meaning is only the first stage of genuine knowledge of the text. The literal points beyond itself.

Meditatio

Meditation (or "consideration") of the text is the second stage of *lectio divina*. This is the discipline of imaginatively entering into a text, learning to inhabit it. "Meditation" means "to chew" on a text the way a cow chews on its cud: slowly, in no rush, and with great deliberation. Meditative reading is repetitive, even (if we push the cow metaphor farther), regurgitative. It involves the consideration of the text from beginning to end—taking it in, chewing it, swallowing it. And then it involves bringing the text back up (to mind, not stomach!), reconsidering it, taking it in again, chewing it again, and swallowing it again. Each time you do this, the text takes on new and richer meaning.

Meditation involves reading the text with your whole self, especially with the imagination. It means reading the text as if it were a particularly involving and evocative novel—placing yourself within the text, inhabiting it, binding yourself to it. This is where the reader begins to understand the text within a larger framework, yet one that draws them personally into the text in dynamic, and perhaps even transformative, ways.

How do we do this in class? When I teach the three books I listed above (*Confessions*, the *Comedy*, and Julian's *Revelation*), I tell my students to place themselves in the narrative. Each of those texts invites such participative reading, as I showed earlier. *Meditatio* means putting yourself in the text. One of the exercises that I use when teaching the *Comedy* is to have students place themselves in the various realms of Dante's afterlife. I ask them where they would find themselves among the damned, the purged, and the blessed? Why? This exercise fuses their analytical understanding of the literal meaning of the text together with an imaginative and personal meditation on themselves in light of the text. Here they move beyond thinking about the text and begin thinking with it. They treat the text as a vehicle for self-knowledge that is necessary for growing in wisdom and holiness. They begin to experience the text in a more direct, more personal way.

Oratio

Oratio is prayer. Professors cannot force students to read in this way, but I think it is important for the professor to model this step of *lectio divina*, despite being unable to assess students on it. At this point, the professor's job is to sow seeds and await a harvest that she may not witness herself. *Oratio* is where our reading opens up our minds *and* our souls. Our minds are drawn to wonder and our souls to humility before God.

This is where a specifically theological or religious imagination enters and we see our text opening up into the larger cosmic, theological story of God's creative and redemptive work.[28]

Let me give an example of the progression of these first three stages as they apply to the way I teach the opening of Dante's *Inferno*. As the poem opens, we meet the main character, lost in a dark wood, threatened by fierce beasts. Trembling, alone, and vulnerable, he spots a shadowy figure approaching him and cries out, "Have mercy on me!" We learn that this is the shade of Virgil who has come to guide Dante from his state of misery to happiness. In *lectio*, the students look at this scene, considering the characters, setting, and conflict. They exegete the passage in order to understand the way Dante's exile is reflected in the situation of his character, how Dante's identity as a poet and a Christian bears on his use of Virgil, and so on. From this, they situate themselves in the text in their *meditatio*, feeling themselves lost and abandoned and desperate for salvation. Dante's exile becomes their own. And then, suddenly, it is not Dante alone calling out to Virgil *Miserere dei!* [Have mercy on me]; the student is saying it as well. Dante's *miserere dei* is a conscious invocation of Psalm 51; the first word of dialogue in the poem is a prayer that the reader has also prayed. Look at what has happened: the student has performed a text which is itself a performance. By performing the *Comedy's* opening prayer, the student has also performed the cry of the Psalmist David. Dante has taught the reader how to perform, not just his text, but Scripture as well. The reader is invited to pray a prayer that is as ancient as it is new.

Contemplatio

Lastly, there is *contemplatio* or contemplation. This is the summit of the practices of *lectio divina*. It is where reading, meditation, and prayer result in personal transformation. This is the proper end of education: the love of God in Christ, or what St. Augustine calls wisdom (*sapientia*). It is identical with love, or charity (*caritas*).[29] Contemplation is the loving enjoyment of God that comes about by means of our intellectual and spiritual pursuit of truth; contemplation where we are drawn into the life of God. This is where we become what we were truly meant to be: image-bearers of God, reflecting the wisdom and love of God.[30] It is where we become the love that God is.[31]

This turn to contemplation reminds us that the summit of higher education in the Christian tradition does not lie in the acquisition of information, in earning a degree, or landing a lucrative job. Its summit is the *formation* of the soul, the *conformation* of the mind and the soul to Truth, which is to say, to Jesus Christ who calls himself the way, truth, and life (John 14:6). Conformation to this image of Christ the truth signals a necessary change in all of our habits and practices of knowledge. *Contemplatio* is the act wherein all of the various horizons of knowledge and study collide in a series of transformations. It is where knowledge becomes wisdom, and wisdom (*sapientia*) becomes tasting (*sapere*). "To know much," St. Bonaventure once said, "and yet taste nothing—of what use is that?"[32] *Contemplatio* takes us beyond the discursive and into the *dilectio* of love. In contemplation, truth, knowledge, and love perfectly coincide in our enjoyment of God.

Contemplatio also transforms the student from *consumptive* self of "closed reading" to the *doxological* self. Matthew Treherne describes the doxological self as "the redirection of one's being to its creator, in an act of gratitude and recognition." In contemplation, knowledge of things shifts from being "the subject of academic discussion, to being the condition in which praise occurs."[33] In contemplation, knowledge becomes celebration and praise; and celebration and praise become ways of knowing. Finally, in contemplation, pedagogical stewardship becomes the act of tradition (*traditio)*—a handing on from one to the next, as in a relay race. Teaching becomes what Thomas Aquinas describes as passing on the fruits of contemplation. But in a pedagogy open to contemplative fulfillment, what we hand over is not simply *ideas* but a person, the one who is the truth in his incarnate flesh.

Contemplation occurs when our knowledge becomes love, when the fragmented parts of our mind, our affections, and our wills are brought together in transformative conformity with Christ. The contemplative reader echoes the prayer of St. Augustine, "as for me, though, I am broken apart in time, whose shape and meaning I do not know; and my thoughts, the most intimate organs of my soul, are split up by time's stormy changes, until, purified and melted by the fire of your love, all of me will flow together into you" (*Confessions* XI. 29). It is here in contemplative union with God in Christ that we become truly wise.

Like my students discover at the end of the *Comedy*, wisdom comes not so much in the act of reading—even performative reading—but rather in the silence that follows that reading, when we stand before the truth made known to us in the great cloud of witnesses, caught up by the beauty and splendor of truth. We become wise, Augustine tells us, when our knowledge becomes love, and our words become the adoration and praise of the Truth, Goodness, and Beauty that is ever ancient and ever new.[34]

* * *

In closing, let me caution that performative reading is not safe. It cannot be tidily parceled out in a reading schedule at the end of a syllabus and then graded on a 10-point scale. In performative reading, students and instructors risk the possibility of being personally challenged and transformed. Performative reading resists the impulse to control, master, or dominate the text. No longer do we read a text for its utility for our projects of self-aggrandizement. No, we read out of the brokenness and hope that constitute our lives, handing ourselves over to the text in patient and humble apprenticeship, a willingness to be challenged, to be transformed, to *be* mastered, rather than to master.

It is a dangerous thing to open the pages of a book. There's no telling who we might be challenged to become in and through those pages. But this possibility of a transformative encounter with God's love is the wellspring of joy that comes in reading and teaching the Christian tradition. To read in this way challenges the rushed and consumptive styles that use and exploit texts. Performative reading carries our vision through the text until we behold the "Love that moves the sun and the other stars"[35] and find ourselves transformed and made wise in that vision.

Notes

1. T.S. Eliot, "The Rock" in *The Complete Poems and Plays: 1909–1950* (Orlando: Harcourt Brace Jovanovich, 1971), 96.
2. Cf. *Confessions* X.34.51. See also Paul Griffiths, *Intellectual Appetite: A Theological Grammar* (Washington, DC: The Catholic University of America Press, 2009), 19–22.
3. Descartes, *Discourse of Method* 6.2.
4. Hans Urs von Balthasar, *Love Alone is Credible* (San Francisco, Ignatius Press, 2004), 142–143.
5. Though the structural issues of the university play an important role in the problem I am describing, tackling them in any significant way is beyond the scope of this essay.

6. This judgment is important. We misunderstand the Christian tradition if we think that it is utterly beyond critique and reproach. We must not be *pious* readers of old books, but neither need we be strict deconstructionists. There is a wide space between fundamentalist and skeptical reading. See Alan Jacobs for a characteristically winsome and balanced narration of the relationship between political readings and nostalgic reading ("To Read and To Live," *First Things*, 1993). My point, however, is that both nostalgic and political readings, whether positive or negative, read and assess books as "closed" objects. This is an important part of the academic task, but it cannot be the *only* way of reading and teaching these texts.
7. Wendell Berry, "The Loss of the University" in *Home Economics: Fourteen Essays* (San Francisco: North Point Press, 1987), 79.
8. Eugene Peterson, *Eat This Book: A Conversation in the Art of Spiritual Reading* (Grand Rapids: Eerdmans 2009).
9. The dominance of technology in our lives accentuates these two characteristics that Peterson identifies. Technology also nurtures a third major characteristic of malformative reading, distraction. This topic is exceedingly important for understanding the intellectual situation of contemporary students. The more distracted we become by the constant demands of social media, the less we are able to sit patiently under the tutelage of difficult texts that cannot be reduced to a sound byte. Further, the more we streamline our intake of knowledge so that it comes to us through highly curated channels of self-selected resources, the more superficial our thinking and understanding become. For an insightful essay on technology addiction and distraction sickness, see Sullivan, Andrew. "I Used to be a Human Being." New York Magazine. September 18, 2016. Accessed October 1, 2016. http://nymag.com/selectall/2016/09/andrew-sullivan-technology-almost-killed-me.html.
10. Cf. Joseph Pieper, *Leisure: The Basis of Culture*, trans. Alexander Dru (San Francisco: Ignatius Press, 2009). Pieper reminds us that our word "school" comes from the Latin "*schola*," often translated as "leisure." Learning occurs within a culture of leisure that makes space for the slow, contemplative work of reading and knowing. The hurry that students feel is often the result of well-meaning teachers who think that more work means more learning. Pieper challenges us to consider the importance of leisured silence for deeper understanding of course material: "Leisure, it must be clearly understood, is a mental and spiritual attitude—it is not simply the result of external factors, it is not the inevitable result of spare time, a holiday, a weekend or a vacation. It is, in the first place, an attitude of mind, a condition of the soul, and as such utterly contrary to the ideal of 'worker'…Leisure is a form of silence, of that silence which is the

prerequisite of the apprehension of reality: only the silent hear and those who do not remain silent do not hear. Silence, as it is used in this context, does not mean 'dumbness' or 'noiselessness'; it means more nearly that the soul's power to 'answer' to reality of the world is left undisturbed. For leisure is a receptive attitude of mind, a contemplative attitude, and it is not only the occasion but also the capacity for steeping oneself in the whole of creation" (46–47).

11. Peterson, *Eat This Book*, 6. In his *Confessions*, Augustine grows dissatisfied reading the books of the Platonists, despite how important a role they played in his intellectual and moral growth, because they "fail to present a reality that is 'not just to be looked at but to be lived in' (VII.xx.26)'" quoted in Rowan Williams, *On Augustine* (London: Bloomsbury, 2016), 11. Despite Augustine's earlier distaste for Scripture, one of the things about the Bible that wins him over is precisely this performative dynamic of the sacred texts.
12. Rowan Williams, *On Augustine*, 47.
13. Ibid. This is especially true when it comes to the way we read Scripture, but Williams sees the way we read *other* books as directly formative of the way we read Scripture.
14. I'm grateful to Dr. Jeffrey Bilbro for this image of the vampire.
15. This is not to say that new books are immune to this kind of reading. Humans have the impressive and disturbing ability to exploit anything they encounter. But I think old books that are read primarily in the classroom are especially vulnerable to this kind of reading.
16. One thinks of Franz Kafka's 1904 letter to Oskar Pollak, in which he asks, "If the book we are reading does not wake us, as with a fist hammering on our skull, why then do we read it?... A book must be like an ice-axe to break the frozen sea within us." This letter can be found in Franz Kafka, *Letters to Friends, Family and Editors*, ed. Richard Winston (New York: Schocken Books, 2016), 15–16.
17. Lash, "Performing the Scriptures" in *Theology on the Way to Emmaus* (London: SCM Press, 1986), 39. Lash resists the claim that there is a clearly "definable" meaning to texts. This might strike us as a first step toward a kind of postmodern relativizing of meaning. But that is not Lash's point. Instead, he wants to resist seeing texts as "containers" of some concrete "meaning" that we the reader can "comprehend" and possess as *data* of knowledge.
18. This does not mean that just *any* interpretation goes. As Lash puts it "there is a creativity in interpretation which, far from being arbitrary (the players [of Beethoven] cannot do whatever like with the score) is connected in some way with the fidelity, the 'truthfulness' of their performance" (40).

19. Ibid., 41.
20. I am grateful for conversations with Jeffrey Bilbro who suggested to me that there is a parallel here with C.S. Lewis' account of friendship in *The Four Loves*. Different friends bring out different aspects of who I am. All of those aspects of my personality are present in me but they are drawn out through my encounter with others. If books are, in a sense, "alive" then perhaps there is a kind of friendship that exists between text and reader. This is the case that Wayne Booth makes in his *The Company We Keep: An Ethics of Freedom* (Berkley, CA: University of California Press, 1988). This notion of friendship also highlights the importance of reading specifically *old* books: if different friends bring out different aspects of myself, then the difference of old books that I addressed above also brings out neglected aspects of the reader.
21. *Confessions* is not unique in this case; in Augustine's day, *all* texts were read aloud. Think of Augustine's scandal at seeing Ambrose reading silently in *Confessions* 6.3.3. How does the fact that *Confessions* was meant to be read aloud change our understanding of it as an autobiography? If we take the orality of *Confessions* seriously, then Augustine's use of first-person plurals means that Augustine is writing an autobiography, yes, but he is also writing the spiritual biography of all of his readers. The particularity of Augustine's life is thus opened up as the story of his readers. My thanks to Jeffrey Bilbro for this keen insight. On the orality of ancient texts, see Ivan Illich, *In the Vineyard of the Text* (Chicago: University of Chicago Press, 1993).
22. A readily accessible English translation of Julian's visions is published in the Classics of Western Spirituality series: Julian of Norwich, *Showings*, eds. Edmund Colledge, O.S.A. and Fr. James Walsh, S.J. (Mahwah, NJ: Paulist Press, 1978). For those unfamiliar with Julian's work, there are two versions of her *Revelation* (also called *Showings*): a short version, published first, and a long version, published after a season of reflection and discernment.
23. Frederick Christian Bauerschmidt, *Julian of Norwich and the Mystical Body Politic of Christ* (Notre Dame: University of Notre Dame Press, 1999), 193.
24. One of the ways that I teach my students how to read the *Comedy* existentially is by showing them how to see themselves in each character they meet. Seeing themselves as those characters in their strengths and their flaws is the discipline of reading with compassion. As they read, they suffer with, or journey alongside of the characters. Then, as we in class sit and analyze the *characters*, we are also interrogating those aspects of *ourselves* that we find in them. This is part and parcel of the profoundly humane approach that Dante takes in creating his characters. He does

not offer us "types" or "symbols" of things; he offers us human beings and invites his readers—as fellow human beings—to meet his characters, human to human. To quote Terence, "I am human. Nothing human is foreign to me."

25. The examples that I have used in this essay all make generous use of the first-person plural, "we" or "our." What about texts that do not use this kind of language? Can they be performed? I would certainly think so, though perhaps not as straightforwardly as the three texts I have used as illustrations in this essay. One strategy for discovering and delving into the performative dimension of other texts might be adopting and adapting something like the way many ancient Christians read the Bible according to a fourfold sense: the literal, the allegorical, the tropological (or moral), and the anagogical (or the spiritual) senses of the text. The latter two senses, the tropological and the anagogical, ask these questions of the text in question: how does this text indicate that I should I live? and how does this text show me how I might come to know God? While the early Christians adopted the fourfold sense specifically for *biblical* reading more often than for merely *literary* reading, I think the model has the potential for being adapted and more widely applied to practices of reading. A pagan example from antiquity was the philosophical or neoplatonic ways of reading Homer's *Odyssey* as the story of the soul's return to its divine homeland. One example of this from the medieval Christian tradition is the way Christians read Virgil's *Eclogues*, specifically the fourth, as an allegorical prophesy of the coming of Christ.
26. Hugh of St. Victor, *Didascalicon*, 113–116, quoted in Rita Copeland, *Pedagogy, Intellectuals, and Dissent in the Later Middle Ages: Lollardy and Ideas of Learning* (Cambridge: Cambridge University Press, 2001), 90.
27. Lash, "Performing the Scriptures," 41.
28. Positioning *oratio* in a typology of academic reading may seem strange. How can prayer and knowledge connect? This is an issue that vexed twentieth-century Roman Catholic theologian and priest Hans Urs von Balthasar. At the conclusion of Balthasar's *Theo-Logic* 1, he says: "If truth were ultimate in God, we could look into its abysses with open eyes. Our eyes might be blinded by so much light, but our yearning for truth would have free reign. But because love is ultimate, the seraphim cover their faces with their wings, for the mystery of eternal love is one whose superluminous night may be glorified only through adoration." Because God is love, the way we come to know God is through adoration. Balthasar's German term is "*Anbetung*." Balthasar is not particularly original here. Of course the way that we know God most truly is through worship. What I find interesting is that earlier in *Theo-Logic* 1, Balthasar uses the term *Anbetung* to describe the proper epistemological attitude

of the subject to its object of knowledge. One does not know the object properly if one approaches it with an attitude of reckless curiosity (what Augustine would call *curiositas*), or an exploitative, utilitarian attitude that wants to conquer the object and put it to use. No, the proper attitude of knowledge is an adoring one that praises and celebrates its object. What I find striking is the implied analogy Balthasar draws between philosophical knowledge—the immanent knowledge between subject and object—and theological knowledge, or knowledge of God.

More significantly, though, is that Balthasar adds to this in *Theo-Logic* 2. Balthasar describes the relationship between the eternal Son and Father as "a relation in which the Son turns to the Father in knowledge, love, *adoration*, and readiness for the Father's very wish" (*Theo-Logic* 2, 126). He again uses *Anbetung* again, but it is applied to the dynamic of love and knowledge in the life of God. Further, Balthasar describes this adoring attitude as "prayer," both in terms of human knowledge of God, and of the triune life.

Through his use of term *Anbetung*, Balthasar has analogically associated three things: God's self-knowledge, human knowledge of God, and human knowledge of the world. The latter two are primordially grounded in the first, and so I think it is fair to say that the latter two are oriented to each other. Knowledge of the world is ordered to knowledge of God, and knowledge of God is ordered to participative knowledge that comes from sharing in the divine life. Balthasar offers a thoroughly mystical theology in which knowledge of God is the hidden correlative of every act of knowing. But more significantly, you have knowledge and love linked together in prayer. Balthasar rescues prayer from the narrow confines of "spirituality" and returns it to the very center of Christian existence. Prayer is the performance, and thus a source, of *all* knowledge: humanistic, scientific, metaphysical, and religious. On this point, see Matthew Rothaus Moser *Love Itself is Understanding: Hans Urs von Balthasar's Theology of the Saints* (Minneapolis: Fortress Press, 2016).

29. Rowan Williams defines Augustine's account of wisdom as "the contemplation of the eternal, God's delight in God; as such, it is what we hope to receive by grace, so that we acquire a share in that reflexive contemplative love which is God's very life," *On Augustine*, 142.
30. Genesis 1:26–27. For Augustine, the "image of God in us… is realized when the moments of our mental agency all have God for their object" (Williams, *On Augustine*, 173).
31. See Dante's image of a representative contemplative, Peter Damien, as having become divine love in *Paradiso* 20.82.
32. *Hexaem.*, XXIII, 21.

33. Matthew Treherne, "Reading Dante's Heaven of the Fixed Stars (*Paradiso* XXII–XXVII): Declaration, Pleasure, Praise" in *"Se mai contiga…": Exile, Politics and Theology in Dante*, eds. Claire Honess and Matthew Treherne (Ravenna: Longo, 2013), 23–24.
34. Augustine, *Confessions* 10.27.38.
35. *Paradiso* 33.145.

CHAPTER 7

Pedagogical Practices: Lessons from Augustine of Hippo

Jennifer L. Howell and T. Laine Scales

For a number of Christian universities and colleges in the USA, a sharp delineation occurs between a student's spiritual life and academic life. There remains within Christian higher education an assumption that the spiritual life and the intellectual life exist in their own distinctive spheres, and that religion has very little to do with the way in which intellectual formation occurs. However, as the intellectual formation of Christian scholars in higher education has received a resurgence of attention, this assumption has been called into question.[1] Following this recent vein of scholarship, our chapter will pursue the idea that Christian faith is not divorced from the cultivation of the student's intellect, but resides at the very heart of the way in which educators are to cultivate students' minds. Specifically, in this chapter, we want to address the formation of doctoral students, a category of student that merits its own particular examination, as doctoral students are training to enter the academic life as a vocation.

J.L. Howell (✉) · T.L. Scales
Baylor University, Waco, TX, USA

T.L. Scales and J.L. Howell (eds.), *Christian Faith and University Life*,
DOI 10.1007/978-3-319-61744-2_7

Our interest in the Christian formation of graduate students began initially as we explored research findings offered by the Carnegie Foundation for the Advancement of Teaching. The Carnegie Foundation has recently devoted a significant amount of time and resources for studying the state and future of doctoral education in America. In 2001, the Carnegie Initiative on the Doctorate was formed in order to conduct a five-year study of the diverse paths to the Ph.D. as practiced in the fields of chemistry, education, English, history, mathematics, and neuroscience. This work has resulted in two timely and thought-provoking publications, *Envisioning the Future of Doctoral Education: Preparing Stewards of the Discipline* (2006) and *The Formation of Scholars: Rethinking Doctoral Education for the Twenty-First Century* (2008), in which the authors seek to draw attention to the problems and promises of American doctoral education. Three main themes have risen to the fore in the CID's research: scholarly integration, intellectual community, and stewardship.

According to the CID, three convictions are central to an account of stewardship as a proper vision for graduate student formation. First, stewards must cultivate a set of knowledge and skills that provide the expertise necessary for accomplishing their research as well as a set of principles that provide the moral compass academic work requires.[2] Second, stewards are responsible for more than their own work and intellectual output. They have a vested interest in the field as a whole and thus are stewards of a discipline rather than managers of a career.[3] Third, stewards are able to function in three areas: generation, conservation, and transformation.

The generative function of the stewardship model points to the role that scholars do best—furthering their field through original and important research. This role signifies that the Ph.D. is able to ask significant questions, conduct highly competent investigations, analyze and evaluate the ensuing results, and communicate the results in order to advance the field. The student has thus learned the grammar of her discipline.

Conservation implies the understanding that new ideas are not created ex nihilo, but evolve out of previous knowledge and content areas. It means understanding the traditional, fundamental ideas of the discipline while discerning what ideas are worth keeping and what must be reframed with new insight. Conservation, in the best sense, passes on the wisdom a graduate adviser has gleaned from years working within the discipline. This material is communicated (and received) with the hope that the student may contribute knowledge that will refine or extend what has already been accomplished in the field. Conservation also entails understanding the relationship between one's particular area of expertise within the field and the discipline as a whole. Conservation attends to the larger intellectual landscape beyond any one discipline.

Transformation carries this thinking further. To transform learning is to recognize the importance of representing and communicating ideas effectively.[4] To learn is, in turn, to share with others what is known.

The Intellect as Appetite

As we laid out in the introduction to this volume, we propose that graduate education can be conceived of in this vein of stewardship. When we think of graduate school education in terms of stewardship, we come to recognize that our graduate students are not simply trained to manage their own brilliant careers, but rather, we hope that they will come to see that part of their task in graduate school is to embrace a larger sense of purpose, as they are entrusted with the care of an intellectual discipline that reaches beyond their own interests and agendas.

The language of "discipline" is not arbitrary, and it would serve us well to pause for a moment and consider what it means when we speak of our work as scholars as a kind of discipline. In his book, *Intellectual Appetite: A Theological Grammar*, Paul Griffiths considers this precise question.[5] The language of discipline suggests that acquiring knowledge in a subject matter does not happen accidentally. Rather, to enter into a discipline requires that we acquire knowledge in a certain way. Discipline entails the formation of particular habits of study and employs a particular grammar that must be learned. In short, learning a discipline does not occur the same way we might download a new program onto our computer. Rather, discipline entails a holistic, embodied approach to learning.

Griffiths points us toward a long history of educators, from as far back as Aristotle, who have conceived of teaching along these lines by suggesting that the teaching of an intellectual discipline can be understood as the cultivation of a kind of appetite in our students. The pursuit of knowledge is something we hunger for, much like we hunger for food. Just as appetites for particular foods or even particular ways of eating can be developed, so too, following this analogy, can the appetite for learning be developed and cultivated.

If the development of the intellect is a training of an appetite, then, Griffiths asks, is there anything distinctively Christian about the ways that we tend to the cultivation and discipline of intellectual appetites?[6] Griffiths' question suggests that the task at hand for Christian institutions of higher education is not simply to determine *what* students should study and learn (though certainly that matters), but also *how* students are to learn. How are we forming graduate students in Christian programs to pursue their academic studies?

The question of how we are to train the intellectual appetite goes back to the earliest days of Christianity. As early as the third century, theologians like Tertullian attempted to develop language to distinguish between different intellectual appetites. From these early days, Christians began to use the language of *curiositas*, a problematic form of pedagogy that regards knowledge as a possession to be consumed. In contrast, *studiositas* was a term used to describe a catechized appetite for knowledge, directing learners to enjoy the gift of learning, and through the process of learning come to participate in the communal life of God. We might conceive of the difference between these two appetites as the difference between quickly eating a meal from a drive-thru alone in the car to satisfy a growling stomach and enjoying a meal prepared with care with friends over the course of an evening, or even, in the fullest sense, preparing and enjoying the highest meal, the Eucharistic feast.

The intellectual appetite was not a hunger that Christians sought to quell, but rather to develop in a particular way. Recognizing the inherent dangers that reside within *curiositas*, not least being the example of Adam and Eve in the Garden of Eden, who pursued a kind of knowledge beyond the boundaries of knowledge established by God, the question that emerged was how to train the intellectual appetite toward its proper end. There is a long existent (but seemingly forgotten) Christian tradition of examining this question of *how* the intellectual appetite for knowledge is to be cultivated, and we will turn in a moment to one example of the tradition: Augustine of Hippo.

The Grammar of *Curiositas* and *Studiositas*

Before we turn to Augustine's pedagogical schema, we first need to clarify what these two historical terms, *curiositas* and *studiositas,* are trying to describe. To aid us, we turn once again to Paul Griffiths as our guide. According to Griffiths, *curiositas* is a particular appetite that orders our loves and affections toward new knowledge.[7] Experiencing "the new" is the end goal, and the desire for control or mastery over the new is the motivating hunger. According to Griffiths, the curious want to know that which they do not yet know, and often they want to know it with an all-encompassing and passionate desire. This appetite for new knowledge "ravishes them."[8] The knowledge they seek is pursued as though it were the only thing to be had. The curious student, moreover, desires to obtain knowledge of an object by enclosing it, keeping it from others, for their own personal use, so that they may fully master the object to a higher degree than others.[9]

Like the curious appetite, *studiositas* has knowledge as its object. However, the studious do not to seek to own the knowledge they seek. The catechesis of *studiositas* leads a student to engage deeply with the object of study as part of a larger picture. Griffiths employs the language of participation. We participate in forms of knowledge and respond to the object of knowledge in love, rather than as a possession. The studious appetite may be just as intense as the curious appetite, but the studious appetite treats the object of knowledge as a gift: a gift that opens the possibility that the studious may participate in the goodness, not only of the gift of knowledge but also in the goodness of the Giver of the gift.

An important implication of this shared connection is that the studious are committed to treating the intellectual commons as common—open to others and not "as a field of conquest, a set of objects to be sequestered."[10] While both appetites seek knowledge, the two different forms of appetite serve different purposes—where curiosity wants possession; studiousness seeks participation.[11]

Readers may be asking, "Isn't a curious mind a valuable asset to a graduate student?" Certainly, an inquisitive attitude would motivate a learner. However, using Paul Griffith's distinction, we describe the curious as those scholars seeking to possess what they know in a way that others cannot share in that possession. To own something, one must first sequester that which one wishes to own. The owned is a passive object. Griffith's defines learning in this world as *mathesis*. "To be mathetized is to be inducted into the world of knowables construed in a particular way: as discrete, transparent, passive, and infinitely manipulable by their knowers."[12]

Within the modern university, graduate students are oftentimes encouraged to pursue knowledge from this approach. We have one colleague who shared with us his frustration that when attending conferences on new discoveries in his field, the data shared is oftentimes deliberately distorted to guarantee that no one at the conference can steal the presenter's findings and claim them as their own. One of us recalls that while in graduate school fellow students complained about having to share their seminar papers in class with fellow classmates, for fear that someone might steal an idea before the graduate students could publish new material in their own name. When knowledge is understood as a possession that is passive, and when graduate education is structured in a way that the end goal is to be the preeminent "expert" on a subject, the tangible result is a world of competition and distrust over and against fellow learners.

In contrast to the world of the *curiositas* and *mathesis*, the world of the *studiositas* is a world of wonder. While the new or novel will surely occur, the aspect of novelty is not the motivation for the pursuit of knowledge. Instead, the studious inhabit a world of gift, of things created and given by God, which can be known, but not possessed. To better understand this form of learning, we will now turn to Augustine, who provides an account of *studiositas* in one of his earliest works: *The Cassiciacum Dialogues.*

The Cassiciacum Dialogues

Set in a villa at Cassiciacum, outside of Milan, the *Dialogues* pursue various philosophical discussions between Augustine and his family and friends. Of particular interest in our examination, Augustine's group includes Licentius, a young and promising poet, who has joined these discussions as a new initiate into the study of the philosophical life. Licentius is, as is obvious from our first encounter with him, eager and hungry to ingest these new teachings, much like our modern graduate student. Augustine must continually direct, tame and nurture Licentius' passions, a continual drama that reveals to us the nature of this particular form of student formation.

Pursuing Knowledge: The Form of the Dialogues

Augustine begins his pedagogy into the studious ways of knowledge in the form of a dialogue. There is historic precedence for this form of teaching. For Plato, the dialogues served as the highest philosophical method for ascertaining truth. Cicero, claiming he followed in the teaching method of Socrates, noted the difference between written and oral teachings. While written teachings were beneficial in the sense that they could be passed out in a widespread manner, they also were susceptible to falling into the wrong hands. Once published, written teachings could be misused by the unwise. In contrast, oral teaching was considered the superior form of pedagogy. Through discourse, a teacher is able to assess her student's moral character, and can subsequently adapt the material to the intellectual needs and capacities of her student, determining at any moment what could profitably be taught.[13] Feedback from a student can sharpen the focus of the teacher, bringing clarity to particular aspects of the material being taught that may be generating confusion. Through the *Cassiciacum Dialogues*, the reader is invited to participate in the ensuing conversation between teacher and pupil.

The *Dialogues* intentionally display everyday life. What a participant in the discourse says or does not say is contingent upon who is present or absent, along with the usual slew of motivations in their contingent forms. The quotidian kinds of conversations that occur between two people over the course of a day help us as readers see how intellectual formation unfolds over the course of time. Here we can even find comedy. Indeed, laughter is a central feature of the *Dialogues*. The *Dialogue's* comic structure both challenges the student to "get the joke," and overrides the propensity to view the world from the perspective of inevitable tragedy.[14]

Licentius, the Student

Within the *Dialogues*, Licentius is located in the epicenter of an unfolding drama that depicts the pursuit of knowledge, and the means by which that pursuit is cultivated by a teacher.[15] Specifically, to look at Licentius' narrative will be to pay attention to the basic framework Augustine is presenting his novice student. In the beginning, Licentius will not engage with some of Augustine's more sophisticated thoughts regarding Plotinus or Plato, Skepticism or Cicero. First, there is work to be done to build up Licentius' morals and virtues, so that he may be ready for the more rigorous and grueling learning that is to come.[16]

While Augustine is delighted that Licentius is beginning to philosophize, he initially regulates Licentius's eagerness for learning so that "after being cultivated by the requisite disciplines, he may rise up more vigorous and strong."[17] By restraining Licentius in his pursuit of knowledge, Augustine is pruning him. Even in the good, there is moderation, for if one dives into the pool of learning too quickly, there is danger of drowning. One must first cultivate the proper muscles to swim. The pursuit of knowledge is not merely an acquisition of given known objects, but rather a way of living, a *vocatio*.

These "muscles" that Augustine is attempting to cultivate must have their proper attunement with one another. To achieve such attunement, Augustine must actually know Licentius—his loves, his strengths, and also his weaknesses. This form of pedagogy also requires Licentius's willingness to follow the protocol of discipline Augustine is setting up for him. We see this work of "attunement" unfold as Augustine works with Licentius's love of poetry. At one point, Licentius becomes so consumed by tragic poetry that he is far too distracted to drink or eat.[18] Augustine momentarily worries aloud that it was perhaps a mistake to restrain Licentius from pursuing philosophy, as philosophy could perhaps temper Licentius's fevered obsession.

In the same way that a doctoral advisor might need to moderate the rash enthusiasm of a new doctoral student, Augustine wants to challenge his impassioned student to properly order his love of poetry. To do this, Augustine does not banish poetry from Cassiciacum, even though at times, Augustine views this love as a distraction or even a hindrance in Licentius' studies. Augustine does not banish poetry from Licentius's pedagogical structure because he understands that poetry is a part of the greater framework of learning, and could ultimately aid in leading Licentius toward wisdom. Poetry as such is not the problem in this context. Rather, what concerns Augustine is the ways in which Licentius's love of poetry overwhelms his attention for other disciplines that are part of the comprehensive whole of his intellectual development.

Rather than prohibiting Licentius's reading of poetry, Augustine gives him an intriguing assignment. He urges Licentius to transform the tragic love poem he is writing into a comedy. At the point where the two lovers are set to commit suicide, Augustine tells Licentius to instead write a poem where the two lovers flee death to participate in "the most happy life."[19] Though we as Christians worship Jesus Christ, who suffered deeply and died on the cross, Christ's resurrection is our rejoinder to live in the profound joy and hope that the world has been reconciled to God. Comedy parallels the wonder of discovery and comprehension that are components of life in Christ's resurrection.[20] In contrast, Augustine believes that tragedy leads Licentius to contemplate the world solely from the human point of view and the cosmos as inscrutably fated.

By leading Licentius to contemplate the nature of comedy over tragedy through the writing of poetry, Augustine takes what Licentius knows and loves, but directs it away from the temptation of self-pity toward a way of seeing his own loves and actions in the larger framework of God's hope and mercy.

At this moment in the *Dialogues*, we see precisely how Augustine wants to cultivate all the liberal arts. That is, we see here the *telos* of the liberal arts. The love cultivated in the liberal arts is not merely for our own enjoyment, but rather should cultivate in us the love of God, which is the only way to attain true happiness. The liberal arts become the means through which Licentius's muscles are fine-tuned toward this end.

Eventually, there is a breakthrough in Licentius' progress. It is a scene that conveys the depth of Augustine's commitment to the moral formation of his student. One night, in the middle of the night, Augustine questions Licentius about the order by which God governs the universe. Licentius, in a way that surprises even himself, finds inspiration and clarity of mind to respond to Augustine's important question. Licentius sees the truth in the midst of darkness of the night. He catches a glimpse of the way in which all of the cosmos is held in God's loving order. Leaping out of bed with joy, Licentius exclaims:

> Who can deny, O great God, that You administer all things by order? How all things hold together! How by fixed successions are they nudged into their own grooves! How great and how many are the things that have been done, that we may speak of them! How great are the things that have been made that we may find You![21]

In this dramatic moment, the knowledge being imparted to Licentius does not come in the form of discussion. Rather, Augustine has guided Licentius to the moment where he is prepared to "see" clearly the telos of his education. What Licentius is experiencing in this important moment is beyond words for the young poet. Licentius has transitioned from talking about the meaning of life to participating in it. In this moment, there is no need for Augustine to be Licentius' teacher.[22] Rather, it is a moment for gratitude and thanksgiving. The morning after, we find Licentius explicitly giving thanks to Christ, announcing that he has now found a love for philosophy over poetry. Joyfully, Licentius breaks into song, singing Psalms of thanksgiving, even (much to the dismay of Augustine's mother, Monica) while he is in the bathroom.[23]

We can imagine the modern doctoral student having a similar dramatic experience as he or she experiences a dramatic realization about the academic life. That experience may come in a moment of breakthrough related to one's subject area, perhaps while writing a dissertation. Alternatively, such a breakthrough moment may occur while the doctoral student is teaching an undergraduate student about his or her subject or in a lunch conversation with other doctoral students. Wherever the breakthrough moments may appear, the student's graduate advisor is challenged to acknowledge the moment for the good gift that it is, and encourage and cultivate the proper ordering of the student's passions with care.

Pride and *Curiositas*

The doctoral student who has had a series of experiences in which the mentor rejoices in the student's understanding may be tempted to feel prideful or arrogant. Augustine realizes Licentius's profound midnight insight is not a permanent revelatory experience, and he must tend to his student carefully "the day after" to prevent Licentious from slipping into error as he basks in the aftereffects of such an experience. To begin, in the light of day, Augustine asks Licentius to provide an account of order. Thus begins a most disastrous exchange; Licentius is unable to articulate clearly any account of order. A heated debate arises between Licentius and fellow student Tyrgetius, a debate that eventually Licentius wins. Pleased with himself, Licentius insists that Tyrgetius' failure be recorded in Augustine's *Dialogues.* When Licentius is rebuked for this desire, Trygetius laughs at his embarrassment. This prideful exchange enrages Augustine:

> This isn't the way you act, is it? Are you not moved by the fact that we are oppressed and overwhelmed by massive piles of vice and shadows of ignorance? Is this your recent attentiveness and ascent toward God and truth over which a little while ago I, fool that I am, rejoiced?[24]

Augustine goes on to tell his students of his own struggles with vainglory. Indeed, he says, this is the reason he left his teaching of rhetoric. This temptation to win debates for the sake of pride does not lead to wisdom: "It is the common lot of all foolish and unlearned minds to be submerged, but wisdom doesn't extend a helping hand to those who are submerged in one and the same way."[25] Tempered by his chastisement, Augustine's pupils settle in for more learning.

Through the interplay between Augustine and Licentious, we have a better sense of the ways in which studiousness can be cultivated, and the temptations toward *curiositas* that can arise. For Augustine as a teacher, to cultivate studiousness demands an engagement with his student precisely where his student is, taking the loves and resources the pupil offers, and attentively cultivating them, harnessing them, pruning them, and at times unleashing them. Augustine knew in the dark of night that what Licentius recognized was not something Augustine himself could teach through a lecture or a reading. When his student reached profound insight, Augustine knew simply to step back. However, Augustine was also aware of the great temptation to then attempt to *own* such an encounter (*curiositas*), and the following day, he made certain to assess where Licentius was apt to fall into that temptation. The best mentors speak honestly with students about their own mistakes and provide helpful feedback about the dangers of *curiositas* in an attempt to set the student back on the path toward studiousness.

Seeking the Self, Seeking God

Raw from the chastisement he has unleashed on Tyrgetius and Licentius, Augustine's own propensity to want to "win" a discourse determines the shape of the final dialogue. Here, Augustine offers fellow teachers profound insight, as he engages in a dialogue with Reason. Augustine incorporates this conversation into the *Dialogues* to remind teachers of their own temptation toward ownership of the kind of knowledge he was attempting to impart to Licentius. In this final exchange, Augustine ultimately turns to prayer as a way to make public what he has learned in his intimacy with wisdom. Any allusion toward mastery is deflected, as Augustine makes clear the true source of knowledge is God.

> O God, O Truth, in whom and from whom and through whom all the things which are are true:
>
> O God, O Wisdom, in whom and from whom and through whom all those who are wise are wise:
>
> O God, O True and Supreme Life, in whom and from whom and through whom all those who truly and supremely live do life:

> O God, O Happiness, in whom and from whom and through whom all those who are happy are happy …
>
> Hear, hear, hear me, O my God, my Lord, my King, my Father, my Cause, my Hope, my Reality, my Honor, my Home, my Salvation, my Light, my Life.[26]

Augustine's humility does not deny his intellectual accomplishments, but rather, humility properly orders them, preserving the posture of gratitude and wonder necessary for seeing the world rightly.

Some Thoughts for the Christian University

Augustine's pedagogical practices revealed in the Dialogues may serve as an important witness as we consider the aims and goals of Christian education, particularly as we focus on forming graduate students who will carry on our intellectual disciplines to the next generation. Over the course of the *Cassiciacum Dialogues*, Augustine, as both teacher *and* learner demonstrates for us the studious pursuit of knowledge. Augustine taught his students not merely *what* they may know, but *who* they are. If we follow Augustine, these two elements are inseparable. The end result of such studies is not a loquacious account of acquired knowledge. It may at best lead us to worshipful silence.

The Dialogues can serve as a challenge for those of us who live academic lives within the walls of the Christian University. Augustine has revealed the depth of knowledge, its participatory nature, and importantly, its *telos*. For teachers and mentors of doctoral students, Augustine's work should challenge us to engage our students in the fullness of their being, not reducing our pedagogy to the dispelling of information to be consumed and spit back. We should be looking, as stewards of the discipline, for the ways in which we can trigger love of learning, understanding that with the cultivation of the intellect comes a fuller love of God. As Augustine demonstrates, pursuing wisdom is not merely acquiring information; *it is cultivating a way of living*. Only when the body, mind, and soul are rightly ordered can one participate more fully in the knowledge of Wisdom, and only then that we may rightly see the ordered nature of the world and all that is within it.

Notes

1. For example, see *Christianity and the Soul of the University*, eds. Douglas V. Henry and Michael D. Beaty (Grand Rapids: Baker Publishing, 2006); Stanley Hauerwas, *The State of the University* (Oxford: Blackwell Publishing, 2007); David I. Smith and James K.A. Smith, *Teaching and Christian Practices: Reshaping Faith and Learning* (Grand Rapids: Eerdmans, 2011).
2. *Formation of Scholars*, 12.
3. *Envisioning*, 13.
4. *Formation*, 12.
5. Paul J. Griffiths. *Intellectual Appetite: A Theological Grammar* (Washington, DC: The Catholic University Press of America, 2009).
6. Ibid., 2.
7. Ibid., 20.
8. Ibid., 21.
9. Ibid.
10. Ibid., 21.
11. Ibid., 22.
12. Ibid., 144.
13. Ernest Fortin, "Transmission of the Christian Message," *Ever Ancient, Ever New* (Lanheim, MD: Rowman & Littlefield Publishers, 2007), 45.
14. We are grateful to Michael Foley for pointing this out to us.
15. Phillip Cary notes that this is a distinction from Cicero's *Dialogues.* In Cicero's *Dialogues*, the nature of teaching and learning is discussed. In Augustine's *Dialogues*, they are actually dramatically lived out. See "What Licentius Learned: A Narrative Reading of the Cassiciacum dialogues," *Augustinian Studies* 29, no. 1 (1998): 142.
16. When Augustine does engage in some of the more weighty discourses regarding the Academics and Skepticism, Licentius is not his interlocuter, but instead becomes another spectator of the debate. This is because the discourse is beyond the depth of Licentius' and Tyrgetius' intellectual abilities. Where Augustine is more rigorously examining the Skeptics, his interlocuter is Alypius, a friend who is both older in age and more seasoned in the pursuit of knowledge. See *Against the Academics* III.6.13. Trans. Michael P. Foley (Forthcoming).
17. *Against the Academics* II.3.8.
18. *Against the Academics* III.4.7.
19. *Against the Academics* III.1.24.
20. For a contemporary treatment on the comedy of our life in Christ, see Ralph Wood's *The Comedy of Redemption: Christian Faith and Comic Vision in Four American Novelists* (Notre Dame, IN: University of Notre Dame Press, 1988).

21. Augustine. *On Order* I.5.14.
22. Augustine writes, "It is not necessary for me to be a teacher now when you, who have already professed to be certain about so great a matter, have still not yet taught me anything- I who am so keen to learn and have subsequently been keeping vigil day and night." *On Order* I.5.12.
23. *On Order* I.1.22.
24. *On Order* I.10.29.
25. *On Order* I.10.29.
26. *Soliloquies* I.3.1–15; I.4.54–56.

CHAPTER 8

"Expound This Love:" Forming the Next Generation of Christian Teacher-Scholars Through the Lilly Graduate Fellows Program

Jane Kelley Rodeheffer

In canto XVIII of the *Purgatorio*, Dante exhorts his teacher, Virgil, to expound on the nature of the great love that seizes the mind and will and is "the seed of every virtue" and every sin (XVII. 104).[1] Following Aristotle, Virgil describes this love as "a movement of the spirit never resting /as long as it enjoys the thing it loves" (XVIII. 32–33). Nevertheless, the soul can easily be led astray, because although "such love seems always good/ ... every seal is not a good one, /even if imprinted in good wax" (XVIII. 37–39). Indeed, the soul requires the exercise of free will to direct that love to its proper end, which is God. Using Dante as a touchstone, I would like to ask how a Christian

J.K. Rodeheffer (✉)
Pepperdine University, Malibu, CA, USA

T.L. Scales and J.L. Howell (eds.), *Christian Faith and University Life*,
DOI 10.1007/978-3-319-61744-2_8

graduate student might be mentored into the proper direction of her love in the practice of teaching and learning. Before moving on to that question, however, let us set the stage by returning to the *Purgatorio* for a moment.

At this point in their journey, Virgil and Dante are on the fourth terrace of Purgatory. Love of evil objects has been corrected on terraces one to three, and excessive love, in the form of avarice, lust, and gluttony will be confronted on terraces five to seven. In a moment that mirrors the very beginning of the *Commedia*, Dante, the pilgrim, once again finds himself in a middle place, and it is here, on the fourth terrace, that he and his mentor, Virgil, pause to consider the problem of insufficient love. Indeed, throughout Purgatory there occurs an intense scrutiny of the self and the objects of its love, and while that self-scrutiny is coupled with a gazing on divine art as the penitents progress around the terraces, we must recall that the pilgrim has only recently left those souls who looked upon their fellows with *invidia*, a kind of "seeing against" that is the heart of envy. As a result, they find themselves in Purgatory with their eyes sewn shut, forced to rely on their inner vision if they are to begin to glimpse the divine "love that moves the sun and the other stars" (*Paradiso* XXXIII.145). As a kind of pivot in the process of purification, from outer seeing to inner vision and from *amor sui* to *amor Dei*, the fourth terrace seems an apt metaphor to describe the place many Christian graduate students find themselves in as they struggle to claim a larger horizon in which to understand their journey through the intense and often dispiriting process of professionalization.

In what follows I will suggest that the tradition of Christian humanism, in which the *Divine Comedy* plays an important role, has much to offer the graduate student who is searching for the right direction of her love. At its best, the tradition serves not merely as a shield against the existential isolation and disciplinary narrowness that can lead to disillusionment, but an invitation into a deepening of both interiority and community. As a founding Mentor in 2008 of the Lilly Graduate Fellows Program (LGFP), I have been privileged to work with over thirty Fellows in the first cohort and the sixth cohort. In what follows, I will highlight a number of ways in which the LGFP provides one such model for nurturing those practices and virtues that enable a graduate student in the humanities or arts to name her heart as a teacher-scholar, and, thus, to expound that great love that Dante speaks of. In particular, I will focus the LGFP's three-pronged approach to enhancing graduate education through conferences, colloquia, and individual mentoring. This approach is made manifest in the cultivation of interior reflection and shared inquiry into texts from the tradition of Christian humanism, as well as the practices of *lectio divina*, Christian hospitality and intentional community, and together these provide a model through which graduate students might recover that inexhaustible inner domain that gives our lives meaning, while at the same time bringing them into a community whose shared love of the Christian tradition, *and of one another in loving that tradition*, provides a larger horizon in which to situate their love of teaching and scholarship. In the conclusion, I will suggest several resources and strategies for Christian graduate students, faculty mentors, and administrators, at both Christian and secular institutions, that might be useful in developing a similar initiative.

The Lilly Graduate Fellows Program: A Trinitarian Approach

The Lilly Graduate Fellows program is built on a cohort model, and each group of ten to sixteen members is comprised of young men and women who have bachelor degrees in the humanities or arts from schools within the Lilly National Network and are interested in becoming teacher-scholars at a church related college or university upon completion of their doctoral studies. As I noted above, the program utilizes a three-pronged, or Trinitarian, approach to enhancing graduate education through conferences, colloquia, and mentoring. Over the course of three years, two senior scholars from Lilly network schools lead a cohort of Fellows; together these mentors implement four conferences and facilitate a biweekly online colloquium, as well as forming mentoring relationships with individual Fellows through frequent phone conversations. The online colloquia draw on classical works of literature, philosophy, art, and theology, including authors such as the Desert Fathers and Mothers, Augustine, Dante, Dostoevsky, Tocqueville, Flannery O'Connor, and Simone Weil, as well as books and articles by contemporary authors like George Marsden, Marilynne Robinson, Charles Taylor, Rowan Williams, Stephanie Paulsell, Paul Griffiths, Rebecca DeYoung, L. Gregory Jones, and Christine Pohl. The colloquia and conferences focus on themes ranging from Christian hospitality and the vocation of the Christian teacher-scholar to virtues, spiritual friendship, secularism and belief, the history of higher education in the USA, and models for composing a life both within and outside of the academy. Mentors provide counsel and aid to individual Fellows, as needed, about all aspects of their graduate education, their sense of vocation, and their eventual placement.

Reflecting on the first seven years of the LGFP, Program Director Joseph Creech writes,

> From the very start, this has not been a program intended to shelter graduate students from the academy; rather, the Lilly Graduate Fellows Program is the only *purposefully ecumenical* program dedicated to fostering a deep theological engagement between academic professionalization and Christian ideas and practices. Fellows… gain perspective on the ideas and practices of Christianity that can inform a life of teaching and scholarship well lived. Perhaps, most importantly, they gain a glimpse of the long view—how to succeed not only in the academy but in life more generally. This all happens in a community of Mentors and Fellows reading and learning together.[2]

This larger horizon is indeed important. To conjure the landscape in which such a horizon figures, in what follows I will draw on the written reflections of LGFP Fellows themselves, as well as the texts that have nourished them. Regarding the need for a broader horizon, one Fellow stated in a recent reflection,

> The LGFP has challenged me to take a much longer, more complex view of what it means to become a Christian scholar-teacher and to see it as a process. L. Gregory Jones's "Negotiating the Tensions of Vocation," which we read at the conclusion of our final semester, emphasized the difficulty of pinning down a lasting, exacting definition of "vocation." Instead, Jones argued that Christians ought to "continually narr[ate] and re-narr[ate] the dramas of [their] lives in relation to God" in order to embody a continually adapting and ever-changing conception of vocation."[3]

The adapting and renarrating of one's Christian vocation within the academy provides an essential metanarrative for young scholars negotiating the increasing professionalization of faculty in the American academy, whose primary allegiance is too often to disciplinary standards rather than institutional mission, student learning, and faculty collaboration. The need for excellent teacher-mentors informed by the particularly Christian practices of vocation, community, and service, as well as an understanding of the challenges and choices facing Christian higher education in the current academy, was the driving force behind the imaginative reformulation of the training of the professor that the LGFP seeks to kindle.

In Search of the Perfect Egg Sandwich: Metaphor as a Stay Against Isolation and Despair

Perhaps the most immediate need the LGFP strives to meet is the sense of isolation experienced by many graduate fellows as they transition from a church related undergraduate college to the very different atmosphere of an R-1 university. This isolation can become even more intense in the third year of study, when many fellows are finished with coursework and find themselves forced to adhere to a punishing and solitary schedule of studying for comprehensive examinations. In our online colloquia, discussion of the character of Ivan, the author of "The Grand Inquisitor" in Dostoevsky's *The Brothers Karamazov* inevitably invites comparisons to the life of a graduate student, who often undergoes an acute hypertrophy of the intellect with its attendant emotional stress, which can cut one off from the human goods of friendship, family, and spiritual life.

To cope with her own isolation, one recent fellow, whom I will call Laura, reached for an aesthetic metaphor from Marilynne Robinson's novel *Gilead*, which we had read and discussed in the online colloquium. When her initial goal of writing her dissertation nestled in the comfort of her extended family was thwarted by a rare Fulbright opportunity, she found grace in egg sandwiches, just like John Ames, the protagonist of Marilynne Robinson's novel, *Gilead*. In her final reflection on the program, Laura writes,

> Like John Ames, I get by on egg sandwiches. Thanks in large part to Marilynn Robinson they have become far more than just a stipend-friendly, no-hassle dinner on a busy weeknight. To me, egg sandwiches mean waiting for real life to begin. Now, I do understand the importance of this time in my life. I am an apprentice; I am learning a craft. My physical and intellectual needs are all met. But again, just like John Ames, I am lonely. I sometimes feel like I am eating an egg sandwich in a dark kitchen while everyone else is living her life. My community is so transient. People graduate, drop out, or move away. They are too overwhelmed by work to make time for a lunch date.

Laura goes on to tell of an "epiphany" she experienced, one she credits as resulting from the Lilly fellowship, which forced a turn inward—one that she had heretofore resisted following:

> I woke up one morning, ABD, and dissatisfied with the way I had spent the last three years. I was proud of my work but not much else. I decided to start over. I would move back to my hometown and commute to the university two days a week. I would live close to my family and I would finally have that 9–5 life with a bright kitchen devoid of egg sandwiches. I thought I was meant to go backwards. God had other plans. In *Gilead*, he sent Lila. He sent me a one-way ticket to New Delhi. I was excited to get the Fulbright of course but also a bit miffed. How was I supposed to rebuild my community if I was 7500 miles away? By extending it, apparently. John Ames recalled the dark days of egg sandwiches to his son as a way to show him how grateful he was to have a family. To say that his son was "God's grace to him." Like Ames, my life won't always consist of egg sandwiches. The Lilly Graduate Fellows Program calls me to be a better academic, to have high standards for community, hospitality, service, and character. The next year in India gives me a new chance to strive toward these standards. I need to be more intentional about community. Most of all, I need more patience with myself, more grace.

In a recent letter from New Delhi, addressed to our Lilly cohort, Laura relates a harrowing situation in which she was indeed called to the high standards of community and character she speaks of above. The Prime Minister of India had recently demonetized India's currency, namely the five hundred and one thousand rupee note, in a measure aimed at eliminating corruption. Residents were given four hours notice before their cash would become worthless. Ninety percent of all Indian economic transactions are in cash and of those transactions eighty-five percent use one thousand or five hundred rupee notes, so this move brought Indian society to a virtual standstill. For Laura, however, it was a call to action, a moment in which she could be intentional about community through the simple act of abiding with the strangers who surrounded her in a most unlikely place: an early morning queue at an ATM machine.

Standing in line, Laura was caught up in a maelstrom when a wealthy Indian woman wearing a Western suit and expensive gold jewelry cut the queue at an ATM machine, causing an uproar among those who, with Laura, had been waiting for hours for their turn to withdraw currency. When both bank officials and eventually, the police, were called to the scene, they defended the wealthy woman. A young man turned to Laura and said, "When you go home, you tell your country, you tell them. Indians are shameless. The rich have no shame." Out of respect, Laura looked him in the eyes but remained silent. He pointed to the wealthy Indian woman, and shouted, "You have no shame!" Finally, in a tone of despair, he whispered to Laura, "India has no shame." An elderly man in the crowd began pointing to Laura and stating loudly to the others in the queue that although she was a white American and, therefore, privileged, she was waiting patiently along with everyone else instead of claiming her rightful place at the front of the queue.

Reflecting on the comment of the elderly man, Laura writes that she has struggled with his kind of logic from the first moment she set foot on Indian soil: "Even as a scholar of gender and cultural imperialism, it is difficult to wrap my mind around the totality of a cultural imperialism that even seventy years after Independence still warps the minds of the colonized to think white means right." Disgusted not only by the presumed entitlement of the queue-cutting wealthy woman but by the elderly man's suggestion that her own white skin granted Laura a similar privilege, she writes, "Realizing that my very whiteness had become a weapon in the class warfare of Delhi, I almost left the queue." But something, some grace, made her stay. Offered the opportunity to escape the isolation and despair of those around her, Laura merely pointed to her spot on the ground, repeating over and over, "I will wait, I will wait." When the shouting began to escalate, however, the bank officials pulled Laura into the bank and exchanged her currency there. Having expressed her need to rise to the high standards of personal integrity and community she experienced as a Lilly fellow, Laura nevertheless found herself graced with both of these gifts.

> As I left the bank, I spotted the old man. I pushed my palms together in a salaam and bowed as low as I could. I then reached out to the young man who found India so shameful. I took both of his hands in both of mine. I told him, "I would have waited. I would have waited." He smiled and shook his head. "I know," he said. I let go of his hands and walked to the metro clutching my purse containing the cursed two thousand rupee note.

In reflecting on what this experience means in terms of her own vocation as a Christian scholar, Laura concludes her letter with the following plea: "Lilly friends, please pray." She notes her own helplessness in the face of an unstable country and her frustration with having to spend valuable research time in a daily queue at an ATM, but her prayer rises not from the metaphor of egg sandwiches and its attendant self-pity but rather, like prayers of Alyosha in *The Brothers Karamazov*, from the deep well of the Gospel: "But please, friends, more than that, pray for my neighbors across India. Think of how drastic economic measures come with a price, think of those left behind by progress, think of the least of these."

Smallness of Soul and the Ancient Practice of Lectio Divina

While Laura's immersion in Christian humanism bore fruit among the disenfranchised of New Delhi, another former Lilly fellow, whom I will call Margaret, found a remedy for chronic stress in the ancient monastic practice of *lectio divina*. In the unrelenting struggle to stay on top of an increasing amount of research involving complicated equations, Margaret found that her stress became a fertile soil in which the vice of pusillanimity, or smallness of soul, began to grow and fester. In a recent reflection, she searches for an antidote:

> Maybe chronic stress requires a treatment plan … I am reminded of Rebecca DeYoung's *Glittering Vices,* which we read alongside the *Purgatorio* in colloquium, and in particular her opening account of pusillanimity, the vice of "smallness of soul." According to DeYoung, 'Those afflicted by this vice, wrote Aquinas, shrink back from all that God has called them to be. [The] pusillanimous rely on their own puny powers and focus on their own potential for failure, rather than counting on God's grace to equip them for great work in his kingdom--work beyond anything they might have dreamed for themselves.[4]

In the midst of a crushing deadline for completing the portfolio that would determine whether or not she would become a doctoral candidate, Margaret overcame pusillanimity—her fears of inadequacy and failure in the face of such a career-defining milestone—through the daily practice of *lectio divina*. She recalled how her Lilly Cohort had prayed the Divine Hours during the season of Advent the year before, taking time to bookend the day, morning and evening, in quiet prayer. She writes,

> The discipline of daily prayer reinforces our un-worldly motivations, our call to serve God with gladness and singleness of heart. That singleness of heart is the pattern I wish to cultivate: to subsume all my motivations under the single mission of following Christ in my present circumstances.

Taken together, the experiences of Laura and Margaret suggest that reading and discussing texts like *Gilead*, *The Brothers Karamazov*, and *Glittering Vices*, as well as the practice of praying the liturgical hours can serve as an occasion for reflection on the narrative arc of one's own vocation. Insofar as it is intended to sanctify the life of the entire Christian community, the Divine Office in particular is a practice into which the lonely and stressed graduate student can lean and through which she can perceive a larger horizon because she finds herself, as another Fellow suggested (quoting the end of the *Purgatorio*), "renewed with new-sprung leaves, /pure and prepared to rise up to the stars" (XXXIII:143–45).

Hospitality, Humility, and the Horizon of Well-Ordered Love

While the practices of shared inquiry, reflective writing, and *lectio divina* can provide an initiation into the right direction of love in such a way that, as Augustine points out, things become evident that would otherwise remain hidden, the LGFP also seeks to introduce various communal Christian practices. Along with keeping Sabbath and communal worship, the practice we have found to be most central to the fellows experience is that of Christian hospitality. We begin the inaugural conference with this theme as it is expressed in the Gospel of Luke, and it is built into the very fabric of the program, in particular, the theme of hospitality to the stranger (*xenia*), which is familiar to many of the fellows from their reading of Homer's *Odyssey*. The code of hospitality is important for understanding the theme of table fellowship in the Gospel of Luke, where Jesus is at table eight times, more than in any other gospel. Indeed, hospitality is central to his ministry.

The focus of our conversation on the Gospel of Luke is chapter twenty-four, which takes place on the road to Emmaus, as two of the disciples leave Jerusalem, disappointed and disillusioned, having abandoned "the way" on the very day that the promise of Jesus' entire life was being fulfilled (the day of the resurrection). Jesus draws near and walks with them, but he is a "stranger" to them: "their eyes were prevented from recognizing him" (24:16; NAB). In this passage, Luke stresses the disciples, not the change in Jesus' appearance: "**their eyes** were prevented from recognizing him." The notion of being a stranger to a new place and community, as well as that of welcoming the stranger in the faces of the many undergraduate students and colleagues they encounter is one that graduate fellows can easily identify with, but the question of truly recognizing Jesus is one that requires an understanding of Luke's use of the Greek word *epiginosko*. It means to "realize" or "really know" and suggests thorough, unassailable, and trenchant knowledge, not of a fact or metaphor or concept, but of a person. Knowing a person thus presupposes an intimate relationship, one based not on an external appearance but on mutual disclosure and inner attunement.

The final transition from seeing to truly knowing Jesus (24:32–35) occurs in the context of hospitality, when Cleopas and his companion, following the example of Jesus facing the crowd of five thousand, invite him to "stay" (*meno*: to dwell or make his home with them). The true test occurs when the three are at the table. Given the centrality of Jesus' meal ministry in Luke's Gospel, it makes sense that the disciples would recognize the stranger as the resurrected Christ in the very moment "he took bread, blessed and broke it, and gave it to them" (24:30). Luke goes on to state that, "their eyes were opened and they recognized him (*epignosan*)" (24:31; NAB). When the two disciples return to Jerusalem and join the eleven, they tell "what had happened on the road, and how he had been made known (*egnosthe*) to them in the breaking of the bread" (24:35; NAB). Practicing hospitality with the living Jesus turns out, for Cleopas and his companion, to have been merely a rehearsal for the real test of recognizing him, a test not of seeing, but of *having their eyes opened*. Like Penelope at the end (also Book 24) of the *Odyssey*, who "felt her knees go slack, her heart surrender, /recognizing the strong clear signs Odysseus offered" (23:231–32),[5] the disciples thus bear witness to the axis upon which true recognition depends: a conversion of heart on the part of the knower, a process that unfolds within the context of hospitality. Such a reading of *Luke* can become a guiding metaphor for graduate students seeking to pursue their vocation as Christian teacher-scholars amidst the competing claims of dissertation advisors, disciplinary guilds, and the cynical culture that permeates graduate study in the humanities.

Hospitality is modeled over the course of four conferences and a reunion conference that takes place in the graduate fellows fifth year. Mentors "set the table" in such a way that one full day of each summer conference is devoted to shared worship and prayer and to cultivating friendships via shared activities from hiking and canoeing to city walks and even fly fishing. Friendships are resumed, stories told of trials overcome, and gestures of commiseration proffered back and forth. Much of this dialogue takes place over long, leisurely meals. As Scales and Howell point out in the Introduction to this volume, all practices are initially rehearsals. Quoting Craig Dykstra, they go on to suggest that true Christian practices like hospitality eventually "become arenas in which something is done *to* us, in us, and through us that we could not of ourselves do, that is beyond what we do."[6] That is certainly an apt description of the transformation Laura underwent while sharing hospitality with the disenfranchised people of New Delhi as they stood in line at the ATM. The community that is created around the practice of hospitality informs and illuminates the lives of these young teacher-scholars for years to come.

A Fellow from cohort one, whom I will call Karen, shared the following reflection upon completion of her first year of teaching at a large secular university:

> Graduate training can often instill in us a sense of colleagues as competitors for scarce resources. The LGFP provided an alternative view of colleagues as friends and mentors in a shared intellectual effort and helped us to adopt practices, like hospitality, that would develop those relationships. While it seemed an odd choice to me at the time, I have drawn heavily on this idea in my first year.

Karen goes on to relate how discussions of war and peace in her International Relations course inevitably bring about disagreement and discomfort among her students. As a counter to this predictable response, she tries

> to create an atmosphere of honest inquiry rather than contentious debate. Thinking about Virgil's hospitality to Dante or the hospitality the desert fathers offered to pilgrims has helped me think about the hospitality I want to show my students and encourage them to show one another. The LGFP provided a space in which I was able to develop a set of practices and relationships with other scholars that, I hope, have translated into a rich classroom experience for my students.

As a young teacher-scholar, Karen already understands that hospitality is at the center of a nexus of practices including collegiality, curriculum development, and teaching. Such an understanding will allow her to remain faithful to her vocation despite the inevitable twists and turns her career may follow.

Perhaps it is the receptivity that hospitality opens up that accounts for the Fellows preoccupation with pride and its antidote—the virtue of humility. In keeping with Gregory the Great, Aquinas, and other medieval thinkers, Dante depicts the vice of Pride in his *Purgatorio* as the gravest of all sins, one that is woven into the very fabric of the human condition. Addressing all Christians who have turned away from God in pride, the poet cries, "What makes your mind rear up so high? / You are, as it were, defective creatures, / like the unformed worm, shaped from the mud" (X:127–29). This canto provokes spirited discussion in the biweekly colloquium as Fellows grapple with the kind of self-promoting culture into which they are being initiated. From showing off the depth and breadth of one's knowledge in seminar to name dropping and ceaselessly talking about one's "work," proud academicians are far from the corbel-like figures depicted by Dante, stooping penitentially under the crushing weight of boulders, "hunched over more or less /depending on the burdens on their backs" (X:136–37). The discussions of pride highlight its attendant virtue of humility, which is for many of the Fellows rooted in the same soil as Christian hospitality. A soul receptive to the presence of God in hospitality is a soul that is at least attuned to the vanity of pride in its own accomplishments.

The Virtuous Practice of Teaching

While the readings, online colloquia, and conferences do much to inspire and sustain Fellows as they enter the professoriate, attention to the more technical aspects of teaching is also a need frequently expressed in mentoring conversations and conferences. Graduate students in the humanities, most of whom are required to work as either teaching assistants or instructors of introductory courses, often find themselves both unprepared and uninspired by the theory-based "pedagogy seminars" that many graduate departments have instituted, in response to criticism that they are not preparing their students for the increasingly diverse and complex milieu of the contemporary college classroom. Eight years into the LGFP, one of the most important findings regarding the formation of the Christian scholar-teacher is the importance of a mentoring relationship with an experienced and hospitable professor, one who is willing to listen to and hear vulnerability; the questions and fears that lurk behind even the most confident posturing in the classroom. In one rather humorous reflection, a Fellow I will call Jason speaks of the dawning insight that he talks too much, but his self-knowledge and determination to experiment with new pedagogies are themselves rooted in a commitment to the practice of hospitality:

> My experience leading discussion sections suggests I have much to learn. First of all, I like talking. This can be a virtue, enabling me to thrive in discussions. But it can also be a vice, causing me to crusade into every silence and confidently plant the flag of my opinion on the matter. This is especially dangerous as a teacher. I do well with those students who resemble my undergraduate self: eager to talk, willing to interrupt. But those students who need a bit more space, a bit more time—do I make my classroom hospitable to them?

Jason goes on to enumerate the various ways in which the discussion section format to which he has been assigned as a Teaching Assistant actually works against the virtues of humility and hospitality to which he aspires. "So," he writes,

> I am fighting back. I am trying to talk less, to relinquish control over the direction and outcome of the conversation. My Lilly mentor is a storehouse of wisdom on this front, and our conversations have helped immensely. Surely I can better help all students if I attempt to understand how they work and provide them with opportunities to thrive. Practically, this has challenged me to welcome different learning and communicating styles, and to provide greater variety in class formats, including in-class writing, pairing off, and small group discussions. Personally, I hope these attempts at sympathetic imagination will form me into a more selfless, hospitable person.

Another recent Fellow, whom I will call Anna, speaks of the ways in which her practice of teaching writing underwent a sea change after a conversation with her Lilly mentor:

> The continual realization that students are loved deeply by Christ has changed my approach in structuring classes. A truly great day in the classroom is one that bends to answer student questions as they arise and flexibly meets students' needs by taking into account their complexity as humans—not as vessels to pour knowledge into. My Lilly mentor once advised me to interrupt the usual pattern of the course and just offer hospitality to my students at a particularly difficult point in the semester. As a result, rather than rushing into new content with my freshmen (which was my inclination), I brought them cookies and we talked about their being homesick and overwhelmed by college for ten minutes before moving into the lesson.

Anna goes on to say that she will be forever grateful for this advice not only because her effort at cultivating hospitality in the classroom paid off, but also because

> it made me stop and think deeply about how it feels to be a freshman student during the first semester of college, and it enabled me to approach the complexity of my students in a helpful way. In writing a syllabus, I have started to think about the rhythms of the academic year and the natural cycles that students go through instead of just counting out the number of pages to assign for each class. These are small examples, but they reveal an overarching theme: while fear is limiting, love opens up new possibilities, especially for how one thinks about teaching. I want to be the sort of teacher who is willing to change—however slowly or awkwardly—in order to love students more authentically and fully.

The practices and habits of reflection inculcated by participation in the Lilly Graduate Fellows Program often bleed into the Fellows evolving philosophy of teaching. For most of these young teachers, that philosophy is inherently incremental. As a Fellow I will call James points out,

> It is often tempting to think that we can only serve God through some ambitious mission, like building a cathedral. Yet cathedrals are built over decades by a myriad of architects and artisans. Each individual contributes his or her particular skills, working every day on one facet of the larger whole. Abraham Joshua Heschel suggests that the Sabbath is a "cathedral in time," and we should take this attitude into our teaching: to teach is to build a cathedral, stone by stone, student by student.

> Teaching belongs to the realm of the quotidian; it cannot be performed once and for all, but can only be practiced day by day. Preparing lessons and grading papers do not lend themselves to a single burst of inspiration, but rather require persistent effort and focus. As an art it requires one to cultivate virtues through quotidian actions, rather than perform a single heroic act. Insofar as it demands patience, gentleness, and charity, teaching is a kind of spiritual discipline.

In expounding her teaching philosophy, another recent Fellow, whom I will call Sarah, questions the value of hospitality as a mere ideal. She writes, "I am increasingly concerned about how *ideals* (such as a belief in the value of Christian hospitality in the classroom, for example) can actually be put into *practice*." Now a doctoral candidate at a Jesuit University whose values are grounded in the life and works of St. Ignatius, Sarah has been inspired to embrace an Ignation version of incarnational pedagogy as "a useful vehicle for mobilizing that ideal of a genuine and hospitable culture of inquiry." She finds herself called to take seriously the Ignatian ideal that education of the whole person should embody both the ability to judge thinking that is superficial or undermining of the human community, and that education of the whole person ultimately must lead to action. Jesuit education is directed toward societal structures, the global community, and the transformation of students through increasing self-scrutiny and self-knowledge that leads if not immediately to action, at least to further reflection on the subject matter at hand. In support of the values of her Jesuit context, Sarah created her own introductory-level literature course centered on the theme of inter-faith relationships among Jews, Christians, and Muslims. Drawing primarily on English texts from the sixteenth through the eighteenth centuries, her course sought to provide students with the tools necessary to read closely, analyze carefully, and master key literary terms, while at the same time exploring how writers of an earlier era navigated many of the complex questions of religious tolerance, intolerance, unity and diversity that we face today. We see her teaching philosophy in the following remarks:

> As global citizens of the 21st century, students find that they are confronted with the reality of violence that comes from uncompromising religious intolerance while even domestic politics seem to be increasingly affected by professed religious identity, and they are often at a loss as to how to respond. My course maintained that an ability to think productively and peacefully about religious difference is necessary if students are to be responsible members of a diverse society.

What is remarkable about the evolution of Sarah's philosophy of teaching is that the leaven provided by the Christian practice of hospitality led her to develop a truly integrative approach to college teaching that belies her years. She not only offered hospitality to her students but engaged them in hospitable reading and analysis of texts featuring relationships among people of various faiths. It is an approach which, as Parker Palmer and Arthur Zajonc ask us to consider in *The Heart of Higher Education: A Call For Renewal*, not only "recognizes the whole human being and his or her place in community and the world,"[7] but also "embraces both the great web of being on which all things depend and the fact that our knowing of those things is helped, not hindered, by our being enmeshed in that web."[8] Furthermore, it is a pedagogy that is receptive to, and animated by, the presence of God and his ongoing relationship to the world in Christ.

As the hospitality of mentors toward our graduate fellows bears fruit in more inventive pedagogies and hospitality to their students, so our stewardship of foundational ideas and themes from the Christian tradition gives rise to reflections on teaching, like those above, which are themselves models of Christian Stewardship. In its Trinitarian approach to enhancing graduate education through conferences, colloquia, and mentoring centered on the tradition of Christian Humanism, the Lilly Graduate Fellows program does indeed represent "an imaginative reformulation and implementation… of an agenda for church-related higher learning in the twenty-first century."[9] At this point, however, the experiences of the LGFP give rise to the following question: How might such an initiative be replicated, in whole or in part, by Christian graduate students, faculty, and administrators who are not members of the Lilly Fellows Network but find themselves desirous of a community steeped in the readings and practices of the Christian Humanistic tradition?

Conclusion: Resources and Strategies for Broadening the Initiative

After 10 years of planning and implementation, the experience of the Lilly Graduate Fellows Program has reached a point at which it can serve as a model that can be modified to suit the needs of like-minded Christian graduate students in Humanities and Fine Arts programs across the country. To this end, the Lilly Fellows program should make resources for developing cohorts like those of the LGFP available on its website. Such resources include the syllabi and discussion questions developed for the online colloquium, which could easily be amended for use in face-to-face reading groups or colloquia. A list of LGFP Mentors and former Graduate Fellows willing to serve as consultants to faculty, administrators, or graduate students seeking to develop a cohort could also be posted on the Lilly Fellows program website. The staff of the Lilly Fellows program could offer a series of webinars on developing a cohort, the role of the Mentor, and possible topics for conferences on themes related to the fostering of Christian teacher-scholars within the wider academy. Finally, the LFP should provide a list of potential funding sources for underwriting a cohort.

As a model of active love that brings Christian academics together across several generations, as both debtors and stewards of the Christian tradition of higher learning, the cohort model described here is worthy of duplication, modification, and renewal, and the resources and strategies that nourished the initiative and help it to flourish should be disseminated to those who are interested in furthering the development of this model. In this way, the long view provided by the Lilly Graduate Fellows program, of "how to succeed not only in the academy but in life more generally,"[10] becomes an even longer and, dare I say, eschatological view. For as a Christian beacon of hope, this model for training the next generation of Christian teacher-scholars connects us not only to the Christian tradition and its future on earth, but to those "mysterious other worlds" that Fr. Zosima suggests, in *The Brothers Karamazov*, beckon to us from eternity. "Certainly we shall rise," says Alyosha, speaking of his hope in the resurrection to the young boys gathered around him at the end of the novel, "certainly we shall see and gladly, joyfully tell one another all that has been."[11]

Notes

1. All quotations are from *Purgatorio*, trans. Jean Hollander and Robert Hollander (New York: Doubleday, 2003).
2. Joseph Creech, *Network Communique*, vol. 30 (Valparaiso, IN: Valparaiso University, 2015), 20.
3. L. Gregory Jones and Stephanie Paulsell, *The Scope of Our Art: The Vocation of the Theological Teacher* (Grand Rapids: Eerdmans, 2001), 209.
4. The Fellow is referring to the Introduction to a text she read as part of the Graduate Fellows program. See Rebecca DeYoung, *Glittering Vices* (Grand Rapids: Brazos, 2009), 9–10.
5. Text from *The Odyssey*, trans. Robert Fagles (New York: Viking, 1996).

6. C. Dykstra, *Growing in the Life of Faith*, 2nd ed. (Louisville, KY: Westminster John Knox, 2005), 56.
7. Parker Palmer and Arthur Zajonc, *The Heart of Higher Education: A Call For Renewal* (San Francisco: Jossey-Bass, 2010), 60.
8. Ibid., 101.
9. Creech, *Network Communique*, 30: 20.
10. Ibid.
11. Fyodor Dostoevsky, *The Brothers Karamazov*, trans. Richard Pevear and Larissa Volokhonsky (New York: Farrar, Straus and Giroux, 1990), 776.

CHAPTER 9

Intellectual Humility & Higher Education

David T. Echelbarger

Engaging students in an examination of life's big questions is becoming increasingly difficult. Ostensibly, one of higher education's central aims is to prepare students for the personal, ethical, and social challenges of life by providing the opportunity to explore questions of meaning and value. Forming a coherent view of goodness, truth, and beauty, it is thought, will help emerging adults decide how they ought to carry out life's journey. And yet, today's students often doubt whether questions about value, meaning, and importance fall within the domain of rational inquiry. Many hold that deciding what ultimately matters in life is left to the individual and that personal opinions are not subject to evaluation. Consequently, they are reluctant to engage life's big questions, because, as they see it, there is nothing about meaning, value, and purpose that warrants discussion.

For the students who inhabit such a worldview, courses in the humanities serve little purpose. There is nothing to be learned from studying canonical texts because they merely inform us of the author's point of view. Whether that point of view holds true is not up for debate, as the categories of truth and falsity do not apply. At best, the humanities

D.T. Echelbarger (✉)
University of Mary, Bismarck, ND, USA

T.L. Scales and J.L. Howell (eds.), *Christian Faith and University Life*,
DOI 10.1007/978-3-319-61744-2_9

offer the opportunity to master the art of description. Students learn to provide coherent accounts of great ideas and movements, such as the worldview of the ancient Greeks, the moral vision of Dante's *Divine Comedy*, the philosophical foundations of the European Enlightenment, Marxism, and various forms of critical theory. While they are capable of articulating detailed taxonomies of how these ideas relate to one another, they are hesitant to engage questions of meaning and value, which leaves them lacking the skills to evaluate these competing visions of the good life. Consequently, a fair number of students pick and choose from these rival accounts as they see fit, while the criteria of selection remain opaque to them. The process of moral choice occurs in the same way one may identify something as salty or sweet—without a full understanding of how this selection occurs.

Put simply, decisions about what to value and how to act are subject to the whim of their appetites. Most worrisome is that when emerging adults act according to what "feels right," they behave as adolescents during what are intended to be the most formative years of their lives.

Certainly, one can arrive at an informed understanding of what makes life worth living without taking a single class in the humanities. Nevertheless, this fact does not diminish higher education's ability to transform lives. Thus, those who maintain that higher education can guide students toward a coherent view of the good life are entrusted with the challenge of finding a way of overcoming contemporary students' intellectual malaise. For, only then can students benefit from one of the true luxuries in life: the opportunity to explore, seriously and in depth, questions that will forever inform how they live.

Importantly, the work of educating students for a life well-lived belongs to all members of the university. In what follows, I contend that no matter what one's discipline, stewards of the academy must practice the virtue of intellectual humility in order to form students who are receptive to searching for and arriving at a vision of what is good, true, and beautiful.

Lost in Transition and Reluctant to Engage

A recent study published by Christian Smith supports the above characterization of today's students.[1] Interviews with 230 18–23-year old Americans reveal that the majority of emerging adults are ill-equipped to think coherently about matters of value. When asked to describe experiences they had facing moral dilemmas, about two-thirds (66%) of the emerging adults interviewed proved unable to engage the questions asked by Smith and his team. The first third (33%) were unable to identify any difficult moral decisions that they might have confronted. Approximately, the second third (29%) provided examples that turned out to be more practical than moral, such as deciding whether to buy a second litter box for one's cat, whether to rent a particular apartment, or if it is worth risking a ticket by parking illegally.[2] For Smith, "These cases make it clear that many emerging adults do not have a good handle on what makes something a *moral* issue or what the specifically moral dimensions of such situations are."[3] Instead of deliberating about what is morally good, bad, right, or wrong, they appeal to considerations that are "straightforwardly practical, utilitarian, financial, and psychological."[4]

Questions that forced emerging adults to reflect on the nature of morality revealed even deeper confusion. Six out of ten (60%) embraced "a highly individualistic approach to morality."[5] In their eyes, what makes something right or wrong is "entirely a matter of individual decision."[6] As one young woman put it, if a person does not believe that what she is doing is wrong, then by definition she cannot be acting immorally.[7]

Smith observes that emerging adults who believe that individuals must decide morality for themselves typically fail to distinguish between two interpretations of moral individualism. According to the stronger interpretation, individuals must decide for themselves what is moral because moral claims are not objectively true.[8] By embracing certain moral claims, they take on a quasi-truth status for that individual. The stronger interpretation is reflected in claims of the following sort, "Personally, for me, it would be wrong to cheat on an exam, that's how I look at it."[9] According to the weaker interpretation, moral claims are objectively true, but individuals must choose to embrace them on a personal level in order to intentionally act morally. Ultimately, this latter interpretation of moral individualism is common sense. The personal endorsement of moral claims is a necessary condition for moral action. However, the personal nature of moral conviction and action is often used to support the former, stronger interpretation of moral individualism which is indicative of a kind of moral relativism—the view that moral standards are not objective, but rather is determined by individual persons or distinct groups of persons.

Smith suspects that most emerging adults who identify as moral individualists embrace the stronger interpretation. Paradoxically, while strong moral individualism entails moral relativism, only about 30% of interviewees believed that relativism is true. Yet, those who wanted to resist moral relativism also struggled to identify non-relative moral claims that they would be willing to defend, which for Smith, is an indication that a significant number of today's emerging adults are, at least presently, unable to think clearly and coherently about important moral issues.

Along with showing that emerging adults desperately need to be taught how to think critically about matters of value and importance, the students in Smith's study also revealed that they were reluctant to take seriously even the most modest forms of moral education. Learning how to reason well about right and wrong requires discussing substantive moral issues and evaluating moral claims, yet the participants interviewed by Smith and his team consistently claimed that one's moral beliefs ought to be kept private. In fact, a recurring theme was that letting one's moral position be known is itself immoral. For many of today's emerging adults, almost any open discussion of right, wrong, good, or bad is seen as an attempt to impose one's moral beliefs upon others. Or, as Smith puts it, expressing one's own moral view is taken to be "synonymous with dominating and controlling others, a kind of pathology that violates other people's dignity and rights."[10] Thus, expressing one's position on matters of value is not just distasteful, it is morally abhorrent. Consequently, many students are often reluctant to discuss, let alone practice making explicit evaluations about competing visions of goodness, truth, and beauty.

Smith argues that emerging adults have adopted this stance at least in part because they mistake all moral judgments for being *judgmental*. That is, they view all appraisals of another's way of life and practices as essentially denouncing and disparaging. As such, moral judgments are social weapons: Their purpose is to shame, separate, and ostracize those who are different. There is a difference, of course, between making a moral assessment and "judging" in a negative, condemning way. Smith reminds us that moral evaluations can be made "with great humility, openness, reciprocity, care, and even love for the idea or person being judged."[11] What emerging adults do not realize is that, when used appropriately, moral assessments are meant to preserve relationships. For example, usually, we do not tell our loved ones that they are doing something wrong as a way of cutting them out of our lives. Rather, we do so because we want to repair and strengthen our bond with them. From this, it seems to follow that one way of encouraging students to engage life's big questions on a substantive level—one which ultimately requires some critical assessment and appraisal—is to show them that moral and critical evaluations are charitable, not judgmental.

My own experience in the classroom confirms Smith's assessment. Yet, as he admits, it is only a partial explanation for why today's emerging adults avoid making value assessments and voicing their moral beliefs. Thus, I would like to suggest another, deeper cause which, I contend, can help explain emerging adult's reluctance to engage questions of value and importance, as well as identify why many often struggle to think carefully and coherently about morality. Specifically, I contend that there is a principled reason *why* today's emerging adults have a negative view of moral evaluations. Their disapproval of moral assessments flows directly from their tacit endorsement of moral individualism.

Smith notes that 72% of those interviewed claimed that knowing what is right or wrong is based on "instinct."[12] According to one emerging adult, "You know what to do and you go with your common sense. Go with your intuition." Another said, "You can kind of just tell instinctively. You can feel if it's good or bad." Similarly, one claimed, "I can usually just tell right away, don't have to think about it very hard, you just know. It's hard to describe."[13] The view that morality is instinctual, or known by intuition, plays a major role in emerging adults' aversion to discussing moral questions. If right and wrong are "in the strands of our DNA," as one emerging adult put it, then evaluating another's moral beliefs is as uncouth as criticizing one's preference for dark chocolate or one's aversion to spicy foods.[14] According to this view, the stances that we take in response to life's big questions are, in large part, out of our control, and thus it is improper to make any substantive judgments about them. Additionally, the moral intuitionism of emerging adults helps account for many of those who are bad at identifying moral dilemmas and thinking about morality in general. If what is right or wrong is determined by our individual tastes (so to speak), then deliberating about what's right, wrong, good, or bad, is as foreign as deliberating about whether ketchup tastes good on fries. It is no wonder that when asked to identify a situation that required serious moral reflection, the emerging adults from Smith's study appealed to practical, utilitarian, and financial considerations. For, in their minds, these are the only sorts of things that one can truly reason about. Thus, the tacit endorsement of moral individualism by emerging adults explains, at least in part, why they are reluctant to engage life's big questions. First, moral individualism implies that all critical assessments of one's worldview are equivalent to the criticism of persons. Second, it implies that the answers to life's big questions are the products of individual preference, and thus they are not suitable subject matter for discussion.

Supposing that I am correct, then, in order to engage students in a discussion of life's big questions, stewards of the academy must first overcome the moral individualism of today's emerging adults. Deciding on a tenable solution, however, requires first identifying why emerging adults hold this view, to begin with. One might think that the reluctance of today's youth to rationally engage questions about what ultimately matters in life is a relatively new phenomenon. What I want to suggest, however, is that students are not skeptical about our ability to rationally discuss matters of value because they have bought into moral individualism per se, nor because they have carefully reasoned to the conclusion that moral individualism is in fact true. Instead, I want to suggest that the problem is, ironically, rooted in the hyper-rational pursuit of knowledge, or in what might be characterized as a kind of intellectual hubris. Interestingly enough, this is a problem that educators recognized as far back as Socrates. As he warns, the methods of the academy are tools that can cut both ways. The practices and techniques that bring us to knowledge can also draw us into skepticism if their various roles and purposes are not properly understood. My hope is that stewards of the academy will benefit from revisiting Socrates' warning to the academy, as we look for ways to reengage many of our students.

A School of Stunned Fish: Socrates' Warning to the Academy

It is natural to read Socrates as one of rationality's great champions. Not only does his axiom, "The unexamined life is not worth living," inspire us to take up the life of the mind, but also his dialectic method is one that values free and critical inquiry: It takes no past truths for granted and is always looking for new sources of knowledge.[15] At times, his pursuit of the truth is even portrayed as ruthless and unforgiving. For example, after being questioned by Socrates on the nature of virtue, the young Meno claims that Socrates is like a torpedo fish, which leaves its prey stunned and unable to swim.[16] Socrates responds, in part, by claiming that Meno's paralysis is not altogether a bad thing. Before, Meno publicly claimed to be an expert on virtue, when in fact he knew very little. Now, he is aware of his ignorance. Freed from error, Meno will be able to set out on the correct path to knowledge.

While Socrates extols the virtues of his dialectic method in Plato's *Meno*, he admits grave concerns about such a hyper-rational and ungrounded model of education in Plato's *Republic*. There, he worries that after being taught to accept nothing at face value and to constantly be critical of every hypothesis, the students of dialectic are left in a state of great danger.[17] They become incredibly skeptical, especially toward the values that they were taught when they were young. This skepticism takes root in the fact that one can cast doubt upon anything. Every claim, in principle, can be questioned and challenged. When coupled with the tacit implication that the only beliefs worth holding are those which are indubitable, it becomes difficult, if not impossible, to assent to truths of any kind or to form opinions of their own. While knowledge of their ignorance keeps the students of Socrates' dialectic from assenting to false beliefs, they are left at an impasse. Due to the influence of this hyper-rationalization, they are unable to identify and commit to the path that will take them to a true vision of reality. As such, they are unintentionally led into a kind of skepticism (at worst) or agnosticism (at best) regarding answers to life's big questions. Insofar as all rational inquiry into questions of value and meaning are either stymied or inconclusive, there is nothing to be known about human nature, goodness, and how one ought to live.

The effects of this hyper-rational skepticism are disastrous. Without a conception of goodness from which to order their priorities, or even a dependable authority to appeal to, the students of Socrates' dialectic are left vulnerable to the temptations of the practical life. Those who succumb to these temptations abandon the pursuit of what is good in favor of wealth and fame. Here, Socrates' concern is that by pursuing what is practical or useful without a conception of what the useful is supposed to be *useful for*, the merely practical life ultimately leads to a life of slavery.

In Plato's *Theaetetus*, Socrates laments an instance in which a student falls into skepticism and is enticed to abandon philosophy (the pursuit of wisdom and intrinsic goodness) in favor of practical goods. Things go well for the young student at first, as his rigorous intellectual training enables him to gain immediate success as a lawyer. But he eventually realizes that in order to preserve his reputation for winning cases, he has no choice but to follow a set path:

> His early servitude prevents him from making a free, straight growth; it forces him into doing crooked things by imposing dangers and alarms upon a soul that is still tender. He cannot meet these by just and honest practice, and so resorts to lies and to the policy of repaying one wrong with another; thus he is constantly being bent and distorted, and in the end grows up to manhood with a mind that has no health in it, having now become—in his own eyes—a man of ability and wisdom. (173b)

Put simply, Socrates' worry is that the critical and unforgiving method of dialectic, which is needed to yield knowledge, often produces nothing more than a class of stunned students. Intellectually paralyzed and without a way to proceed, they can no longer assent to claims about important matters. As a result, their reasoning becomes purely instrumental, which in turn leads them unwittingly into a life devoid of meaning.

Socrates' warning still applies to the academy today. It continues to emphasize "critical thinking"—which, like the Socratic method, teaches students to come to well-reasoned conclusions by first challenging assumptions and analyzing the use of evidence to support one's views.[18]

While Socrates is chiefly concerned with a misuse of philosophical reasoning, there is also need to be cautious about misunderstanding the role of the academy's wildly successful natural sciences. The natural sciences, which have advanced at an impressive rate, are founded upon observable, empirical claims about the physical world. These "material facts," which can be weighed and measured, are less susceptible to scrutiny, as they are supported by our common experience of our sensory faculties. Moreover, the findings of the natural sciences can be universally duplicated and thus confirmed to be true. When paired with the tacit axiom of hyper-rationality, which holds that the only beliefs worth committing oneself to are those which cannot be challenged, one finds what at first appears to be a promising way of overcoming the *aporia* of critical inquiry. Put simply, one might conclude that the only way to attain knowledge is to apply the scientific method to the physical reality of the natural world.

Such a view is unique in that it makes claims about the kinds of things that can be known. One can know empirical findings, but one cannot have knowledge of abstract theoretical matters—such as the nature of goodness or the meaning of human life. As such, this view lends itself readily to moral individualism. While empirical claims can be known, questions about meaning and value are not subject to rational debate. Instead, they are the products of human choice and desire. It is up to individuals to decide for themselves what ought to be pursued and what ought to be avoided. Thus, while this position makes room for some knowledge (knowledge and mastery of the natural world), it still leaves us unable to rationally address some of life's biggest questions.

Importantly, such a view rests upon familiar foundations. Its success is due to its ability to provide seemingly certain conclusions, which *itself* is made attractive by the acceptance of a hyper-rationalized view of knowledge. If we set too high a standard for what constitutes knowledge by claiming that only perfect certainty will do, then only the natural sciences can provide knowledge and insight and we remain in a state of paralysis with respect to questions that fall outside of the scientific domain. Thus, given these limitations, perhaps moving beyond the misconception of human rationality and knowledge is the first step in recovering the ability to discuss life's big questions.

Finding the Way Again: The Need for Intellectual Humility

In the *Republic,* Adeimantus appeals to examples like the young lawyer from the *Theaetetus* to support his claim that students who begin training in dialectic turn out to be vicious individuals (487d). They are the tyrants who have become slaves to their own immediate desires (577d). It is in light of Adeimantus' poignant criticism that Socrates famously concludes that his hyper-rational method for pursing truth requires good cities—as only then are students safe from being led astray by the non-virtuous. Socrates' response is brief, but one can reasonably interpret him as stressing the importance of stewards within the academy—those who will preserve the pursuit of truth by modeling both moral and intellectual virtue. Unfortunately, Socrates does not explicitly comment on the kinds of attitudes educators will have to adopt or the practices that they will need to exercise in order to keep the skepticism that often follows critical inquiry at bay. We are left wondering how to prevent students from succumbing to this dangerous mindset, to begin with and how to handle those who have already become intellectually scandalized. Fortunately, by drawing upon Socrates' own example, it becomes clear that safeguarding the quest for truth will at least require practicing the virtue of intellectual humility.

Situated between the vices of intellectual hubris and intellectual meekness, intellectual humility consists of an honest appraisal of our intellectual abilities. It accepts that what we can know with certainty is limited (in some contexts more than others), yet it remains confident that we can know some things, and when we cannot, we can form reasonable beliefs about them. Unsurprisingly, Socrates himself is a model of intellectual humility. He believes that he is wise only because he knows what he does not know. He reminds us that knowing the Good is difficult, if not impossible. As displayed in the *Symposium*, he acknowledges that knowledge is ultimately a gift. Yet, Socrates' humility does not dampen his intellectual hunger. It leaves him with a sense of wonder and makes him all the more eager to discuss what is true, good, and beautiful.

If the intellectual humility modeled by Socrates is the solution, how can we cultivate this intellectual virtue within the academy? In the remaining sections, I outline two sources of intellectual humility that will help us to adopt an appropriate vision of what we can know and reason's role in the exploration of life's most important questions.

Humble Beginnings: Starting Out on the Right Foot

The first source of intellectual humility that I want to explore stems from reason's origins. Pope John Paul II's *Fides et Ratio* reminds us that faith supplies reason's starting point. In this context, "faith" is not meant to carry a theological connotation. Aristotle expresses virtually the same idea when he says that reason must proceed, and then return to, first principles that are "indemonstrable."[19] The principle of noncontradiction, for example, cannot be proven. Any such proof would itself depend upon its axiom that the same proposition cannot be both true and false or that the same thing cannot simultaneously exist and not exist. Thus, all rational inquiry and judgment depend upon this foundational starting point, which is not itself supplied by a rational proof.

Once reason has been supplied with its first principles, the life of the mind has a valid aspiration to be, in the words of Pope John Paul II, an "*autonomous* enterprise, obeying its own rules and employing the powers of reason alone."[20] It is crucial to recognize, however, that being "autonomous" is not the same as being "self-sufficient." For, without faith, reason would have nothing from which to begin its inquiry. Nor would it have anything against which to compare what it had discovered.[21]

What plagues Socrates' students, then, is the assumption that reason is both autonomous *and* self-sufficient. The reason that their inquiry never ends (and thus appears futile) is because they fail to recognize that the life of the mind begins with premises that are either not supplied by reason or not immune to scrutiny.

In order to facilitate an environment in which students can confidently pursue the truth about even the most difficult of questions, stewards of the academy should model this aspect of intellectual humility by openly acknowledging the humble beginnings of their own disciplines. Mathematicians, for example, might spend time explaining the significance of Gödel's Theorem, which shows that no mathematical system is complete. In every instance, there are true, foundational statements which the system itself is unable to prove. Those in the natural sciences can draw attention to when empirical findings must be interpreted and placed into context within a larger set of data—something which is not properly the domain of science, but rather falls under the scope of abstract or theoretical reasoning. Professors in the humanities might strive to show how answering certain philosophical fundamental questions in their fields is grounded in a proper understanding of other disciplines.

Finally, those who are engaged in the enterprise of teaching "critical thinking" would do well to examine the manner in which our beliefs are formed and their relationship to the truth. Students are often surprised to discover that even the most, well-formed belief can turn out to be false. This inspires open-mindedness, a kind of intellectual humility in which one recognizes that the certainty of our beliefs is rarely assured. Students who embrace this attitude are more willing to engage difficult questions. First, they recognize that their previously held beliefs may warrant reexamination. Perhaps they were not consciously formed, and thus their foundations are relatively unknown. Or, even if their beliefs were thoughtfully formed, open-minded students are willing to look again, to evaluate the quality of their prior reasoning. Second, such students recognize that the best way to understand one's own position is to listen to the well-formed views of others. Only by listening to others can we discover that what we believe is incomplete, or inaccurate. Likewise, by critically engaging different answers to the same question, we often find corroboration for our views, learn of new evidence to support them, or be more convinced of their truth, insofar as they are able to withstand even the most challenging objections.

Simple practices, such as these, show students that the journey toward knowledge almost never begins with certainty. Instead, it begins with a firm commitment to a claim that it is reasonable—but not indubitable. A correct understanding of rational inquiry's humble beginnings allows students to embark upon paths to truth that might otherwise appear unpromising.

Modest Ends: Keeping Our Destination in Mind

What happens, however, when students encounter challenges and obstacles in their search for truth? How might we help students to resist succumbing to skepticism when answers to life's most important questions seem to evade them or when they are faced with particularly stubborn objections? My suggestion is that here we might help students by calling to mind a second source of intellectual humility, which focuses on reason's ending point.

In his *Intellectual Appetite*, Paul Griffiths stresses that "to perform an act of knowing is to attain a participatory intimacy in what is known."[22] He also notes that participation is a "peculiar relation" in that it is "asymmetrical."[23] The asymmetrical nature of participation stems from the fact that when the *x* participates in *y*, *x* receives a part of *y* but not all of it. In other words, when one obtains knowledge of the natural word, or correctly identifies a piece of artwork as beautiful, one also becomes acquainted with a more fundamental aspect of reality, such as the nature of being itself. This second act of reason, however, is limited, as reason does not fully grasp the essence of this higher order truth. Griffiths describes this relationship as "an intimacy of which that between lovers is a distant, participated shadow, with an equally profound difference and distance between them."[24] If knowing is a participatory act and participation is, in some sense, incomplete, then it is not surprising that we are always able to question whatever we take ourselves to have discovered. Reminding ourselves that, in many ways, our knowledge is only partial is one way to preserve the life of the mind.

Importantly, in order for knowing to be an act of participation, what we are coming to know must somehow transcend us. The very idea that *x*'s participation in *y* is limited seems to presuppose that there are aspects of *y* that extend beyond *x*'s grasp. It seems, then, that in order to exercise this intellectual humility with respect to reason's end, one must acknowledge that reality extends beyond the reach of our human faculties.[25]

There are a number of ways to cultivate this aspect of intellectual humility. First, stewards of the academy must continually remind students of our ability to know and increasingly understand true answers to life's biggest questions. Second, when perfect knowledge does escape us, it is paramount to provide a rational explanation as to why. Students must be encouraged to wonder about our own limitations. What is it about our own intellectual abilities that make answering particular questions so difficult? Why are some questions more difficult to answer than others? Finally, stewards of the academy must celebrate the commitment to well-formed beliefs, which, despite falling short of knowledge, provide us with the justification needed for our views about the world and our place in it.

Conclusion

Overall, understanding that there are limits to both what and how we come to know seems to be a necessary first step for preserving the legitimacy of rationally examining life's big questions.

One question I have not addressed is what commitments learning communities must hold in order to practice intellectual humility. In a volume dedicated to *Christian* stewards of the academy, it might seem odd that I have yet to mention how such a viewpoint fits within the Christian tradition. In fact, some might say that I have gone out of my way to show how the Christian sources I have relied on are either drawing from or at least compatible with non-Christian sources (i.e., Socrates). I have done this because I do not think that there is anything *distinctively* Christian about intellectual humility. It is, I suggest, distinctive of a certain view of transcendence—one which Socrates, Plato, and many others have endorsed. But one can hold such a view without being a Christian.

That being said, I do steadfastly maintain that intellectual humility is *essentially* Christian. As Mark Noll argues, true Christian discipleship requires a commitment to the life of the mind, and such a commitment requires approaching life's biggest questions with humility.[26] As he eloquently puts it, Jesus Christ is the "sure antidote to the moral diseases of the intellectual life" as "Jesus himself confessed… that there were things he did not know, then scholars following Christ should be double aware of how limited their own wisdom truly is. Knowing Christ, in other worlds, means learning humility."[27]

Finally, although I am not convinced that the practice of intellectual humility cannot be incorporated into the secular academy, I am inclined to think that it is more easily practiced within a Christian environment. Part of this is due to the Christian commitment to the transcendence of truth. Knowledge and wisdom require a true conception of the nature of reality. Insofar as reality is grounded in the nature of God, every act of knowing involves participation in the transcendent. While, as mentioned earlier, such a view can be found in the Socratic and Platonic traditions, it can easily be forgotten when not paired with theological commitments and everyday Christian practices. Indeed, the very fabric of the lived Christian life involves constant reminders of God's transcendence and, with it, both a joyful optimism and humble recognition of what we can come to know.

Given this, on might suggest that Christian higher education has a decided advantage over its secular counterparts when it comes to cultivating the life of the mind. Arguing for such a thesis is beyond the scope of this chapter. Yet, it is certainly worth reflecting upon the ways in which Christianity's commitment to the harmony of faith and reason provides a much needed environment in which students are keen to explore and critically engage answers to the questions that will set the course for their lives within and beyond the academy.

Notes

1. Christian Smith, *Lost in Transition: The Dark Side of Emerging Adulthood.* (New York: Oxford University Press, 2011).
2. The remaining three percent declined to answer the question. For Smith's discussion of their responses, see *Lost in Transition,* 56–59.
3. Ibid., 59. Emphasis original.
4. Ibid.
5. Ibid., 21.
6. Ibid.
7. Ibid., 22.

8. The stronger interpretation of moral individualism is also compatible with the view that there are moral truths, but they are unknown to us.
9. Ibid., 23.
10. Ibid., 24.
11. Ibid.
12. Ibid., 52.
13. Ibid.
14. Ibid.
15. *Apology,* 38a.
16. Meno, 79e–80b.
17. *Republic,* 537e.
18. One might reasonably worry that devoid of any substantial commitments to views of truth and goodness, critical thinking is reduced to the instrumentalism that worries Socrates in the *Theatetus.*
19. Aristotle, *Posterior Analytics.*
20. John Paul II, *Fides et Ratio* (Boston: Pauline Books & Media, 1998), 94. Emphasis original
21. Socrates comes to terms with this in the *Phaedo* when he admits that he has no choice but to posit, without proof, the existence of the Forms (99e–100a).
22. Paul J.Griffiths, *Intellectual Appetite: A Theological Grammar* (Washington, DC: The Catholic University of America Press, 2009), 76.
23. Ibid., 77 and 78 (respectively).
24. Ibid., 79.
25. For an example of how intellectual hubris violates the participatory nature of knowledge, consider Wendell Berry's criticisms of specialized language in his essay, "The Loss of the University" (in his *Home Economics* [San Francisco: North Point Press, 1987], 76–97). While furthering our academic pursuits requires refining the way we speak about what we have discovered, it is important to remember that specialized language only expresses one particular way of participating in a greater body of knowledge. When we choose to dwell solely within the linguistic boundaries of our disciplines (as is often the case) we are implicitly endorsing the viewpoint that our way of participating in what is knowable is superior to others. Griffiths reminds us, however, that this is a kind of idolatry. We have stepped beyond the bounds of participation by assuming that we have somehow grasped the entire whole.
26. Mark A. Noll, *Jesus Christ and the Life of the Mind* (Grand Rapids: Eerdmans, 2013), and *The Scandal of the Evangelical Mind* (Grand Rapids; Leicester, England: Eerdmans, 1995).
27. Noll, *Jesus Christ and the Life of the Mind,* 61–62.

CHAPTER 10

How Christian Faith Can Animate Teaching: A Taxonomy of Diverse Approaches

Perry L. Glanzer, Nathan Alleman and David Guthrie

Christian doctoral students and professors share a high calling with every current and future academic. This calling is aptly summed up in a wonderful phrase suggested by a group of authors with the Carnegie Foundation. They describe the goal of those who receive Ph.D.'s as being "stewards of

A version of this chapter first appeared in Nathan F. Alleman, Perry L. Glanzer, and David Guthrie, "The Integration of Christian Theological Traditions into the Classroom: A Survey of CCCU Faculty." Christian Scholar's Review 45, 2 (2016): 103–25 (copyright©2016 by Christian Scholar's Review; reprinted by permission).

P.L. Glanzer (✉) · N. Alleman
Baylor University, Waco, TX, USA

D. Guthrie
Penn State University, PA, USA

T.L. Scales and J.L. Howell (eds.), *Christian Faith and University Life*,
DOI 10.1007/978-3-319-61744-2_10

the discipline."[1] For Christians, this phrase should remind us of our expansive responsibilities that come with the calling to steward. In Genesis 1, God says of humans made in God's own image and likeness, "let them rule over the fish of the sea and the birds of the air, and over all the creatures on the earth" (Genesis 1:26). In what is known as the creation mandate, men and women are crowned with the glory and given the honor of being the vice-rulers over the rest of God's creation. Just as God takes care of his whole creation, humans are to be God's embodied representatives on earth and stewards of all of God's creation, including the creations that humans make.[2] The idea that Christians are stewards of God's gifts is also reinforced in Jesus' parables and other New Testament teachings.[3]

Our academic disciplines are an extended human dimension of God's creation. Humans continue to build up storehouses of knowledge that need to be stewarded. What exactly this stewarding process involves proves complex. Chris Golde in this explication of the Carnegie phrase above argued that it involved three things: (1) generation, (2) conservation, and (3) transformation.[4] This description mirrors what we would suggest are the three tasks of the Christian educator, although we prefer to use a slightly different language that echoes the Biblical story: (1) creating new knowledge; (2) creating new learners and practitioners of the discipline, and (3) redeeming fallen learning and practices within the discipline.[5]

This chapter will focus on the second matter in particular. One of the major tasks of the Christian professor in his or her stewardship will be creating new learners of the discipline as well as classroom environments where learning within the discipline can take place. In other words, stewarding academic disciplines involves more than merely accumulating sets of ideas about things that fill books and journals. It also includes developing a storehouse of wisdom regarding particular practices in which we engage and the way to pass along those practices to other novices. Put another way, it involves a form of disciplinary discipleship.

Yet, for Christians, it involves more than a narrow form of mentorship. After all, Christian educators throughout the ages have believed that an educator does not merely disciple someone in a particular discipline. Being a good chemist, accountant, educator, or historian involves more than merely learning how to be a member of a professional guild and to use the intellectual tools associated with the guild. It also requires helping future professionals to understand how these things fit into a larger understanding of the good life and human flourishing. Neil Postman describes this as distinguishing a technical problem (e.g., how individuals learn best) from a metaphysical problem (e.g., what the purpose of learning is).[6] The latter mission proves wonderfully expansive and vital.

Despite the importance of this task, Christians have not necessarily created scholarship about the particular practice of teaching about a discipline or the good life. David I. Smith and James K.A. Smith contend that the central task of *teaching* has "almost completely dropped off the scholarly radar."[7] Smith and Smith do not mean that teaching has dropped off the radar since most Christian colleges and universities are primarily teaching institutions. The problem, they point out, is the paucity of scholarship related to the practice of teaching and the faith-learning conversation.

This chapter attempts to provide an empirical basis for the conversation about Christian faith and teaching. In particular, we analyze the results of a survey that sought to discover how professors working at member institutions of the Council for Christian Colleges and Universities claim that their respective theological traditions influence a particular aspect of their teaching—the creation of class objectives. We discovered that professors take eight different approaches. Each one of the approaches, we suggest, has important strengths but each one also has possible weaknesses, especially if used in isolation. In light of this conclusion, we contend that this typology can provide a helpful guide for professors. They can determine the degree to which they are only relying upon one strand of a cord that requires multiple strands to maximize its strength. Indeed, our hope is that this article can help professors appreciate and develop multiple approaches to creating classroom experiences infused with a vibrant Christian faith.

The Scholarly Context

Our interest in this topic stems from a weakness with the recent scholarly conversation about the integration of faith, learning, and teaching in Christian higher education. Significantly, much of this conversation has taken place without any broad-based empirical studies from the very Christian faculty whose classroom practices writers either reflect on or critically appraise. In fact, James K.A. Smith and David Smith recently undertook a review of the scholarship on faith and learning and found "only a tiny percentage of the scholarly writing that emerges from Christian higher education is devoted to the development of ... nuanced accounts of how teaching and learning are supposed to work in a Christian setting."[8]

There are some rich individual and institutional statements, of course,[9] but most typologies of how to understand the relationship between faith and learning have related more to scholarship than teaching and a number of them are not empirically based.[10] While each of these works lends valuable insights about the nature, content, and, process, of this contested ground we call "faith integration," the preponderance of evidence thus far emerges primarily from scholars' reflections, informal observations, and small-scale research studies. This article attempts to supplement this recent work by drawing upon empirical research from a large group of CCCU professors. We attempt to explore responses to this central question: What do Christian professors in CCCU institutions say they actually do when it comes to incorporating their particular Christian traditions into classroom teaching? Moreover, how can answering this question help guide future practice?

Learning from Christian Professors

The findings used in this article are part of a larger dataset generated from an online survey of instructional faculty members employed at Council of Christian Colleges and Universities (CCCU) member institutions.[11] Forty-eight institutions (61%) participated in this phase of the study directed at the faculty of these institutions.[12] Participants were asked to identify their own faith perspectives, those held by the institution, and the manifestations of those faith commitments in policy and practice. Among these questions, faculty members were asked to identify the broad theological tradition with which they most closely identify. Survey respondents selected from a drop-menu of faith tradition options that included: Anabaptist, Anglican, Baptist, Catholic, Eastern Orthodox, Evangelical, Pentecostal/Charismatic, Reformed, Wesleyan, or Other (see Table 10.1 for the results).[13] Faculty respondents were then asked whether this theological tradition influenced the following areas of their teaching: (1) Course Objectives; (2) Foundations; Worldview or Narrative Guiding the Course; (3) Motivations for or Attitude toward the Class; (4) Ethical Approach; (5) Teaching Methods. The resulting faculty responses to this question, by percentage, are in Table 10.2.

This chapter addresses the area where only close to half of faculty indicated the impact of their particular theological tradition on their teaching—course objectives. Of the 2313 faculty members who provided a survey response to this question, 48% (n = 1110) said "Yes." Twenty-three % (n = 523) of those responding positively also completed the optional write-in answer.[14]

Table 10.1 Broad theological traditions of faculty respondents (n = 2309)

Baptist	20%
Evangelical	19%
Wesleyan	18%
Reformed	12%
Pentecostal/Charismatic	8%
Anabaptist	7%
Other	5%
Anglican	5%
Catholic	4%
Lutheran	3%
Eastern Orthodox	1%

Table 10.2 Does your theological tradition influence the following areas of your teaching? (Responses by percentage)

Question	*Yes*	*Don't know*	*No*
Course objectives	48	9	43
Foundations, worldview or narrative guiding the course	79	5	16
Motivations for or attitude toward the class	78	6	16
Ethical approach	84	4	12
Teaching Methods	40	20	40

The Eight Types

So what difference did respondents believe their faith tradition made with regard to their course objectives? The results of our coding process led to the emergence of eight categories of activity.[15] Four of the activities were largely understood as undertaken by the teacher and the other four were focused on students. As we will see later, all faith traditions engaged in these activities, although some did so to varying degrees. Furthermore, the themes express both a generic Christian sensibility and the particularities of Christian traditions in the development and delivery of course objectives. Nevertheless, the degree to which professors mentioned a particular faith tradition did vary by category, although often the language or manner of expression could still be linked to particular theological cultures. (Table 10.3)

Table 10.3 Ways of integrating one's faith tradition in the course objectives here

Activities of the teacher	*Student focused*
1. Introduce the Data of Scripture	5. Cultivate Personal Spiritual Growth & Practices
2. Employ Specific Interpretive Views	6. Integrate a Christian Worldview
3. Make Distinctive Curricular Choices	7. Understand & Utilize Theological Traditions
4. Use Unique Methodological Approaches	8. Develop Ethical Thinking or Behavior

We provide explanations and examples of these eight types of activities below.

1. *Introduce the Data of Scripture*
The label for this category was taken from a quote given by a faculty member describing evidence taken directly from the Bible: "Former President [name] challenged us to introduce the 'data of Scripture' into our courses wherever it was relevant. As a philosophy teacher, this was a helpful challenge." Professors' responses placed in this category (n = 70 responses) focused on connecting the subject matter to related Biblical material based upon an implicit view of the authority or relevance of the Bible for the course's subject matter. These professors provide straightforward examples
   - "I may utilize passages of scripture to illustrate point".
   - "I incorporate Biblical scripture into writing prompts and lessons…"
   - "When discussing ethical business practices I bring in the biblical teachings of Christ."

   In some case, these introductions of scripture may be, as sometimes happens with introductions, a little forced or awkward. For instance, this faculty member gave an example of the way he or she tied to course content into a scriptural example:

> I have 2 or 3 short devotionals in Kinesiology where I link Bible stories to the content. For example, when we are discussing muscle fiber, I open with a devotional about Jacob's wrestling match with an angel; the connection here is that the angel touches Jacob's hip and dislocates it. That leads back to our discussion about muscle and bone anatomy.

Yet, this kind of connection drawing between subject matter and the Bible may be an essential first step in considering the relevance of Christianity or a theological tradition for a discipline.

The goal of this incorporation was sometimes understood, as one professor stated, to support a "strong emphasis on the importance of biblical literacy." In other cases, the stated goal entailed making sure that students not only were Biblically literate but also understood the relevance of Scripture. For instance, the following faculty response in which the professor begins with scriptural perspective (content) and ends with the scriptural application (examples):

> "See to it that no one takes you captive through philosophy and empty deception, according to the tradition of men, according to the elementary principles of the world, rather than according to Christ." Colossians 2:8. The relevance of God's Word must be explicitly included in course objectives.

Faculty who emphasized content and example elements operationalized scripture and Christian practices as curricular resources for all subjects.

2. *Employ Specific Interpretive Views*

   This category, along with the following two (*Influence Curricular Choices* and *Form Methods Approaches*) can be thought of as conjoined yet individually distinct aspects of a continuous curricular sensemaking and construction process. In this, the largest of the eight categories (n = 188 responses), faculty respondents discussed the foundational perspectives that lend form to their course objectives. Often, their explanations were given without reference to any impact on students:

> Reformed doctrine emphasizes that the world is good, though fallen, so that very much influences my approach to all my classes. There is lots of good to be found in any area of study, but we must also seek to recognize the fallen-ness in our approach to any subject.

This response illustrates the essential elements of this category: a prior theological perspective or belief (frequently rooted in an identified tradition), a particular principle drawn from that commitment, and an implicit or explicit expectation that course objectives are yet one more area where said commitment can find expression. In another example, a respondent spoke for his or her academic unit in describing the conceptualization that guides their collective purpose: "We believe that God made us to be dialogic creatures with the ability to communicate; therefore, we take the approach that communication studies are important."

Many faculty responses began with a kind of personal credo or theological testimony, and then transitioned to either the implications of that commitment or the curricular target:

> I believe that we are all fallen sinners, but that we can all be redeemed. Those that come to saving faith in Christ are gifted to serve Him. All of us need to be held accountable to give a good and honest effort to tasks that are presented to us. As faculty members, we need to see the potential in each student and do all that we can to help our students grow in faith as well as in our academic discipline and in the ability to use their gifts more fully for Christ's service.

Others emphasized a particular theological tradition and some aspect of it that directs their curricular approach or sensemaking: "The Wesleyan Quadrilateral understanding of religious authority influences both my beliefs and my pedagogy, which is interdisciplinary, contextual, and integrative." Another faculty member similarly responded from his or her tradition, this time pointing to course objectives as a means to meeting tradition-informed ends:

> The Anabaptist theological tradition places great emphasis on discipleship and "following Jesus." I view my course objectives (learning to read and exegete the Scriptures faithfully) as a tangible means to assist my students in that overarching calling.

The nature of the relationship between theological commitments and course-shaping perspectives diverged for faculty along several lines. Most clearly, some respondents framed the issue as a compulsive response and natural outgrowth of their desire for consistency across all facets of professional life:

> [My theological tradition] serves as the thread holding together my reason for teaching, for knowing my students, and for guiding them into the

worlds beyond this university. My learning outcomes derive from my view of God and who He is in my life (my theology).

Others described it as a deliberate process:

I attempt to incorporate an evangelical worldview into the course objectives. I teach business and leadership and most definitely come from an evangelical perspective throughout while allowing for other opinions and viewpoints to share space and time.

As in this case, some respondents did not specify any particular content focus when mentioning their perspective.

3. *Make Distinctive Curricular Choices*
The prior category (*Employ Specific Interpretive Views*) is the antecedent to category three, in which theological beliefs, values, and perspectives are translated into a course plan. Many respondents in this category (56 total responses) made this connection by highlighting a curricular aspect selected or focused on as a result of this theological tradition: "I teach economics, which means I teach about stewardship over everything entrusted to us." The following lengthier response connects the sensemaking of a Reformed perspective to both the selection of course topics and to a theologically informed approach that the faculty member wishes to convey:

In the Calvinist tradition there is a strong emphasis on the universal claim of God over all creation and culture making. As such all areas are legitimate areas for study and research. Rather than rejecting certain areas, such as genetic modification of organisms out of hand, therefore my course objectives emphasize how various technologies can be applied to God's honor and glory.

In some responses, faculty members emphasized how their theological tradition influenced their selection of course materials, texts, examples, and experiences. This influence was also sometimes described in indirect terms, as a source of motivation:

Church of the Brethren and Anabaptist traditions value service to others, living out your beliefs and pacifism. These are not directly course objectives but may motivate me to include certain books, examples, articles rather than others.

And in other responses, the process of influence was less circumspect: "Since I teach Ministry courses, my own tradition cannot help but come through in the way I teach. Specifically, I tend to favor textbooks that represent an evangelical point of view."

4. *Use Unique Methodological Approaches*
   Some respondents extended their explication from the influence of their theological tradition to the implications for classroom practice. Though technically departing from "course objectives," faculty respondents described classroom approaches, structures, and behaviors as the end produce of course objectives informed by their theological tradition(s). Here, a faculty member's class tactics (listening, supporting, and offering accountability) are shaped by his or her perspective on students as humans deserving of personal regard and care:

> The syllabus gives broad objectives that must be met. Because I know life and walks of life can be different, I ask my students what their needs are and how I can serve them during this journey. I listen carefully, help support them and hold them accountable. We meet the course objectives, while also meeting personal objectives, which allows a living example of God in the classroom.

Similarly, the following respondent sought to translate a curricular goal ("serve students well") into a worshipped-centered classroom approach:

> As an evangelical Friend, my goal is to serve my students well; that is why I work them hard and seek to engage them in the subjects I teach. I am a servant-teacher. As a believer in the present Christ, accessible wherever two or three are gathered in his name, I have sought to design several of my courses as "the meeting for worship in which learning is welcomed"—facilitating the student's being enrolled in the school of Christ…

Other respondents suggested that how they taught reflected a general tone or point of emphasis resulting from their faith tradition perspective: "Yes—A Reformed education tradition influences both intellectual formation and the shaping of an entire self. Thus it can be intellectually rigorous." And another faculty member responded in kind: "Teaching Bible & Theology, I seek the transformation of each student, seek to teach rather than indoctrinate, and attempt to clarify and encourage concepts that reflect a Wesleyan/Arminian perspective." In these examples, "rigor" and clarification over indoctrination describe not only interpretive approaches, but also the roots of classroom practice as well.

5. *Cultivate Personal Spiritual Faith and Practices*
   This category of responses (n = 65) marks the turn from responses that implied a focus on faculty tasks or perspectives, to those that aimed to influence student beliefs, perspectives, or behaviors. In this category, professors primarily indicated a desire for their students to further a personal commitment, understanding, or relationship with Christ. Often their objectives reflected the faith orientation of the faculty member ("As an evangelical I emphasize the importance of individuals having a 'personal relationship' with Christ.") or the institution ("We always ensure at least one course objective focuses on a spiritual formation objective and this will be constructed from a Wesleyan perspective."). Unlike the last quote, the variety of stated goals in this category often did not mention a particular faith tradition directly, although the language or manner of expression could still be linked to particular theological cultures. Generally, responses focused on some form of personal encounter ("Students will grow in their appreciation of Jesus"), internal change and growth ("To help students better understand the saving grace of Jesus and to grow closer to him"), or personal development resulting in associated behaviors ("Fundamentally I want students to embrace the sacrifice of Christ and have that play out in their best thinking and their daily lives in ways that bless them and draw others to Christ.")
   Within this category, a set of alternative perspectives emerged from respondents who included spiritual formation as a course objective and those who were committed to encouraging faith development but did not include it as a stated course purpose. Some respondents questioned whether these purposes were appropriate for course objectives even as they sought to infuse them throughout the course ("It's not an objective I would state in the syllabus, since it's not one that can be assessed, but I tell students in courses that my primary objective is that they encounter Jesus Christ and grow as his disciples in love of God and neighbor."). Other respondents saw faith as implicitly embedded throughout all facets of the course and thus perhaps unnecessary to state as a singular objective: "Being evangelistically missions-minded is an assumption underlying many of the goals of my classes."

6. *Understand and Critically Integrate a Christian Worldview*
The use of worldview language as one way to understand the integration of faith and learning has a long history of the Christian traditions within the CCCU.[16] Not surprisingly, we found this language prominent among a subsection of responses (e.g., "I use a Christian worldview as a foundation for all I teach."), but we did not place professors' comments in this category merely for the use of that language. The characteristics of this category (n = 96 responses) are summarized by one professor's response: "Every course has an objective of relating Christian faith to the subject matter of the course (but nothing related to a particular theological tradition within Protestantism)." In other words, the actions suggested in this category by professors usually related it to helping students understand or critically apply a theological way of thinking that would be shared by all Christians (e.g., "Appreciate the beauty of mathematics as an extension of the Creator."). We could not be sure if or whether professors saw these approaches as directly arising from their particular theological tradition (although if they answered the question as intended they would).
Professors generally mentioned four types of broad activities that we placed in this category, all of which are also aspects mentioned in the literature of distinctive Christian scholarship.[17] In this respect, visions for Christian scholarship and Christian teaching shared much in common. First, some professors simply emphasized the spiritual dimension of a subject or making sure a subject is not reduced to its materialistic components.

- "For a nursing pediatrics course: identify psychological, spiritual, ethical, and cultural variables that impact the delivery of education and care to members of the child-rearing family. This is done with the understanding that the spiritual dimensions are a fundamental component of nursing care."
- "I cannot teach without regarding both the spiritual nature of humanity, including the literature I teach my students and the very nature of my students and me."

These professors apparently sought to counter the view sometimes promulgated through naturalistic reductionism that reduces humans merely to physical entities.[18]

A second set of responses discussed common Christian beliefs that involved emphasizing some aspect of the doctrine of creation

- "Examples of objectives include helping students to understand the world as God's creation, or understand their responsibility in regards to the world based on the fact that God created it and he created us as his image bearers."
- "I believe God has given each of us purpose, gifts, and talents. Course objectives should accomplish the goals of the institution while incorporating the interests of the students."

In other words, these responses focused upon the common doctrine of creation that Christian scholars recognize as shaping one's approach to a subject.[19]

A third set of responses focused upon Biblical revelation and making sure students understood its authority or trustworthiness. These two teachers provide examples of this approach:

- "One's world view has a dramatic influence on how one structures and teaches. Believing the Bible is God's Word is imperative."
- "One of our department's objectives is to enhance the student's commitment to the trustworthiness of scripture."

These respondents were different than the "Introduce the Data of Scripture" approach in that their focus was less on including Scripture and more upon students coming to particular theological conclusions about Scripture.

A related and final set of approaches tended to emphasize the broad theological parts of the narrative included in Scripture that starts not only with creation but also reaches beyond it:

- "The Reformed (or broadly Augustinian) theological tradition informs our institutional mission which speaks of inspiring and equipping learners to bring renewal and reconciliation to every walk of life as followers of Jesus Christ, the Servant King. An emphasis on the goodness of God's creation, the pervasiveness of sin and evil, the cosmic sweep of redemption and the reign of God, and on our human calling to participate in God's redemptive work are characteristic of this tradition, and provide orientation for the entire curriculum."
- "Understand environmental issues within creation/fall/redemption approach."

As can be seen, those in the latter category often identified with the Reformed tradition.

7. *Promote Understanding and Critical Use of Theological Traditions*
   The seventh category of responses involved applying a particular theological tradition to the subject matter (n = 68). The responses in this category clearly identified a Christian faith tradition either explicitly or through strong theological referents. Professors would then identify a particular objective related to that tradition and the academic enterprise. It is in this category that one can see confirmed a point made by the Jacobsens that each theological tradition will bring to this task particular theological emphases that result in unique approaches to the integration of faith and teaching.[20] We placed these elements on increasing levels of complexity in a way that comprises a kind of taxonomy of learning:

   A. Understanding a tradition or traditions:

      - "It is very important to me that my students have a broad understanding of Christian history, in particular the Anabaptist insights—as these views have been frequently eclipsed by louder more strident voices.... Therefore my objectives often read something like: Students will grasp the complex and textured historical purposes of baptism; or students will gain a broader understanding of salvation–not as simply a moment in time, but an ongoing stepping into discipleship that accompanies one's putting on Christ."
      - "In courses in history and religion, I want to ensure the students understand the high church traditions since almost all come from low church backgrounds."

   B. Seeing its benefits:

      - "I teach French foreign language and culture; I hope that students will understand better after my courses that Christian community does not exclude all things Catholic."
      - "One objective is to introduce evangelical Christians to the richness of their Protestant tradition as expressed in Anglican patterns of worship and theology."

   C. Using it to guide one's interpretive lens:

      - "I want students to be able to express the issues we cover in class from an evangelical orientation."

- "The Baptist tradition emphasizes the freedom of the conscience under God, which is necessary for the educational enterprise. My course objectives are designed to help students learn how to search for truth and evaluate truth claims independently following their own consciences."

D. Applying it to one's discipline:

- "In a Finance class I start out by trying to help my students see how religious orientation, creational structure, and the various ways that people have developed the creation affect what happens in business and finance. I then challenge them to think about how finance needs to be "reformed" to become what God expects of his people."
- "Quaker approaches to ethics, servant leadership, respect for all persons, [and] openness to individuals serving in any role to which God calls them are essential frameworks for teaching Management and leadership principles."

Although one might be critical of the fact that professors often only mentioned one part of a learning taxonomy instead of the full range of objectives that would entail understanding and applying a theological tradition in a critical manner, we should note that professors were only asked to give one example.

8. *Develop Ethical Thinking or Behavior*

This category (n = 120 responses) included the responses from faculty that reflected a desire for students to think or act ethically. More specifically, they usually sought to help students understand or practice a particular virtue or set of virtues (e.g., "Promote [the] character development of students to enhance the integrity of higher education by stressing respect, honesty, fairness and responsibility"). Indeed, professors rarely mentioned moral principles or rules (e.g., "My objectives include Biblical principles, such as the Golden Rule when teaching ethics."). The dominant virtues including the following:
Service or Servant Leadership (18 responses)

- "The idea of being a servant in education."
- "In many courses, we conduct service-learning projects serving the poor and homeless."

Love (7 responses)

- "Love of enemy, how to relate to those who disagree."
- "Teaching counseling and psychology courses with an emphasis on the Christian value of love in relationships is fundamental to my approach to meeting the teaching objectives of my courses."

Social Justice (6 responses)

- "Making sure my objectives reflect my sense of community and social justice."
- "Focusing on social justice and cultural humility in nursing care."

Integrity (4 responses)

- "Inclusion of issues related to integrity, honesty."
- "Punctuality, integrity, living with hope and faith, and teaching in that light."

As can be seen from these responses, many comments did not mention a Christian doctrine and instead exhibited a generic form of moralism. As a result, it is not always clear what role a Christian theological tradition plays unless one knows the background Scripture or theology. This proved particularly true in several references to the "Golden Rule," an ethical concept that is not exclusively Christian (e.g., "The concept of the Golden Rule can be found in everything I teach including principles, scenarios, examples, etc."). Indeed, one could argue that almost all of the virtues listed above are also emphasized in secular literature and practices pertaining to moral development in higher education.[21] Only when combined with a particular Scriptural or theological referent would the Christian distinction emerge (e.g., "Character Education course includes a goal on the fruit of the spirit and character."). Only in some rare cases was a whole different approach set forth (e.g., "Responsiveness to the Holy Spirit rather than rely on professional society ethics code books").

Responses by Faith Tradition

Since the focal question for this inquiry asked faculty whether and how their theological tradition and course objectives related, analyzing the intersection of claimed faith traditions and the eight thematic categories may illuminate how those from particular faith traditions tend to conceptualize how faith ought to shape course objectives. Although, about one-half of all participant faculty responded "Yes" to this question, written responses varied by faith tradition. The most frequent positive responses by faith tradition were from Reformed (60%) and Evangelical (57%) participants, followed by Wesleyan (51%), Baptist (48%), Anabaptist (47%), and Pentecostal/Charismatic (40%). Faculty members with the smallest positive response rate were Lutheran (30%), Catholic (23%), and Anglican (21%), though their total participant responses were smaller as well. Nevertheless, results suggest that faculty from high-church faith traditions may make different sense of the question at hand. These percentages may indicate that as a group, faculty from high-church traditions were much less likely to attempt the integration of their faith tradition into course objectives. However, it might also be the case that they conceptualize the role of their faith tradition in the academic setting differently, or they may simply have interpreted the question differently than those from other Christian traditions.

The tally of responses by theological tradition within the eight thematic categories were as follows: Evangelical (150), Baptist (134), Reformed (105), Wesleyan (126), Anabaptist (63), Pentecostal/ Charismatic (36), Other (39), and a High Church Combined (30) made up of Anglican, Catholic, Lutheran, and Eastern Orthodox respondents.[22] We acknowledge that some respondent groups, once divided by faith tradition, are small enough that findings only suggest implications for faith traditions and require further investigation to validate. However, since the data we are using is qualitative and our purpose is exploratory, individual responses as examples of faculty meaning making are of greater importance than if generalization were our sole aim.

In aggregate by category, *Employ Specific Interpretive Views* (28%; 188 responses) was the largest response group, followed by *Develop Ethical Thinking or Behavior* (18%; 120 responses), *Integrate a Christian Worldview* (14%; 96 responses), *Introduce the Data of Scripture* (10%; 70 responses), *Understand and Utilize Theological Traditions* (10% 68 responses), and *Cultivate Personal Spiritual Growth and Practices* (10%, 65 responses), all of which were at or above 10%. The remaining categories were *Make Distinctive Curricular Decisions* (8%, 56 responses), and *Form Unique Methods Approaches* (3%, 17 responses).

Responses by faith tradition showed a similar convergence of emphasis, with a few distinguishing variations (See Table 10.4, below). *Employ Specific Interpretive Views* was the top category of response across all theological tradition groups (22–34% of responses) except the "Other" category. Evangelicals' responses were similar in most categories, varying between 12% and 17%. Baptist' responses were similarly distributed, with *Develop Ethical Thinking or Behavior* (20%), *Introduce the Data of Scripture* (19%), and *Integrate a Christian Worldview* (15%) as the next top categories. Only 5% of Baptist responses were in the *Cultivate Personal Spiritual Growth and Practices* category, a rate half of their peers. Responses from Wesleyans were the most frequent in the *Employ Specific Interpretive Views* category at 34%, trailed by *Develop Ethical Thinking or Behavior* at 19% and *Understand and Utilize Theological Traditions* at 15% of their responses. The Wesleyan response percentage for *Integrate a Christian Worldview* was dramatically lower than all other surveyed traditions at 5% of their responses. Perhaps not surprisingly given this tradition's strong emphasis on God's sovereignty in all parts of life,[23] Reformed responses were strong in the *Integrate a Christian Worldview* category (21%), followed by *Understand and Utilize Theological Traditions* (15%). As with Baptist responses, interest in *Cultivating Personal Spiritual Growth and Practices* was quite low (3%) for Reformed respondents.

The remainder of the theological tradition groups had below 100 responses, causing us to redouble our caution against unwarranted generalizing from these findings. Nevertheless, the findings may be suggestive, if not instructive: Anabaptists showed little concern for *Introducing the Data of Scripture* (2%), emphasizing instead *Cultivating Ethical Behavior and Practices* (22%), perhaps reflective of historic focus on the practical implications of following Jesus. By contrast, Pentecostal/Charismatic responses were evenly distributed among three categories, emphasizing practical application, personal faith, and a broad-based Christian worldview (17% each). The catchall "Other" tradition category contained many faculty members who had embraced multiple theological traditions (what might be called "theological omnivores"), perhaps reflected in the relatively high 13% response percentage in *Understand and Utilize Theological Traditions.* Their responses were also most often pragmatic: 28% were in *Cultivate Ethical Thinking and Behavior* category. Finally, the summative "High Church Combined" cluster of theological traditions showed strong interest in *Forms Methods Approaches* (20%) and *Understand and Utilize Theological Traditions* (17%). Responses suggest that many faculty members in this group, like the "Other" category, recognize that their theological tradition or combination of traditions may be less familiar to students, resulting in a special point of emphasis in their course objectives.

Table 10.4 Eight categories by theological tradition

	Introduce the data of scripture	*% of total*	*Cultivate personal spiritual growth and practices*	*% of total*	*Employ specific inter-pretive views*	*% of total*	*Make distinctive curricular decisions*	*% of total*		*Use unique methods approaches*	*% of total*	*Integrate a christian worldiew*	*% of total*	*Understand and utilize theological traditions*	*% of total*	*Develop ethical thinkng or behavior*	*% of total*	*Total*
Evangelical	18	12	26	17	39	26	7	5	Evangelical	3	2	26	17	7	5	24	16	150
Baptist	25	19	7	5	34	26	12	9	Baptist	1	1	20	15	7	5	27	20	133
Wesleyan	8	6	12	10	42	34	12	10	Wesleyan	2	2	6	5	18	15	24	19	124
Reformed	10	10	3	3	32	30	9	9	Reformed	3	3	22	21	16	15	10	10	105
Anabaptist	1	2	4	6	19	30	9	14	Anabaptist	0	0	9	14	7	11	14	22	63
Pentecostal charismatic	4	11	6	17	8	22	3	8	Pentecostal charismatic	0	0	6	17	3	8	6	17	36
Other	4	10	5	13	7	18	2	5	Other	2	5	3	8	5	13	11	28	39
Anglican	0	0	1	8	3	23	0	0	Anglican	3	23	0	0	4	31	2	15	13
Catholic	0	0	1	13	3	38	1	13	Catholic	1	13	0	0	1	13	1	13	8
Lutheran	0	0	0	0	1	14	1	14	Lutheran	1	14	4	57	0	0	0	0	7
Eastern orthodox	0	0	0	0	0	0	0	0	Eastern orthodox	1	50	0	0	0	0	1	50	2
High church combined	0	0	2	7	7	23	2	7	High church combined	6	20	4	13	5	17	4	13	30
Totals	70	10	65	10	188	28	56	8	Totals	17	3	96	14	68	10	120	18	680

Evaluating and Synthesizing the Types

What can be learned from this typology to inform our practice? In looking over the responses and the tendencies of different traditions, we suggest that we should avoid the danger common with certain typologies associated with theological traditions of identifying one best approach.[24] Indeed, we would argue that all of these approaches have their strengths and should be considered when thinking about how a/the Christian theological traditions are incarnated in the classroom. Each one, to use Biblical language, is part of the body of Christian teaching. And like different parts of the body, each one is necessary.

Furthermore, all of them have weaknesses when practiced in isolation. We will suggest a few. First, introducing Scripture into the subject is often a reasonable first step, but it may revert to proof-texting without attention to worldview and theological considerations. Second, being conscious of how a/the Christian tradition influences one's views, curricular choices and methods proves helpful, but modeling this type of integration exhibits the weakness of all other types of "I just model" strategies. Students may not understand the motives or rationale for a professor's actions unless the related worldview or theological rationale is articulated to them. Third, if one focuses on students' personal devotional growth, it is not always clear what relationship the Christian tradition has to the subject matter being taught. Fourth, exposing students to the Christian worldview proves vital for understanding foundational issues, but as critics have rightly identified it can become too heady. Finally, the popular ethics approach, as can be seen from the examples offered, can be easily secularized when divorced from the worldview and narrative approach. The golden rule, service, and social justice are all valued at many different secular campuses, and it may not be clear how Christianity can or should transform these ethical practices. Indeed, we would argue that the ethics category, although it is for some faculty members the dominant way that they claimed it influenced their course objectives, also demonstrates the most danger of being misunderstood if used alone. Although discussing ethics is perhaps an easy way to address what one envisions as Christian subject matter, it is the approach most likely to discard overt Christian references.

Thus, we would suggest that the best approaches would attempt to make sure that all types of integration are at least considered and possibly addressed, at least by type if not extent. In fact, the most noteworthy examples we noticed were often ones that combined a variety of approaches. This Reformed professor provides a helpful example.

> I teach history, and coming from a Reformed perspective it influences my course objectives because I try to teach in such a way to develop empathy for our historical figures among the students. I try to help them see that our historical forbearers were image bearers just as we [are], and they deserve our courtesy and respect.

Although the respondent suggests that they are applying a distinctive theological tradition (e.g., the Reformed perspective), we would suggest that an emphasis upon the fact that "historical forbearers were image bearers" fits more with the Christian worldview category. What we find noteworthy is that an ethical objective (e.g., "teach in a way to develop empathy for our historical figures…they deserve our courtesy and respect") is given a clear theological rationale ("our historical forbearers were image bearers [of God]").

Not surprisingly, we often found this kind of combination with ethical objectives. In these cases, the professor usually listed a Scriptural, worldview or theological rationale for the ethical outcome being promoted. For example, one responding professor identified the virtues of humility and servanthood exemplified in the Last Supper narrative, but applied it to a way of being and behaving as a teacher in a future professional position:

> The Church of the Brethren teaches a simple life style and a life of servanthood, modeled after Christ who humbled Himself to wash the feet of the disciples at the Last Supper. In the same vein, I advocate to my students through the course objectives that as public school teachers they are answering God's calling to teach His children in our public schools. I emphasize through the course objectives the importance of differentiating instruction to meet the learning needs of every child they teach.

Similarly, in the following example a faculty member describes an outcome related to teaching a particular reasoning skill that is based upon a Scripturally grounded Christian worldview:

> In Business Ethics, the reason I insist that students need to be able to make a case for asking a non-Christian colleague in a secular business setting to do the right thing by using a secular argument rather than "Bible-thumping" is that, based upon Rom 1:18ff; 2:14, all persons have a moral

> awareness. Hence, secular ethics, at best, focuses on some aspect of this God-given moral awareness all persons have or had until they repressed it (Rom 1).

Another professor discussed the role that a particular theological tradition shaped his or her course objectives in ways that influenced ethical beliefs and practices:

> Quakers have a narrative of living a HOLISTIC life with integrity. Quaker theology is as much seen in practice as it is spoken in theological belief statements. And I try to live and teach according to this, using practices to guide and check beliefs, and beliefs to guide and check practices. So I often have course objectives that involve "living a more holistic life" or "living a life with more integrity" or "putting into practice what I believe to be true."

In these examples, making sure students understand the connection between theology, ethics, and classroom practice remains vitally important. Combining several strands in this way creates a stronger Christian understanding and presence in the classroom.

Although this type of synthesis often involved ethics, in some cases it involved the merging of two other types. For instance, this professor took what is often considered a matter of personal spiritual growth (the practice of witnessing to others) and combined it with academic goals and a focus on Christology that made for a unique classroom practice.

> At the core of my faith is a need to live out being a Christ-follower; one of the ways we do this is through our witness to others. One objective in a biology course I teach states that students will wrestle with an area where their faith and science may seem to be in conflict (and no, this is not always evolution), and reflect on how their response to this area of dissonance may be perceived by non-Christians. They then reflect on what image of Christ they are portraying through this interaction and whether or not their interaction will compel people towards Christ or repel them away.

Connecting one's witness to how one engages in the academic intellectual struggle, we believe, would likely be a new and invigorating experience for students.

Conclusions

What do faculty responses reveal about the influence of faith traditions on course objectives? Several fairly straightforward lessons emerged, though with complex implications.

First of all, the eight categories that we identified suggest that there are a variety of ways that faculty members conceptualize integrating their faith tradition content, if at all. Since the typology is based on short responses, we cannot know the degree to which individual faculty members may draw upon these eight, but we would hypothesize that most individual faculty members do not think about all eight types when considering how their theological tradition may influence their teaching. We suggest that faculty development courses at Christian colleges could help faculty and prospective faculty be conscious of these eight types and consider how to apply them all. We actually believe that such an activity would be quite freeing to faculty, some of whom may not recognize the variety of ways to think about and practice Christian teaching.

Indeed, we note that sometimes faculty thinks they are failing in this endeavor but in reality, they simply are not conscious of the ways their teaching is shaped by the Christian faith in general, their particular faith tradition, or both. We think this kind of typology can prove helpful for doctoral students and new faculty in a number of ways. First, they can perhaps identify an area where they already engage in integration efforts. Second, they can perhaps use this typology to help others understand and appreciate the various approaches.

It is also clear that when parsed by faculty member's faith tradition, these various categorical inclinations both cut across historical faith tradition distinctive and reflect their points of theological emphases (for example, Baptists favoring introducing Scripture, Evangelicals and Pentecostals favoring personal faith development, Reformed favoring integrating a Christian worldview, Anabaptists favoring ethical thinking and practice). Although we believe such differences result from the particular strengths of these traditions, we also believe those who identify with those traditions may need to consider if other categories within our typology are being unduly neglected.

Finally, we would suggest that doctoral students and faculty may want to consider how to balance two possible needs. We would propose that doctoral students and those overseeing them should be encouraged to pursue styles that work for them while maintaining a holistic approach.

It often proves difficult to adopt a strand that may not be familiar. Yet, we would also encourage Christian educators to make sure they include and synthesize many of the different strands into their course objectives and their teaching as a whole. In this way, the Christian nature of their teaching does not rest on one or two strands that may easily become weak and tattered when left to themselves. Instead, they should weave together a thick cord of several strands to provide a strong and robust line of help to students seeking the wisdom of faith-shaped course objectives in the classroom.

Notes

1. Chris M. Golde, George E. Walker, and Associates, *Envisioning the Future of Doctoral Education: Preparing Stewards of the Discipline Carnegie Essays on the Doctorate* (San Francisco: Jossey-Bass, 2006).
2. This aspect of being placed as stewards of creation is aptly captured in Psalm 8, where David asks a poignant question. "What is man that you are mindful of him, the son of man that you care for him? You have made him a little lower than the heavenly beings and crowned him with glory and honor. You made him ruler over the works of your hands; you put everything under his feet: all the flocks and herds, and the beasts of the field, the birds of the air, and the fish of the sea, all that swim the paths of the seas" (Psalm 8:4).
3. Matthew 25:14–30; Luke 16:1–15; 1 Peter 4:10.
4. Chris M. Golde, "Preparing Stewards of the Discipline," in Chris M. Golde, George E. Walker, and Associates, *Envisioning the Future of Doctoral Education: Preparing Stewards of the Discipline Carnegie Essays on the Doctorate* (San Francisco: Jossey-Bass, 2006), 10–12.
5. Perry L. Glanzer, Nathan Alleman, and Todd C. Ream, *Restoring the Soul of the University: Unifying Christian Higher Education in a Fragmented Age* (Downers Grove, IL: Intervarsity Press, 2017).
6. Neil Postman, *The End of Education* (New York: Vintage Books, 1996).
7. David I Smith & James K.A. Smith, eds. *Teaching and Christian Practices: Reshaping Faith & Learning* (Grand Rapids: Eerdmans, 2011), 2.
8. Ibid., 3.
9. Chris Anderson, *Teaching as Believing: Faith in the University* (Waco, TX: Baylor University Press, 2004); Jean B. Elshtain, "Does, or Should, Teaching Reflect the Religious Perspective of the Teacher?" in *Religion, Scholarship, and Higher Education: Perspectives, Models and Future Prospects*, edited by Andrea Sterk, 193–201 (Notre Dame, IN: University of Notre Dame, 2002); various essays in Stephen R. Haynes, ed., *Professing in the Postmodern Academy: Faculty and the Future of*

Church-Related Colleges (Waco, TX: Baylor University Press, 2002). For a helpful institutional statement see: Azusa Pacific University, "Faith Integration Faculty Guidebook, 2012–2013, *The Center for Teaching, Learning, and Assessment, the Office of Faith Integration, and the Faith Integration Council.* Retrieved from: http://www.apu.edu/faithintegration/resources/guidebook/.

10. Ken Badley, "The Faith/Learning Integration Movement in Christian Higher Education: Slogan or Substance?" *Journal of Research on Christian Education*, 3, no. 1 (1994): 13–33; Todd C. Ream, Michael Beaty, and Larry Lion, "Faith and Learning: Toward a Typology of Faculty Views at Religious Research Universities," *Christian Higher Education*, 3, 4 (2009): 349–172; Stephen Moroney, Where Faith and Learning Intersect: Re-Mapping the Contemporary Terrain, *Christian Scholar's Review*, 43, no. 2 (Winter 2014): 139–155.
11. Seventy-nine of the 110 institutions that were CCCU members at the time of the survey participated in Phase I of the study. The first phase surveyed institutions about their denominational affiliations. For a report based upon some findings from this survey see Perry L. Glanzer, Jesse Rine, and Phil Davignon, "Assessing the Denominational Identity of American Evangelical Colleges and Universities, Part I: Denominational Patronage and Institutional Policy," *Christian Higher Education* 12, no. 3 (2013): 182–202.
12. For a summary of the method for this portion of the study see Jesse Rine, Perry L. Glanzer and Phil Davignon, "Assessing the Denominational Identity of American Evangelical Colleges and Universities, Part II: Faculty Perspectives and Practices," *Christian Higher Education* 12, no. 4 (2013): 243–265. It should be noted that the results reported in the above article pertain only to the faculty respondents working with denominational institutions.
13. This list of faith traditions reflects those used in other national religion surveys, such as the Baylor Religion Survey. We do not suppose that we know all that each respondent assumes about their selected tradition. Nevertheless, most traditions do include important points of convergence, each requiring more explanation than is possible here. We recommend readers interested in better understanding the implications of these faith traditions consult the following resources: Richard T. Hughes *How Christian Faith Can Sustain the Life of the Mind* (Grand Rapids: Eerdmans, 2001); Richard T. Hughes and William B. Adrian, *Models for Christian Higher Education: Strategies for Success in the Twenty-First Century.* (Grand Rapids: Eerdmans, 1997); Richard J. Foster, *Streams of Living Water: Celebrating the Great Traditions of Christian Faith* (San Francisco: HarperCollins, 2001); Douglas Jacobsen and Rhonda Hustedt

Jacobsen, *Scholarship & Christian Faith: Enlarging the Conversation* (New York: Oxford, 2004).

14. Due to the branching structure of the survey, no faculty members who answered "No" or "Don't Know" completed the write-in response. Consequently, the findings discussed below are explanations of ways that faith tradition relates to course objectives for those faculty members that believe that it does. The 52% of respondents who said "No" to this survey question represent a population worthy of further study. That up to half of CCCU faculty respondents might not believe that their faith tradition (which is not necessarily synonymous with Christian faith generally) is relevant to the formation of course objectives might imply that faith tradition is a concept of little value to many faculty members, or that the particulars of those traditions are not sufficiently distinctive to meaningfully inform this aspect of instruction. The survey included quantitative data about theological positions, as well as professional attitudes, values, and perceptions of their employing institution that may be mined for a future project. However, because of the branching nature of our qualitative survey data we do not have qualitative responses for faculty that responded negatively to this question. The focus of this paper, consequently, does not allow us to take up this worthwhile question further.

    Of faculty who provided a short-form answer, 61% were male (2% unassigned), and most (58%) held a PhD as their highest degree, followed by an MA (14%). Those with a doctoral degree most often received it from a public institution (45%), with almost 20% receiving a terminal degree from a religious institution of some kind (including 8% "Other Protestant," 7% CCCU Member, and 3% Catholic, though 16% did not respond to this item). Respondents tended to be those more firmly rooted in the profession: 85% were employed full-time (with 14% part-time or other) and 39% had achieved full professor rank, followed by associate (27%), assistant (18%), and nontenure system faculty (14%, through a combination of various titles). By discipline, 23% were in some professional program, 21% were in philosophy, religion, or theology, 13% were in the social sciences or history, 10% were in the STEM fields, 9% were in business and related fields, 8% were in English and associated subfields, 6% were in communications and technology fields, 5% were in the visual and performing arts, and 3% were unassigned. Respondent's undergraduate alma maters reflected a strong preference for religious institutions generally (60% combined) and CCCU institutions in particular (48%). Public institutions ranked second at 28%, followed by "Other Protestant" (10%) and "Secular, Private" (8%). Catholic institutions constituted 2% of undergraduate alma maters.

For perspective on this cohort, data for all faculty at 45 of the 48 institutions (not all institutions reported data to IPEDS) that participated in the phase two faculty survey show that the same percentage (61–61%) were male, fewer (61% compared to 85% of respondents) were employed full-time, and fewer (32% compared to 39% of respondents) had achieved professor status. The biggest gap was among assistant professors (33% compared to only 18% of respondents). This variance might be indicative of a generational difference in faith integration thinking between veteran and early career faculty members, or it may simply be a reflection of the time pressures associated with pre-tenure status. National Center for Education Statistics, *Integrated Postsecondary Education Data System* (Washington, DC: U.S. Dept. of Education, Office of Educational Research and Improvement, National Center for Education Statistics, 2013).

15. We used an inductive approach to analyze the short-form responses since our desire was to generate frameworks from the particulars of faculty responses, rather than to impose theory upon them. To do this we used a two-cycle coding process through which descriptive categories could emerge (first cycle) and then be combined into thematic categories (second cycle). The result was eight thematic categories and a summative ninth reflecting synthesis between them.
16. For the origins of this use see David K. Naugle, *Worldview: The History of a Concept* (Grand Rapids: Eerdmans, 2002).
17. For a summary see Todd C. Ream and Perry L. Glanzer, *Christian Faith and Scholarship: An Exploration of Contemporary Developments* (ASHE-ERIC Higher Education Report; San Francisco: Jossey-Bass, 2007), 47–57.
18. See George Marsden, *The Outrageous Idea of Christian Scholarship*, 72–77.
19. Ibid., 84–90.
20. Douglas Jacobsen and Rhonda Hustedt Jacobsen, *Scholarship & Christian Faith*.
21. See Anne Colby, Thomas Ehrlich, Elizabeth Beaumont, Jason Stephens, *Educating Citizens: Preparing America's Undergraduates for Lives of Moral and Civic Responsibility* (San Francisco: Jossey-Bass, 2003).
22. Note: one respondent's data may appear in more than one category, thus, this tally represents instances of category appearance and not the number of individual respondents (n = 523 respondents; n = 680 response appearances).
23. Hughes, *How Christian Faith Can Sustain the Life of the Mind*.

24. We are referring in particular to the controversy surrounding H. Richard Niebuhr's famous typology in *Christ and Culture* (San Francisco: HarperSan Francisco, 2001). See for example Perry L. Glanzer, "Christ, Culture and Heavy Metal: Can Either Niebuhr, Marsden, or Yoder Make Sense of the "Rock n' Roll Refuge?" *Journal of Religion and Society* 5 (2003): 1–16.

PART III

Church and Academy: Stewarding our Faith and our Universities

CHAPTER 11

The Mind Is Its Own Place: Gnosticism and Why Scholars Need the Church

Rev. Kyle Childress

In the spring of 1968, a mere three days after the assassination of Dr. Martin Luther King, Jr., five young faculty members of Stephen F. Austin State University in Nacogdoches, Texas, and their families, gathered on a Sunday morning to organize a new congregation they later named Austin Heights Baptist Church. A historian, a mathematician, an economist, a psychologist, and a physicist, all young Baptists, wanted a church without a racially segregated membership policy where church members could speak openly about the civil rights movement as well as discuss how to be people who followed the Prince of Peace while the Vietnam War raged overseas.

In their previous congregation, they were told these concerns were outside the boundaries of acceptable Baptist and Christian beliefs. Proper Christian belief, they were informed, was that Jesus Christ died for their sins, saved them, came to live in their hearts so they would one day live with him in eternal life in heaven, and their job was to tell others of his salvation. Furthermore, they were told discussions, much less actions,

R. Kyle Childress (✉)
Austin Heights Baptist Church,
Nacogdoches, TX, USA

T.L. Scales and J.L. Howell (eds.), *Christian Faith and University Life*,
DOI 10.1007/978-3-319-61744-2_11

regarding civil rights and the war were not only unchristian but also un-American and put them perilously close to hell and far from good society. Young history professor Archie McDonald responded, "Hell, if I'm going to put up with a church like that!" and promptly joined with the others in the work of forming a new congregation.[1]

The identity and ministry of Austin Heights Baptist Church have sought to stay true to its birth as a congregation full of thinking people, people at home in the world of ideas, who at the same time have been very involved in the world. Not content with ideas abstracted from material practice, instead it has tried to live in the tension of thinking people who know that the gospel is to be incarnated.

In what follows I suggest that such a congregation exists through attentiveness to that tension between the head and the hand, of ideas and of practice, and is committed to working in that tension helping scholars and other intellectuals, especially graduate students and young faculty members, who are at home in the world of ideas and knowledge, to become more faithful members of the fleshly body of Christ, the church.

But first, I suggest that living in and working through this tension puts a congregation, and perhaps especially intellectuals, in the crucible faced by much of American evangelical Christianity: gnosticism. People who live and work in the world of ideas and knowledge are particularly (but not exclusively) susceptible to the dangers of gnosticism. When the scholar is immersed in research and study day after day, isolated in a cubicle in front of computer screens, abstracted from relationships beyond other students and scholars immersed in the same mental and technological world, with little time to tend to the mundane and material life of relationships, place, and service, the Christian life can easily shrink to one more idea in the scholar's head. If Descartes said, "I think, therefore I am," then the Christian scholar can be tempted to say, "I think of God, therefore I'm faithful."

In John Milton's *Paradise Lost*, Satan, having just been exiled from heaven and suddenly finding himself in hell, proudly announces:

> *A mind not to be chang'd by Place or Time.*
>
> *The mind is its own place, and in itself*
>
> *Can make a Heav'n of Hell, a Hell of Heav'n*
>
> *What matter where, if I be still the same …*
>
> (I. 253–56).

In other words, Satan will live in his head and outward circumstances of place or time make no difference. This is what historic and orthodox Christianity has called gnosticism and is the most persistent and subtle of heresies throughout the church's 2000-year history. It is a heresy because it takes elements of Christianity and distorts them, twisting them, and taking them to extremes, so that they become the polar opposite of the heart of the Christian faith: incarnation.

Gnosticism first began to show itself during the time of the early church concurrent with the end of the New Testament, with evidence that some of the later writers, especially the Johannine epistles and the Gospel of John, were partly written in response.[2] What Sam Wells calls "perhaps the central verse of Christian faith," John 1:14—"And the Word became flesh and lived among us, and we have seen his glory, the glory as of a father's only son, full of grace and truth"—speaks directly to what became the orthodox teaching of God becoming flesh and blood in Jesus Christ, living with us, in relationship with us and with this world, all of which are counter to gnostic claims and tendencies.[3]

One of the characteristics of gnosticism (note the lowercase) is its ability to morph into various permutations depending on context over the centuries. Not so much a particular school of thought or tradition with clearly defined lines and institutions as tendencies and emphases and analogies that are similar to earlier variations in Christian history.[4] This is what Thomas G. Long calls "the gnostic impulse" rather than Gnosticism in a formal sense.[5] Gnosticism, or whatever terminology it goes by, sees the spiritual as good and the material as bad, a dualism that shows up in contemporary American Christianity in everything from spiritualizing salvation so that the work of Christ becomes an inner, spiritual event in the individual's heart to the goal of Christianity being eternal life in a spiritual heaven. This otherworldly understanding of Christianity denigrates work and service in the world and considers it beneath the true spiritual calling of the Christian, usually interpreted as evangelism—inviting others to be saved spiritually.

Another key characteristic of gnosticism is the centrality of a kind of private or special knowledge or experience. Indeed, the term gnosticism is derived from the Greek word "gnosis" for "knowledge." Those who were gnostic adherents in the ancient world claimed they received a special revelation or experience with the divine. In our contemporary world, this privatized experience or knowledge is often expressed as something like a "personal experience with Jesus" or "the Lord spoke to me," and so on. This is not to say that New Testament Christianity denies personal experience. Indeed, the Christian life is most assuredly personal but it is never private. The call of Christ is for the person to become a participant in the community of Christ, or what the Apostle Paul calls the body of Christ (I Corinthians 12:12–13). The early church portrayed in the book of Acts shared life, prayed together, studied Scripture together, and even practiced economic sharing (Acts 2:43–47; 4:32–37). The problem of the gnostic impulse in contemporary Christianity is that personal experience or knowledge becomes so central that the shared life of the church is marginalized. Authority becomes "what I think" or "what the Lord told me," my own private interpretation of the Bible, or even my own individual understanding of theology and doctrine rather than how the community of faith across time and around the world has interpreted the Bible and the faith. In privatized Christianity, there is no accountability or guidance from the wider Christian community, and therefore there is no real support or mutual encouragement. Church becomes a gathering place of discrete individuals each seeking spiritual experiences rather than a body of people being formed into the likeness of Christ so they may serve Christ and others in the world.

And finally, with private experience as the linchpin of being a Christian, the believer is oblivious that God works through the mundane, everyday, and the material. Here is the great insight Catholic Christianity has that most evangelical Christianity misses: that God intends the material to bear the mysterious movement of God. So God works in and through bread and wine, for example, to become the very body and blood of Christ feeding, nourishing, renewing, and transforming the church. And God works through water to incorporate us into the church in baptism. This sacramental understanding of faith suffuses throughout life so that marriage and sex, as another example, becomes more than an emotional or private physical act. When the church gathers around a couple in the wedding, it is saying that marriage and sex are public, communal, material, and spiritual all at once.

In Walker Percy's novel *Love in the Ruins*, Doris, Dr. Tom More's wife, asks her Roman Catholic husband, "My God, what is it you do in Church?" More responds:

> What she didn't understand, she being spiritual and seeing religion as spirit, was that it took religion to save me from the spirit world, from

orbiting the earth like Lucifer and the Angels, that it took nothing less than ... eating Christ himself to make me mortal man again and let me inhabit my own flesh and love her in the morning.[6]

One of the early versions of gnosticism in Christianity was called Docetism, which taught that Jesus only seemed to be a human body. In fact, Jesus was so spiritual, one of the Docetic stories said, that when he walked along the shore at the Sea of Galilee, he did not even make footprints in the sand. Spiritualized, privatized, otherworldly faith has no connection with place, this earth, and the creation of God. This is what Norman Wirzba calls a "disincarnate" faith[7]; philosopher Charles Taylor uses the term "excarnation,"[8] both terms referring to this notion of spiritually escaping out of our bodies and out of our world and out of our place in the world. The practical result of our disincarnation is "this world is not my home, I'm just passing through," as the old gospel song says. There is a long history of American evangelical Christianity being unconcerned about the abuse and exploitation of the earth, mountain-top removal for surface coal mining, tar sands mining, oil and gas fracking, massive topsoil erosion, acidifying of the oceans, climate change, and on and on.

At the same time, this disincarnation from the place is accentuated by post-World War II mobility, so that people move from neighborhoods, cities, and places for the next job or at the service of corporations or moving from school to graduate school to another academic job. Poet Christian Wiman remembers that when he was thirty-six years old, he had moved forty times in fifteen years. He said he owned nothing that would not fit easily into his car. When talking about this with some friends, all of whom were in their twenties and thirties, all smart, well-educated and upwardly mobile, they compared notes and realized that between them they had lived in every state and dozens of foreign countries. Not one person lived near where they were born and raised and none of them ever asked anyone else where they're from, "skirting the question as if it were either too intimate or, more likely, too involved to broach."[9]

Contrast this view with Wendell Berry's statement in *Poetry and Place*:

How you act *should* be determined, and the consequences of your acts *are* determined, by where you are. To know where you are (and whether or not that is where you should be) is at least as important as what you are

> doing, because in the moral (the ecological) sense you cannot know *what* until you have learned *where*. Not knowing where you are, you can make mistakes of the utmost seriousness: you can lose your soul or your soil, your life or your way home.[10]

Notice that Berry never mentions what you believe. His concern is the linking of place and practice. Belief comes later. Place, people, and practice are essential to the Christian, not because the "thought police" or some "church lady" is correcting our beliefs or lack of beliefs but because, as Berry says, we can become lost. To be "lost" is most assuredly spiritual, but has a thickness of meaning which includes a lostness resulting from the isolating and abstracting blindness to the consequences of our actions. More, the church of Jesus Christ can become lost, too.

I'm not saying that a graduate student living in the world of ideas is a heretic or that everyone who has moved a lot or who has had a profound religious experience is wrong. I am saying that my vocation as a pastor is to help the church be the church and to incorporate individual members of the church into the body of Christ. Since 1989 I have sought to incorporate many graduate students and academic faculty into Austin Heights Baptist Church and my experience has taught me that people living in their heads, with a faith abstracted from place, people, and practice, are particularly susceptible to gnostic tendencies.

My own assertion is also that a church with gnostic tendencies is correspondingly a dangerous church, one in which the witness of Jesus and his Way are muted or even ignored in this world of bigotry, violence, fear, poverty, and injustice. Let me give a particularly pernicious example from history with repercussions in our world today. What we call the Second Great Awakening in American religious history broke out in upper New York State, around 1790. It was characterized by revivalism and personal experiential religion with practices that transformed social and economic relationships—employers treated their employees more justly, and in many cases, slaves were given their freedom. The movement spread west into the frontier but as it moved into the South, where slavery was much more established and provided the foundation of economic life, many of the social and economic transformations of the religious movement were subdued and even discounted. What had started out as a renewal movement with both personal and social consequences was narrowed to one with only personal and individual ones—"I don't smoke or chew or go with the girls who do" as later male revivalistic converts said. Early on, preachers and evangelists preached against the evils of slavery but over time the emphasis shifted away from slavery to individual sin and individual redemption. Perhaps the slave owner was converted to becoming more "humane" toward his slaves, but the notion that in Christ all are free and slaves should be released was no longer tolerated or taught and certainly not practiced.[11]

On the other hand, African-American Christianity, with a wholeness that retained both the personal and the social embodiments of faith, by the time of the Civil Rights Movement publically challenged the racism of white American religion. The white church's privatized and spiritualized faith was no match for its own racism and bigotry; a social, public, and communal practice of Christ-like faith would have provided a bulwark against bigotry and racial segregation, and at the same time, would have acted as a public witness to the alternative way of Jesus of unity and oneness across racial division. A gnostic white church has proven to be a racist church; private belief, no matter how orthodox, has shown itself to be impotent.

Church historian Alan Kreider points out that early Christianity put its emphasis on transformation of the habits and practices, the behavior, of new converts. During the second and third centuries, the world was an ominous place for Christians and the church needed to be well rooted in who they were in Christ in order to not wilt under the pressure of persecution.[12] "The Christian faith was visible," Kreider says, and he quotes Tertullian who said that the pagan world spoke of Christians, "'*Vide*, look! How they love one another.' They did not say, '*Aude*, listen to the Christians' message'; they did not say, '*Lege*, read what they write.'" The Christian faith "was embodied and enacted by its members. It was made tangible, sacramental."[13] Kreider says, "Floating on the surface of our consciousness are our ideas and convictions. We are thinking creatures, and we may believe that ideas determine our identity and that decision making shapes our ethical behavior."[14] Kreider uses the insight of French sociologist Pierre Bourdieu to interpret how the early church trained its converts. Kreider says that what truly forms us "is more profoundly a part of us than our intellectual knowledge. It is 'corporeal knowledge,' a 'system of dispositions' that we carry in our bodies." Kreider, borrowing from Bourdieu, calls it "habitus." Reinforced by story and example and by repetition, "by the sheer physicality of doing things over and over so that they become habitual, reflexive, and borne in our bodies." He says that we learn kinesthetically—we learn bodily.[15]

According to Kreider, each baptismal candidate was given a sponsor or mentor who trained the candidate in Christ-like behavior—practicing patience, demonstrating love, forgiveness, servanthood, mercy, the nonviolent Way of Jesus, as well as practicing the physicality of standing when praying, making the sign of the cross during the designated times of prayer during the day, and greeting other Christians with a holy kiss—all were among the practices expected to become habitual. Only after the sponsor witnessed the baptismal candidates' changed behavior did teaching of the Bible and doctrine begin. Kreider says, "The teachers wanted to know that the candidates were living in such a way that they were able 'to hear the Word.' Can they appropriate what the teachers are teaching?" He goes on, "The assumption is clear. Inner and outer are inextricable; if you live in a certain way in everyday life, you cannot hear, comprehend, or live the gospel that the Christian community is seeking to embody as well as teach. The church will not baptize people in hopes that they will change thereafter" He concludes that the church was saying, "We believe that people *live their way into a new kind of thinking*. If we admit them as they engage in idolatry, immorality, and killing, they will be unable to 'hear the word,' and they will change the church, fatally compromising its distinctiveness, which is the basis of our witness."[16]

What if the church of the American South had practiced this same way in its life together and with its baptismal candidates? What if it had said, "We're glad to have you and we commit to praying for you, supporting you and loving you. You are here to learn to embody the Way of Jesus Christ; learn Christ-like habits as you unlearn un-Christian habits. So for a start: no slavery. Release your slaves. And no more bigotry. Part of what we're going to do together is to learn to serve with and listen to our sisters and brothers in Christ who are black. Some of them are former slaves; can you do that? We'll help you." What if the white church had not only lived in its head but also practiced the Way of Jesus in the world? I'm under no illusions that it would have solved everything but what a difference it might have made! For starters, instead of a white church and a black church, we might have simply had the church.

Years ago, we had a new faculty member come to our church. She was raised and baptized a Southern Baptist and was now fresh out of graduate school after years of study. She was eager and smart. After a few weeks, we met for coffee and she confessed, "You know, I need to tell you there's a lot I don't believe… In fact, I'm not sure I believe much at all anymore." I didn't react but simply responded to the question, "Does your lack of belief bother you?" She said, "Oh yes! It's on my mind almost all the time. Every Sunday when I come in the door, I'm worrying over it. And during the hymns and prayers and your sermon." I said, "That sounds tiring to me to be worrying over all that unbelief all the time." She agreed, "It does get tiring. It wears me out." So I said, "Why don't you quit worrying about what you don't believe? I'm not terribly worried about it and the church is not worried. In fact, the church is very assured of what it believes so you're freed to believe or not believe and quit worrying about it." She looked at me quizzically, as I went on, "But here's what I want you to do. I want you to keep coming to church and I want you to keep practicing the things of worship: sing the hymns whether you believe any of them or not, say the prayers, including the Lord's Prayer, whether you believe in it or not, read the Bible, whether you believe it or not, listen to the sermon, give to the offering, and all the rest. And I want you to find a place of service. Sing in the choir, or volunteer as a tutor after school, or show up for Habitat, or whatever but I want you to serve. Relax about what you believe or don't believe." She responded, "I've never heard of such a thing but I'll give it a try."

For the next three or four months she never missed a Sunday, she joined the choir, and she served in some other ministries. We met for coffee again and this time with a big grin she said, "I have another confession to make. I'm beginning to believe this stuff." About six months later, she came to me and said, "I want to join the church and renew my baptismal vows I made as a child. I really believe this again." So we started the long and slow journey of reading Jesus' Sermon on the Mount together, praying together, and working in a garden together with some other church folk.

I remember the great theologian Stanley Hauerwas went to his pastor and said, "Tell me where you want me to serve." She told him to mow the churchyard. So every other Saturday, a theologian of the church, teacher, and writer of fifty books got out of his head and pushed a lawnmower up and down the yard of the Aldersgate United Methodist Church, weeded the flower beds, and edged the curbing. Through such mundane acts, God makes us the church.

Notes

1. Archie McDonald, ed., *The Amazing Grace Baptist Church: Four Decades of Service at Austin Heights* (Austin Heights Baptist Church, 2007), 14–17.
2. Philip J. Lee, *Against the Protestant Gnostics* (New York and Oxford: Oxford University Press, 1987), 3–44.
3. Samuel Wells, *A Nazareth Manifesto: Being with God* (Chichester, UK: John Wiley & Sons, 2015), 142.
4. Lee, *Against the Protestant Gnostics*, 45.
5. Thomas G. Long, *Preaching from Memory to Hope* (Louisville: Westminster John Knox Press, 2009), 64.
6. Walker Percy, *Love in the Ruins* (New York: Farrar, Straus & Giroux, 1971), 254.
7. Norman Wirzba, "Placing the Soul: An Agrarian Philosophical Principle," in *The Essential Agrarian Reader: The Future of Culture, Community, and the Land*, ed. Norman Wirzba (Lexington: University Press of Kentucky, 2003), 86.
8. Charles Taylor, *A Secular Age* (Cambridge: Belknap Press of Harvard University Press, 2007), 288.
9. Christian Wiman, *Ambition and Survival: Becoming a Poet* (Port Townsend, WA: Copper Canyon Press, 2007), 5–6.
10. Wendell Berry, "Poetry and Place," in *Standing by Words: Essays* (San Francisco: North Point Press, 1983), 117.
11. Edward E. Baptist, *The Half Has Never Been Told: Slavery and the Making of American Capitalism* (New York: Basic Books, 2014), 198–206. See also Christine Leigh Heyrman, *Southern Cross: The Beginnings of the Bible Belt* (New York: Knopf, 1997).
12. Alan Kreider, *The Patient Ferment of the Early Church: The Improbable Rise of Christianity in the Roman Empire* (Grand Rapids: Baker Academic, 2016), 19, 26.
13. Ibid., 61.
14. Ibid., 39.
15. Ibid., 40.
16. Ibid., 149–52.

CHAPTER 12

Imagining Structural Stewardship: Lessons in Resistance and Cultural Change from the Highlander Folk School

Emily Hunt and João Chaves

In December of 1987, two members of the educational elite, Myles Horton and Paulo Freire, came together to discuss the dynamics between schooling and social change. It is clear from their conversation, outlined in *We Make the Road By Walking*, that despite differences in their respective socio-political contexts and tensions, the two held a common view that education was the backdrop of cultural change. They explained:

> At that time, there was a lot of discussion about whether you should try and reform education, which is what we were concerned about, by

E. Hunt (✉)
Sociology Department, Baylor University,
Waco, TX, USA

J. Chaves
Baptist University of the Americas, San Antonio, TX, USA

T.L. Scales and J.L. Howell (eds.), *Christian Faith and University Life*,
DOI 10.1007/978-3-319-61744-2_12

> working inside the system, because if you worked outside the system, you couldn't influence the system. The argument was that you could change the system. We concluded that reform within the system reinforced the system, or was co-opted by the system. Reformers didn't change the system; they made it more palatable and justified it, made it more humane, more intelligent. We didn't want to make that contribution to the schooling system. But we knew if we worked outside the system, we would not be recognized as educators, because an educator by definition was somebody inside the schooling system.[1]

Horton, a former student of Reinhold Niebuhr at Union Theological Seminary in the 1920s, and Freire, a member of the growing liberation theology movement in Latin America, understood and approached theology through its social dimensions. They shared an understanding of education as formation: that knowledge emerges from experiences and practice. Horton's main work was through the Highlander Folk School, a rural Appalachian educational center, while Freire's was through a popular education model incorporated into state run educational efforts in Brazil. Horton's Highlander model illuminates a particular tactic, or strategy of schooling, that provided supportive structures for change at one of the most divided moments in United States history—the Civil Rights Era. Understanding the success of the Highlander experiment in its own context offers a window through which to consider the possible future of social change in and through Christian higher education.

To the extent that Horton and Freire's respective visions of schooling were inspired by the challenges set forth by their contextual and political theologies, their approaches challenge us to think of Christian action in ways that attempt to go beyond excessively individual, and sectarian terms and to consider social and structural justice. While Schools of Education around the country regularly draw on Freirean critical pedagogy as inspiration for efforts toward equality and inclusion, in considering the conditions under which Christian higher education might steward its vision given the larger social and political dynamics at work, a retrieval of how Highlander and Horton's strategies provided alternative space for critique is illustrative of what it could take to create a counter-witness to status quo if, and when, necessary.

Highlander provided an educational space during the Civil Rights Era where students could both learn and inhabit a new reality that challenged the status quo of divisiveness and stewarded an ethic of love that defied the cultural presses of the day. While the issues plaguing higher education and the particularities of societal pressures in this contemporary moment are different than the ones addressed in Freire and Horton's generation, the prospect of an educational institution that offers significant critique to dominant cultural narratives is absolutely relevant to preparing tomorrow's stewards of the academy.

While Christian higher education is not likely to, nor should it, become Highlander, we argue that the particular critiques and imaginative approaches of Highlander's story may inform future discussions on stewardship and formation. Giving space for an alternative moral vision that embraces the vision of social and structural justice and the practices that follow may allow a university to resist those cultural forces that are at odds with both its vision and its strategies of engagement.

Our argument will progress in a few steps. First, we will address the necessity of a central concern for structural and social justice in Christian higher education. We contend that universities that appropriate the label "Christian" but remain entangled in elitist commitments that ultimately reveal their values and hopes often neglect the appropriate concern for social justice that allows them to use the label with broad plausibility. At the risk of sounding judgmental, we take the radical stance that the plausible use of the term "Christian" comes with a cost. In this section, we also address the state and market entanglements that co-opted American higher education in general and American Christian higher education in particular. This first step helps us diagnose the aspects of Christian higher education that we want to challenge. After this preliminary diagnostic, we look at the role of an educational institution's position in relation to society-wide power dynamics in its ability and interest to enact change. Finally, we lay out the example of the Highlander Folk School and develop thoughts on how their history can shed light on ways in which Christian educational institutions might address social justice concerns effectively.

Structural Stewardship

Our own informal conversations as doctoral students, or stewards in training, have echoed tenets of the conversation between Freire and Horton.[2] Though ours have been focused on higher education specifically, we have found timely inspiration for this chapter in their words. Given the complexity and contradictions of educational institutions, is it best to reform the system from the inside or the outside? What are the longings and apprehensions of both approaches? Discovering the story of Highlander has given us more questions than answers, but this chapter represents our ongoing attempt to answer the questions they pose of the possibility of social change in and through schooling, specifically applied to Christian higher education.

The call for stewards of the academy to remain faithful to their Christian identities has resounded throughout the rapid pace social and cultural shifts of late modernity. Amidst deepening difference and increasing polarization, the challenges faced by Christian higher education are not wholly unlike those faced by their secular counterparts. Administrators are weighing how to stay faithful to their missions amidst increasing competition, and questions of vibrancy, not to mention affordability, remain constant. However, many of the concerns plaguing higher education are affected by a deeper problem: how much autonomy institutions have given the significant influence of the market and the state.

According to Robert Bellah, it is the core tenets of market exchange that guide human interactions—such as those between universities and students.[3] It is against this backdrop that we consider the gravitas of stewardship and are drawn to Highlander's example. While the issues of higher education are ever evolving, an underlying concern for the next generation's change agents in the academy is dealing with the problem of market totality. This tendency to commodify and compete plays out in direct and subtle ways in and through the academy. For example, in *Academically Adrift: Limited Learning on College Campuses*, Arum and Roksa describe a significant problem in higher education as a failure to satisfy the demands of corporate leaders in the private sector.[4] For Arum and Roksa, a serious issue is whether or not alumni will be able to remain competitive in a global economy. To lament the lack of critical thinking because it inhibits corporations from hiring graduates is moreover a lament of the inability of students to be globally competitive. The market mentality is so engrained in the way in which higher education is conceptualized today that even criticisms of the educational system itself may take job placement as the highest standard of educational success.

This concern of the over-reach of markets also plays out in the students themselves and their goals for attaining a college education.

Students approach schooling as consumers, career-oriented efforts are increasingly monolithic and given primacy while consideration for character development diminishes.[5] Other dimensions of citizenship, which have historically focused on identity, purpose, meaning, interdependence and the common good, are subsumed by the utilitarian seduction of job placement. High tuition and substantial debt limit the institution's ability to imbue these "fundamental outcomes."[6]

Considering the relationship built on market logic, Bellah goes on to ask if it is even possible for universities to operate outside of this dynamic. He asks, "Can we construct a vision of the social world that is not dominated by the contemporary economic or political fields but has at least a degree of moral autonomy?"[7] It is both the possibility and extent of moral autonomy necessary for institutions seeking to steward their particular visions that is in question. Yet another related concern is the connection between universities and the state. The policy and legal contracts under which higher education must operate are vast—and the funding contingent upon obedience to laws of the land remains the lifeline of the modern university. Financial pressures and legal constraints, therefore, directly influence the extent to which colleges and universities can act in ways that support their particularity, in this case, Christianity.

Universities are in a difficult position to legitimate themselves in a market culture, but may also inadvertently create or perpetuate some of the problems their students are learning to solve.[8] Since its inception, American higher education has had the transmission of knowledge as well as the transformation of culture as central purposes.[9] However, the capacity to continue these noble humanitarian purposes waxes and wanes. As Wuthnow notes, universities are in an awkward position as they directly benefit from and contribute to competition while attempting to simultaneously be committed to humanitarianism and global values.[10] External and competitive accomplishments are central to the status, prestige, and ultimate lifeline of the institutions, even if they are at times logically inconsistent with more universal and caring values. The tragic irony is that despite their espoused ethic of making the world a better place, they inevitably produce citizens entrenched in a market culture where contradictory tendencies are made to seem coherent and virtuous. This irony is perhaps even more clearly seen in Christian higher education, where institutions often mirror these efforts while also attempting to espouse an ethic of Christ's love and vision for the world.

Christian Identity

As new problems face each generation of scholars, and problems never encountered may require new solutions, stewards in training are called to do the hard work of imagining alternative visions regarding what Christian higher education might be amidst the increasing pressure of entanglement, both institutionally and ideologically, in this market-state dialectic. Not only do universities legitimate and disseminate both state and market agendas, they also reap benefits from their involvement with state and market institutions and ideologies. Christian institutions, broadly speaking, are in no way immune to these cultural presses, and the extent of co-dependency influences the degree of freedom a given institution may have with which to make decisions within the framework of their own identity.

Our view is that the fundamental outcome of cultivating an ethic of Christian commitment requires a particular prioritizing of social and structural justice, an outcome that has, in many cases, taken a back seat partially due to the financial and legal entanglements that such a stance would upset. This specific tension is visible across the university context in areas including, but far beyond widely discussed controversies over diversity politics, prioritizing athletics, or the potentially divisive presence of Greek Life. While these points require awareness and action internal to the institution, might Christian stewardship also require a greater degree of external reflection? This could include greater concern about the ways in which an institution's investment portfolio reflects God's economy and care for the earth or how to respond to refugees and immigrant members of the campus community. Currently, these tensions are illuminated through the hesitancy present in a number of purportedly Christian institutions in taking a public stance for the biblical mandate to welcome the stranger by declaring themselves sanctuary campuses. As we write this chapter, presidential executive orders and governmental policies that will potentially affect millions of immigrants and refugees negatively are rolling out, and, in the world of academia, the most vociferous opposition to these tendencies have come from secular, rather than Christian universities. These are just a few examples among many we could discuss.

We echo Willie Jennings's concern for Christians to "recognize the grotesque nature of a social performance of Christianity that imagines Christian identity floating above land, landscape, animal, places, and space, leaving such realities to the machination of capitalistic calculations and the commodity chains of private property."[11] We are indeed challenged to imagine the Christian identity of universities by emphasizing the material, measurable outpouring of this Christianity in social life. In order for a Christian university to use the label "Christian" with broad plausibility, it must, as an institution, strive for justice in terms of ideological dissemination, public witness, and political commitments. That is to say that there is a cost involved in using the label "Christian" that goes beyond requiring students to attend chapel, take Bible courses, or adhere to particular behavioral codes. While these efforts of individual morality matter a great deal, we would add that at the core of one's plausible use of the term is the question of the direct, intentional, and distinctive contribution of Christian universities to the implementation of justice in contemporary society. If such distinctiveness is lacking, it seems that the qualification "Christian" is dispensable.

When it comes to public witness and political commitments, there is always the propensity for an institution's commitment to self-preservation to trump its ideological rhetoric. As institutions of all types have some focus on reproducing themselves, this is a possible danger of stewardship. Nevertheless, a Christian institution's public witness and political commitments must be guided and measured by its approximation to the life and teachings of Jesus Christ. The potentially revolutionary task that such approximation calls for may, at times, entail direct confrontation against the instrumentalism of state policies and market agendas.

The tension regarding the possibility of a Christian university *vis-à-vis* existing structural entanglements and realistic concerns of institutional vibrancy is central to our concern in this chapter. Although efforts directed toward the disenfranchised cannot mean the neglect of Christian doctrine and its corollary appropriation of a watered-down gospel, it does mean emphasizing Christian-inspired, ecumenical justice over proselytizing and apologetic anxieties. Institutions standing for sanctuary campuses and against aggressive anti-refugee policies or endowments divesting from the fossil fuel industry represents instances of this possibility—though, many other opportunities are imaginable.

As efforts to address social and structural justice might require critical reflection toward the market and state systems that legitimate the very existence of the institution attempting to prioritize justice initiatives, a challenge for today's stewards of the academy is finding ways to creatively resist a total encapsulation of their strategies and ideals in the university-market-state dialectic. Such resistance must contend with the competing goals of prestige and status and requires a particularly formed imagination that itself has not been co-opted by the state or political realm as contemporary American Christian imagination often is. Building the capacity for such resistance of this kind demands both an understanding of cultural change, and a robust alternative vision. The story of the Highlander Folk School gives us an example of a time in history where an institution relinquished these secondary goods in order to create dramatic social change in favor of structural and social justice as higher priorities. While not a story about a religious or overtly Christian institution per se, the story of Highlander inspires us to imagine a Christian witness that, if necessary, would be prepared to press against the state and market systems that ultimately legitimate its existence.

We are convinced by the biblical account, most recently mediated through the herculean theological corpus written primarily by black and Latin American liberationists, that such witness and commitments must manifest themselves as clear action in favor of disenfranchised peoples—the poor, the brutalized, the widow, the undocumented immigrant, and so on. Outside of this, talk of a Christian university, especially coming from privileged sectors of society that can afford themselves the lack of a sense of urgency, falls short of its true substance. We do realize, however, that any talk of a Christian university's call to struggle for structural change in the name of the disenfranchised is complex and dependent on an analysis of historical examples and social dynamics that is too broad to be done comprehensively within a short piece.

While the idea of education-as-resistance and the goals of so-called radical educators may seem unfit for traditional models of Christian higher education, a retrieval of certain tactics and ideals surrounding the Highlander Folk School, are analytically helpful. Through the Highlander narrative, we can imagine a way for Christian higher education to resist being subsumed into the goals or vision that may at some point be at odds with its Christian identity. Christian stewards of the academy would do well to pay attention to the example of Highlander in order to better understand how resistance and change efforts are mitigated by a given institution's social position and to also envision a Christian identity with greater attention to social and structural justice. To that end, a consideration of the way in which educational institutions relate to the dynamics of power in society is indispensable.

Education and Cultural Power

Change in and through education is constrained by the culture of which a given educational institution is a part. Conversations about the role of education in social change and resistance, therefore, must begin with a discussion about how culture tends to operate. According to sociologist James Hunter's theory of culture outlined in *To Change the World*, it is the combination of individuals, networks, and institutions operating in the center rather than in the peripheral locations of society that produces cultural change.[12] These domains are organized by a sense of prestige and the status assigned to a particular structural location and a given institution's influence is directly related to where it fits into this status structure.[13] In short, an institution is bound by its need to be legitimated by society, and greater legitimacy, or power, is afforded to institutions at the center of cultural production.

In applying Hunter's theory to higher education, schools operating at all points of the spectrum of cultural power may be more or less prepared to not only change the world, but also to challenge the status quo, a possibility that is contingent on the extent to which they depend on the center for legitimacy. Various approaches to education reside in the center of cultural power and attempt to change the world from this position—a top-down approach that certainly has its benefits and is attractive for many reasons, not least of which is greater stability and prestige (e.g., Harvard means more, symbolically, than Kaplan). In terms of world changing, higher education institutions located at the center of cultural production have a significant, and often positive, impact on the world. Many facets of the modern university, including research, teaching, and community engagement have been invaluable in addressing the most complex problems of modernity.

However, those institutions holding a centermost position lack an adequate level of detachment from their own legitimation in order to critique it, even if they have the most cultural power to make a change. Even if those near the center have access to power and to countercultural ideas, institutions taking this approach are at mercy of the cultural center, "or nucleus" for their own legitimation and must take care to avoid an ousting to the periphery for fear of losing legitimacy.[14] They cannot be too radical. The periphery lacks the necessary access to the cultural gatekeepers, though it does have the necessary detachment in order to offer critique. If the centermost sphere of cultural production includes the most prestigious universities, then institutions closer to the periphery are those with lower statuses or rankings, making them less powerful and their influence measured in their proximity to the center.

Reform from the center of cultural production often remains more or less a reification of what already exists. While their focus may be on challenging the status quo of what they see as the world's vices, institutions further away from the center vie for the power and prestige afforded to those at the nucleus of cultural production. These institutions and their approaches have as their goal to reform those cultural values, though they often use the same means as those who simply reflect the dominant culture in their attempt to arrive at the center of power. Their product is a version of what was produced by their more centrally located parallel prototype. They may mimic the dominant culture, even in their best efforts to reform it, but fail to detach substantively from the dominant center and thus position themselves in a place, where they can provide an appropriate criticism of the system. The most obvious example of operation from this location in cultural production is the topic at hand of Christian higher education.

These institutions are in a conundrum, constantly being pulled simultaneously toward a religiously articulated self-identity understood in moral terms and toward a market system with characteristics that may not be easily harmonized with such identity. These institutions, specifically those members of the Council for Christian Colleges and Universities (CCCU), have operated historically further away from the centermost spheres of cultural production than have Catholic and other Protestant institutions. Their idea of education is preparing citizens both for this world and the one to come as conceived of in the Kingdom of God. Hunter notes that the Christian Right, with which many of these Evangelical institutions would identify, care deeply about changing the world, but have historically employed and reproduced a "defensive against" mentality to changing culture and, as such, they tend to conceptualize of forms of change that function as attempts to either regain or maintain position of structural privilege.[15]

For our analytical purposes, the work of Freire and Horton is representative of the peripheral sphere in regard to education and cultural power. Popular education models developed by Freire are focused on the education as a means to freedom and liberation from oppressive structures (which are almost always found in the center). Freire argues that there is no conceivable way a liberating education could exist within the dominant system (the center).[16] He notes that cultivating such an institution of critique would require the ruling class to challenge its own dominant position. Schools operating from this position may question the capacity of the center to be critical or reflective in regard to its inconsistencies.

One recent example of an institution operating from this location of power is Freedom University.[17] Freedom University was founded in 2011 following a decision made by the Georgia University system to refuse admission to undocumented immigrants from the top five universities in the state. Faculty from the University of Georgia began teaching students at Freedom University for the purpose of educating them as full citizens with the right to education, yet outside the credentialing system, or, the center of power in this case. Institutions like Freedom University approach change more or less from the periphery of cultural power, outside of the dominant structure of prestige and status (and accreditation). While Freedom U. may have more autonomy to reflect their vision, it lacks the legitimacy afforded to those institutions closer to the center of cultural production and thus may be limited in its change-making efforts.

The Highlander Center and Strategies for Change

The challenge for those operating from the periphery is to develop a new vision of society that still fits and resonates to some degree with the reality of the old, yet maintains sufficient distance to offer challenge and critique.[18] In seeking to answer the question of how might the Christian scholar approach the task of training, teaching, and stewarding amidst and, at times against, this dominant culture, we are inspired by the example of Highlander. The Highlander Folk School operated along the continuum of the center to periphery and formed a unique synthesis for a particular time of cultural crisis. While existing mostly far away from the center, the story of Highlander offers a case study in cultural change through education in line with Hunter's specific proposition that elites working outside of the center and their overlapping networks are most likely to affect cultural change.

Beginning in the 1930s and primarily focused on the development of Citizenship Schools in the South and adult literacy, Highlander acted as an incubator and haven for activists in what eventually became the Civil Rights Movement. In many ways, it was its own social movement.

Operating in the Appalachian region of Tennessee in the southern, rural, and unaccredited context, Highlander successfully gave energy, networks, space, and ideas to individuals like Rosa Parks, Ella Baker, Septima Clark, and Martin Luther King, Jr, among others who visited, and became a place where world-changing ideas were birthed and practiced into action.

From the Montgomery Bus Boycott to the Freedom Rides and Sit-in Movements, many of the well-known strategies and tactics of the Civil Rights Movement came from conversations, trainings, and seminars at Highlander. According to Morris and McAdam, though Highlander was influential beyond one particular movement, Highlander workshops were considered vital components to the "cognitive liberation" which sustained the Civil Rights Movement.[19] Although Highlander was technically considered a school, it did not have a formal curriculum or structure like that of a college or university and in that sense existed on the periphery.[20] The space, both physically and ideologically, was removed enough from the center of cultural production such that it was not bound by the same constraints of those educational institutions operating closer to the center. Because if its more peripheral position it created a space where blacks and whites could meet together and practice being citizens of a world that did not yet exist, one in which their skin color did not define their participation, and one where directly affected individuals and allies could act as equals in visioning and strategizing.

In short, its contribution to social and structural justice was amplified by its unique social position as it was more equipped to offer critique. Though situated on the periphery, it was connected to the center of cultural production. The inspiration for Highlander, as well as a great deal of its resources, originated in what could be considered the center of cultural production during that time. The connections to the center were manifest through Horton's connections with elites and their institutions, such as Robert Park, John Dewey, and Reinhold Niebuhr.[21] Because the networks of elites involved were widespread and influential, it would be wrong to say that Highlander was totally on the periphery. For example, Dewey offered his full support of the effort along with Eleanor Roosevelt, who financially supported the project.[22]

Highlander offered an alternative cultural schema to those made available by the center of cultural production and did so as a network of cultural power bridging the center to periphery continuum. It helped to facilitate a shift in a larger cultural schema on what it meant to be a citizen by enacting a different type of citizenship education than could have occurred at the center, yet backed by the power of the center. Existing as a coalition of power and network of cultural production, Highlander specifically differed from the center of power in its willingness to go to the periphery and resist market and state, and it differed from the periphery in knowing it needed legitimation from the center's cultural elite.

Lessons in Resistance for Christian Higher Education

By the very nature of its position in cultural production, Christian higher education remains more or less beholden to and constrained by the center for its legitimation. Thus, its efforts directed toward stewardship are at the very least, constrained by requirements of prestige and status. Highlander offers a lesson in that it imagined another way that was driven by a theology that took seriously the social and political implications of Christ, but retained its legitimacy through leadership and networks for a greater impact. The mandate of full and equal humanity was embodied through its pedagogies, and it generated new ideas into existence through its structures and programs because it was not beholden to the typical pressures of competitive achievement. The Highlander story acts as an exemplar school, or movement, that can help enlarge our theological vision of moral formation in Christian higher education to one that includes dimensions of social and structural justice, and one that is willing to relinquish certain aspects of worldly success if necessary.

The conditions at the time of Highlander were ripe for a refocusing to take place, and we think that the conditions are similar in the current context for Christian higher education to reimagine a way forward in stewarding its vision, particularly through the formation of new scholars. Sociologically, Highlander offers an interesting take on how the various spheres of cultural production might work together for social change. Schools that want to form students that will change society should consider the way structural location, essentially efforts toward power and prestige, might mitigate their efforts. The Highlander story teaches us that schooling closer to the center is inseparable from the often-oppressive ideologies of the dominant culture and that there is an alternative space apart from the rationalizations of the system.

We conclude that institutions on the periphery are vital when those institutions that once provided a sense of critique are actually encapsulated by that which they were intended to critique, but these institutions cannot operate in isolation without a network that taps into the cultural power of the center. Change more likely occurs when a system is intolerable for those on the periphery and intolerable for some at the center of society who enter into a partnership with one another. In the case of Highlander and civil rights, an opportunity for change existed when a diverse coalition of power, including those directly affected by racism and allies in the movement, organized to enact compelling initiatives for change.

From the case of Highlander, we can learn that a level of attached detachment from the center of power is necessary for educational institutions to implement or energize significant change in society. World-changing institutions need to be independent enough from the center of power to assess power structures with a significant amount of freedom and integrity. A level of connection to the center of power, however, is also necessary so that communication channels between such institutions and those in the center of power is cultivated, and so that the institution is seen as a legitimate authority. Because Horton was attached to elites, he had a sense of status and prestige through his own networks that sustained the vision, even if Highlander itself operated at the periphery.

According to Hunter, cultural change begins with the conceptual and moves to the concrete and remains most "enduring when it penetrates the structures of our imagination."[23] Highlander's existence pointed out that too much compromise with the center, and not enough challenge, can render an alternative vision unfulfilled. This is the challenge for higher education, and particularly, Christian Stewards. Dewey, Niebuhr, Horton, Freire, and the many others who directly or indirectly participated in the ongoing project of Highlander knew that such radical ideas as racial and economic justice were impossibilities from the center of cultural production, despite the fact that they were conceived there. The interdependent networks operating through Highlander offered an opportunity for education toward citizenship and participation as citizens for those who had been denied that opportunity because of legal constraints from the center of cultural production. It offered the structural location and pedagogical conditions for practicing citizenship of a world that did not yet exist.

How exactly Christian higher education should move forward in stewarding its vision remains a bit unclear. Though there is a vast literature regarding Christian higher education and tactics for optimal identity maintenance, we have laid out important cultural conditions for how and to what extent Christian higher education might influence social change by theorizing about the location of schooling within existing power structures as well as suggesting that this identity include a wider vision of structural and social justice. While we recognize the somewhat Utopian nature of the Highlander experiment, we also believe that Highlander was a creative response to a cultural moment and it supported a redefinition of who was a citizen and ultimately facilitated the reimagining of America.

The challenging question with which the example of Highlander leaves us in terms of its expansive vision parallels the one voiced by Leonardo and Clodovis Boff, who asked of the traditional theologians who criticized their liberationist commitments as overly ideological: "what part have you played in the effective and integral liberation of the oppressed?"[24] Highlander challenges us to think about the quality of our commitment to Christian higher education by calling us to go beyond techniques of theological and existential coping with a culture that has deep anti-Christian elements dressed with evangelical piety. Whatever else we call Christian higher education, if it does not imagine ways to change the oppressive and dehumanizing structures of American society, perhaps it is not Christian enough. Highlander, at the very least, offers an example of clever and timely resistance.

Notes

1. Myles Horton and Paulo Freire, *We Make the Road by Walking: Conversations on Education and Social Change*, ed. Brenda Bell, John Gaventa, and John Peters, Reprint (Philadelphia: Temple University Press, 1990), 199–200.
2. Ibid.
3. R. Bellah, "Class Wars and Culture Wars in the University Today: Why We Can't Defend Ourselves," in *The Robert Bellah Reader*, ed. Steven M. Tipton (Durham: Duke University Press, 2006), 402–409.
4. Richard Arum and Josipa Roksa, *Academically Adrift: Limited Learning on College Campuses* (Chicago: The University of Chicago Press, 2011).
5. Arthur W. Chickering, "A Retrospect on Higher Education's Commitment to Moral and Civic Education," *Journal of College and Character* 11, no. 3 (2010): 1–6.
6. Ibid., 5.

7. Bellah, "Class Wars and Culture Wars in the University Today: Why We Can't Defend Ourselves," 409.
8. Robert Wuthnow, *Communities of Discourse: Ideology and Social Structure in the Reformation, the Enlightenment, and European Socialism* (Cambridge: Harvard University Press, 2009), 255.
9. George M Marsden, *The Soul of the American University: From Protestant Establishment to Established Nonbelief* (New York: Oxford University Press, 1994).
10. Wuthnow, *Communities of Discourse.*
11. Willie James Jennings, *The Christian Imagination: Theology and the Origins of Race* (New Haven: Yale University Press, 2010), 293.
12. James Davison Hunter, *To Change the World: The Irony, Tragedy, and Possibility of Christianity in the Late Modern World* (New York: Oxford University Press, 2010).
13. Edward Shils, "Centre and Periphery," in *The Logic of Personal Knowledge: Essays Presented to Michael Polanyi on His 70th Birthday*, ed. Polanyi Festschrift Committee (London: Routledge & Kegan Paul, 1961), 117–130; Hunter, *To Change the World.*
14. Hunter, *To Change the World*, 42.
15. Hunter, *To Change the World.*
16. Paulo Freire, *Paulo Freire on Higher Education: A Dialogue at the National University of Mexico*, ed. Miguel Escobar, Alfredo L. Fernández, and Gilberto Guevara-Niebla (Albany: State University of New York Press, 1994).
17. For more information on Freedom University, see http://www.freedomuniversitygeorgia.com/.
18. Hunter, *To Change the World.*
19. Aldon D Morris, *The Origins of the Civil Rights Movement: Black Communities Organizing for Change* (New York: Free Press, 1986); Doug McAdam, *Political Process and the Development of Black Insurgency, 1930–1970* (Chicago: University of Chicago Press, 1982); Bob Edwards and John D. McCarthy, "Social Movement Schools," *Sociological Forum* 7, no. 3 (1992): 541.
20. Edwards and McCarthy, "Social Movement Schools."
21. John M. Glen, *Highlander: No Ordinary School 1932–1962* (Lexington, KY: University Press of Kentucky, 1988).
22. Aimee Isgrig Horton, *The Highlander Folk School: A History of Its Major Programs, 1932–1961* (Brooklyn, NY: Carlson, 1989), 265; Glen, *Highlander.*
23. Hunter, *To Change the World*, 42.
24. Leonardo Boff and Clodovis M Boff, *Introducing Liberation Theology* (Maryknoll, NY: Orbis Books, 1987), 9.

CHAPTER 13

William James's Pragmatic Pluralism and the American University's Loss of Soul

Karl Aho

Much of the literature on Christian scholarship focuses on research, teaching, and service. In addition to these traditional academic activities, Christian scholars who work in mainstream universities face a further challenge: ensuring that there is a place for faith-informed scholarship in such institutions. As Jenny Howell and Laine Scales note in the introduction, one of the tasks of stewardship is transforming knowledge so that new learners can engage with it. One form of academic stewardship is working to develop and defend the university as an institutional context for the transformation of knowledge. However, Christian scholars who work in universities without expressed faith commitments face a special version of this stewardship challenge. They must defend the university in general and their own faith-based approach to their scholarship in particular. So, how should Christian scholars working in mainstream universities (i.e., private and public secular institutions) advocate for having their distinct perspectives heard? Around twenty-five years ago, George Marsden influentially argued that Christian scholars working in primarily

K. Aho (✉)
Tarleton State University, Stephenville, TX, USA

T.L. Scales and J.L. Howell (eds.), *Christian Faith and University Life*,
DOI 10.1007/978-3-319-61744-2_13

mainstream universities should actively campaign for those universities to be broadly pluralistic. Marsden claims that this sort of intellectual pluralism would provide faith-based intellectual positions a place within these universities. In this chapter, I evaluate Marsden's prescription for pluralism in light of recent developments in higher education. I also discuss some practical implications of Marsden's proposal for Christian scholars at public institutions.

After discussing the many merits of Marsden's view, I will argue that certain developments within contemporary society suggest that pluralism is necessary but insufficient to secure a place for faith-based scholarship. To defend this claim, I will present the 2012 emergence of groups I collectively term "the Newer Atheists" as emblematic of the challenges Christian scholars face today. These successors to the New Atheists, such as Alain de Botton or the Atheism Plus movement, claim that atheists should tolerate religion rather than polemically argue against it. I invoke the Newer Atheists not to suggest that they are a particularly dire challenge to faith-based scholarship, but in order to illustrate that the mere inclusion of such scholarship in the mainstream academy is insufficient. Through developing Marsden's discussion of William James's pragmatic pluralism, I argue that Christian scholars should also present their scholarship attractively and persuasively, lest it be marginalized by other groups—even if those groups do not directly argue against faith-based scholarship. To that end, I argue that faith-based scholarship in a mainstream context should not be promoted through appeals to pluralism alone, of the sort Marsden models. We ought not assume that pluralism is good *a priori*. Furthermore, arguments based on pluralism such as identity politics have been criticized from a variety of perspectives in the wake of the 2016 presidential election. Instead of relying on merely pluralistic or identitarian principles, we should also promote faith-based scholarship in the public university by emphasizing ways such scholarship can contribute to the university. I expand Marsden's discussion of James's pragmatic pluralism as a way to advocate for faith-informed scholarship in the mainstream university in part by demonstrating that certain pedagogical practices of Christian scholars can address concerns in mainstream universities. On the one hand, this pragmatic approach cannot in itself answer the question of how to best promote faith-based scholarship in the mainstream university. On the other hand, this approach can free scholars to respond to the problems they and the communities that they serve may face. One implication of this idea is that

Christian scholars should be free to defend the goods that faith-based scholarship within the particular communities they serve rather than having to defend the place of Christian scholarship in the university broadly construed.

Marsden's Prescription of Pluralism

Before discussing Marsden's position, we need to understand some of his terms. Though his early work (like his influential *The Outrageous Idea of Christian Scholarship*) uses "Christian scholarship" throughout, Marsden has since moved away from this term. His more recent work on religious colleges uses the term "faith-informed" scholarship.[1] I will follow Marsden in using this term whenever possible. I will use "Christian scholars" to refer to academics whose work is informed by their Christian faith. However, many of the arguments of this chapter still apply to scholars whose work is informed by other religious traditions. These arguments may also prove helpful for scholars whose institutions are nominally church-related, but do not place any particular value on faith-based scholarship. Given the existence of such schools, I will use the term "mainstream" to refer to both public and private secular institutions. In order to more fully reconstruct Marsden's arguments, I will rely primarily on Marsden's 1992 essay "The Soul of the American University: A Historical Overview" while referring to later works as is necessary.[2]

In "The Soul of the American University," Marsden prescribes advocating pluralism as a response to the secularization of mainstream American universities. He writes that "despite their rhetoric of pluralism," many academics "want to eliminate from academia those who do not broadly share their outlook." In response, Marsden thinks that Christian scholars should challenge these academics to be more consistently pluralistic. This broad pluralism would be more consistently inclusive, "embracing even traditional Christian views."[3] Being "open to the widest-ranging free inquiry [...] would involve allowing all sorts of Christian and other religiously based intellectual traditions back into the discussion."[4] In short, true pluralism requires including religious perspectives. So "it is fair to ask whether it is consistent with the vision of contemporary universities to discriminate against religiously informed views when all other sorts of advocacy and intellectual inquiry are tolerated."[5] Marsden concludes that we should encourage scholars—whether religious or secular—to openly reveal their perspectives. He claims that this sort of openness would be "more fair and more consistent with the pluralistic intellectual tenor of our times."[6] Furthermore, "the alternative seems to be to continue the cycle of replacing one set of correct views with a new consensus that is to be imposed on everyone—which is not pluralism at all."[7]

What would a mainstream university that adopted the broad pluralism that Marsden advocates look like? Marsden's *The Outrageous Idea of Christian Scholarship* further develops his claim that faith-informed perspectives should be accepted in the university. Marsden appeals to the American philosopher William James's essay "What Pragmatism Means" to provide an image for the pluralistic university. James (borrowing from Giovanni Papini) likens pragmatic discourse to a corridor in a hotel:

> Innumerable chambers open out of it. In one you may find a man writing an atheistic volume; in the next some one on his knees praying for faith and strength; in a third a chemist investigating a body's properties. In a fourth a system of idealistic metaphysics is being excogitated; in a fifth the impossibility of metaphysics is being shown. But they all own the corridor, and all must pass through it if they want a practicable way of getting into or out of their respective rooms.[8]

Marsden writes that he "would be happy if someone like William James were in charge of setting the rules for these corridors."[9] James would be a welcome adjudicator for the university because he would have agreed with Marsden that "there is no adequate pragmatic basis for marginalizing all supernaturalist religious viewpoints a priori."[10] That is, James would affirm that we cannot exclude faith-based scholarship from the university simply because it is faith based. Instead, we need to evaluate particular cases of faith-based scholarship. As Marsden notes in his 1992 essay, admitting faith-based scholarship to the university would not commit the university to a sort of moral relativism in which every view is permissible. It would merely involve permitting expressions of "responsibly presented minority opinions, including some very unpopular ones."[11] Thus, James's pragmatism provides a method for dealing peacefully and equitably with diverse groups, including religious groups.[12]

Marsden's approach is not to claim that all perspectives matter. Instead of appealing to abstract principles like ideological diversity, Marsden introduces what he calls "rules of the academic game."

These rules help to determine what perspectives or disciplinary approaches may find a place in the academy and which may not. The most representative of these rules for the purposes of this chapter is Marsden's version of the golden rule: "How would [religious scholars] want scholars holding other strongly ideological convictions to act in the mainstream academy?"[13] Instead of imitating other groups that violate the rules for civil discourse, Christians should model "what it means to love and respect those with whom one differs, even as they may debate their differences."[14] This love and respect requires affects both the ways that faith-based scholars present religious perspectives, as well as how they listen to the perspectives of others. "In classrooms, especially in state-supported schools, teachers must present [faith-based] viewpoints only as relevant to the academic subject and with great deference and respect for opposing viewpoints, especially opposing religious views."[15] So Christian scholars would both refrain from proselytizing in the classroom, ***and*** teach their students about the views of other religions and nonreligious perspectives. For Marsden, these are some of the rules that Christian scholars must follow to be able to appeal to pluralism to maintain their place in the mainstream public university and secure a room in the Jamesian hotel. Marsden thinks following these rules of the academic game will enable Christian scholars to retain their place within the academy by treating others well and, hopefully, being treated well in return.

Evaluating Marsden's Pluralism

Now that I've presented Marsden's account of how pluralism can help Christian scholars, I will turn to evaluating that account from a contemporary perspective. Marsden's prescription of pluralism has proven its worth in the more than two decades since "The Soul of the American University." In that time, Christian scholars have faced many sorts of challenge—some affecting the university in general and some unique to those pursuing faith-based scholarship. The former sort of challenge has been chronicled at length in books and essays, like Marsden's, that describe the American university's loss of soul. Susan VanZanten lists five books that echo Marsden's concerns (discussed at length in *The Soul of the American University*) about character education, affirmation of spirituality, and respect for and learning about religious institutions and traditions.[16] The latter sort of challenge includes intensifications of the academic secularization that prompted Marsden's prescription of appealing to pluralism. One recent source of this secularization was the emergence of the New Atheism, a group of anti-religion public intellectuals who rose to prominence in the early 2000s. Their position is distinct from the sort of secularization that Marsden discusses in "The Soul of the American University." Instead of viewing pluralism as a default position, the New Atheists view religion as an ideology to be argued against, in the university and elsewhere.

Marsden's prescription of pluralism has helped Christian scholars face both general academic challenges and the challenges specific to faith-based scholarship. Universities have been able to respond to many of the general academic challenges. As VanZanten notes, "the twenty-first century has subsequently witnessed an increased concern for civic virtue, character formation, and spirituality among both public and private universities."[17] For example, theologians like Stanley Hauerwas have argued that all teachers rather than a limited subset of teachers, such as teachers of ethics, should attend to the ways in which they morally form their students' characters. (David Cramer's chapter in this volume addresses this theme in the context of introductory religion or theology courses.) We should not credit Marsden's warnings about loss of soul for causing these changes in the university, although Marsden's work may have contributed to them. However, his prescription of pluralism does seem to have helped at least some faith-based scholars to preserve their places in the university until the culture became more favorable for their work.

Marsden's prescription of pluralism can provide Christian scholars with a response to the New Atheists. As Marsden notes elsewhere, "argument, while it may hearten those who are already sympathetic, usually stimulates those who are inclined against your views to dig in more deeply in their opposition."[18] Since the New Atheism is a more contentious version of the old secularization challenge to faith-based scholarship, the movement relies on proffering arguments against religion (and thus faith-based scholarship). These arguments have had the effect of mobilizing those sympathetic to the presence of faith-based scholarship. Unlike the New Atheist approach, Marsden's prescription of pluralism does not rely on direct arguments for Christian scholarship. Advocating for a truly pluralistic academy like Marsden does not prompt arguments against Christian scholarship. By contrast, more direct apologetic arguments in favor of Christian scholarship might invite criticism. So Marsden's prescription of advocating for and modeling pluralism in the academy can help Christian scholars respond to the New Atheists and other criticisms along similar lines.

The Newer Atheists' Challenge to Marsden's Pluralism

One recent challenge to Christian scholarship in the mainstream university is the New Atheists' successors. For lack of a better term, I will refer to these groups collectively as the Newer Atheists, and refer to specific group according to the name they have adopted. For example, some have dubbed a less contentious group of atheistic public intellectuals as "the New New Atheists." These writers, such as pop philosophers Alain de Botton, think that religion is a source of insight even though religious beliefs like belief in God are false. In his 2012 *Religion for Atheists*, de Botton writes:

> The error of modern atheism has been to overlook how many aspects of the faiths remain relevant even after their central tenets have been dismissed. Once we cease to feel that we must either prostrate ourselves before them or denigrate them, we are free to discover religions as repositories of a myriad ingenious concepts with which we can try to assuage a few of the most persistent and unattended ills of secular life.[19]

De Botton wants neither to exclude religious perspectives by default nor actively argue against them (like the New Atheists). He promotes studying religions as cultural artifacts in order to get at the values those religions gesture toward. Education, on de Botton's view, can help people learn to how care for themselves and their communities, analogously to the way that religions (and by extension scholarship informed by religions) seeks to help people.[20] For example, de Botton concludes his chapter on Education by claiming that "A university alive to the true responsibilities of cultural artefacts within a secular age would establish a Department for Relationships, an Institute of Dying and a Centre for Self-Knowledge."[21] We can see from these representative samples of Botton's work that he and other "New New Atheists" think religion should be tolerated for the sake of its contributions to wholly secular concerns.

Another group of Newer Atheists called itself "Atheism Plus," or "A+." Whereas de Botton and "the New New Atheists" advocate extending some of the benefits of religion to atheists, Atheism Plus approached progressive political concerns from a nonreligious perspective. The movement was especially concerned with issues of equality. Its founder, Jen McCreight, called for a new sort of atheism that "cares about how religion affects everyone and that applies skepticism to everything, including social issues like sexism, racism, politics, poverty, and crime."[22] Atheism Plus's original Frequently Asked Questions page claims that linking atheism with social justice could have the result of "perhaps ultimately driving more people away from religion and toward the methods of secular humanism."[23] Thus, like de Botton, McCreight and Atheism Plus offer secular alternatives to religious groups which advocate for social justice, thus attracting people to adopt secular humanist perspectives.

The Newer Atheists are distinct from their predecessors because they promote alternatives to religion rather than directly arguing against it. For example, de Botton claims that secular forms of education can offer ways to care for the self that are analogous to those found in Christianity. His project explicitly involves replacing religious forms of education with secular equivalents. Likewise, McCreight and Atheism Plus claim that people's passion for social justice can draw them away from religion rather than attracting them to it. Though A+ is not primarily an academic movement, their approach could apply in academic settings. For example, A+ might influence those studying the history of social justice movements to minimize the role that religions have played in seeking social justice. So A+ might also supplant faith-based scholarship without arguing directly against such scholarship.

The Newer Atheists present a new kind of challenge to Marsden's pluralism. They do not seek to exile religious perspectives from the academy, but rather seek to replace those perspectives within the academy. Since Marsden's prescription of pluralism is a response to those attempting to keep faith-based scholarship out of the university, it has little to offer in response to the Newer Atheisms. To clarify some of the specific features of the challenge posed by the Newer Atheists, I will refer back to two features of Marsden's prescription of pluralism: the hotel metaphor he borrows from William James and his rules for responsible Christian scholarship. I will discuss each of these elements in turn.

First, consider what follows from the presence of both Newer Atheist and Christian scholars in the academy. Neither of these groups argues against each other directly. To do so would be to violate Marsden's rules for the responsible faith-based scholarship. However, the groups do engage each other indirectly. They compete with each other to attract teachers, students, sources of funding, and all of the other things needed to work in the university. To see what this might look like, let us return to William James's hotel metaphor. In the metaphor, competing perspectives occupy different rooms of a hotel. These rooms are united by sharing the same hallway. However, nothing in James's metaphor specifies that the rooms must be identical. Perhaps the rooms at the front of the hotel are luxurious and attractive, whereas the rooms at the back of the hotel are shabby and unpleasant. If the Newer Atheists have their way, secular groups will have their choice of the hotel rooms, relegating religious perspectives to the less attractive rooms. At least this gives Christian scholars a home in the academy, but this minimized place is hardly enough to allow them to voice their perspectives. In fact, this marginalized place is in some respects worse than no place at all, since it reduces the Christian scholar's voice to a whisper that is scarcely heard. How might the Newer Atheists compete with Christian scholars? We might arrive at some specifics by comparing the Newer Atheists' claims with Marsden's account of the rules for Christian scholars. Remember, Marsden claims that Christians should model love and respect for those with whom one disagrees. On his view, Christians should appeal to others through this love and respect. This gentler approach contrasts strongly with the vitriolic rhetoric of the New Atheists. But their Newer Atheists successors also model values that students may find attractive. Both Christian scholars and "New New Atheists" like de Botton offer ways for people to live in better relationships with each other. For example, whereas Christians gather together for Eucharistic worship services and fellowship, de Botton recommends sharing meals with strangers as a community-building form of moral education.[24] Whereas Christians may model love and respect, Atheism Plus offers people a passionate commitment to social justice that may also prove attractive. These Newer Atheisms thus indirectly compete with religious perspectives in ways that are more challenging than the antireligious arguments of their predecessors.

Someone might at this point suggest that other parts of Marsden's advice for Christian scholars might provide those scholars with resources to respond to the Newer Atheists. For example, Marsden emphasizes the positive ways in which faith can inform scholarship. Against those who think that the faith makes no difference for scholarship, Marsden argues that faith (alongside other factors like gender and nationality) provides Christian scholars with background beliefs.[25] These beliefs "have a vast influence on the pattern we see when we look at 'the facts.'"[26] They also shape our priorities—what we see as important to study, what we find interesting about our subject, and the sort of questions we ask about that subject.[27] However, the Newer Atheists' claim is not that faith makes no difference for the scholarship. Consider, an analogy with Atheism+'s approach to social justice. Just as Atheism+ sees social justice as a vehicle for promoting secular humanism, so also Newer Atheists might claim that scholarship is a vehicle for promoting atheist approaches. So Marsden's arguments that faith makes a difference for the faith-based scholarship do not by themselves answer the Newer Atheists' challenge. The Newer Atheists such as de Botton are, after all, informed by their atheism much like Christian scholars are informed by their theism. Recall de Botton's claim that an Institute of Dying might replace religious institutions as a way for universities to help people respond to death.[28] Given that Newer Atheists can appeal to pluralism also, Marsden's approach is insufficient to help Christian scholars preserve their place within the Jamesian hotel.

In response to the Newer Atheists, Christian scholars should consider how to develop an account of faith-based scholarship that might prove more persuasive to the mainstream academy than Newer Atheist rivals. Some might think that no such account is needed, given the rich resources of centuries-old religious traditions. But challenges (like the one provided by the Newer Atheists) can serve as an occasion to remind faith-based scholars to discern ways to be good stewards of the intellectual resources provided by their faith traditions. Such scholars should use all of the resources at their disposal to make sure that our place in the academy is at least as attractive as those enjoyed by other perspectives. After all, working out ways to present academic work more attractively—both in the university and beyond—has been a perennial problem for scholars in general and Christian scholars in particular. To suggest ways to present Christian scholarship more compellingly, I will return to Marsden's discussion of pluralism and the Jamesian pragmatism that inspired it.

Pragmatic Pluralism as a Guide to Promoting Christian Scholarship

I propose that adopting a pragmatic pluralism could help Christian scholars be better stewards of their work by presenting that work more winsomely and compellingly. By pragmatic pluralism, I mean an approach that uses James's pragmatism as one standard—albeit not the only standard—for evaluating scholarship. Marsden sometimes calls to his recommendation of pluralism as "a pragmatic pluralism."[29] However, nothing about Marsden's recommendation is indebted to pragmatism. Marsden does invoke James's hotel metaphor to describe the ways in which incommensurable perspectives can coexist in a pluralistic context. However, Marsden's use of this metaphor does not appeal to James's understanding of pragmatism, which is the subject of the essay in which the hotel metaphor appears. The omission of more discussion of James may not be surprising, since Marsden is neither a philosopher nor writing for an audience of only philosophers. However, since one of James's arguments in "What Pragmatism Means" is that pragmatism may help harmonize the empiricism of his day with religious perspectives, James's pragmatism seems a likely source of further insights into how to include such perspectives.

For James, pragmatism is a method that tries "to interpret each notion by tracing its respective practical consequences."[30] Since pragmatism is concerned only with practical consequences of a given view, it requires continually evaluating views according to the ways they help people engage the practical challenges they face. Metaphysical views like the Idealism that preceded James's pragmatism sought a kind of certainty by appealing to concepts like "the Absolute" to help them respond to any challenge they faced. Having one of these concepts allowed one to rest, secure in their possession of that concept. By contrast, James's pragmatism prompts people to continually examine the ways their views help them face challenges. James writes that pragmatism "appears less as a solution, then, than as a program for more work."[31]

Since pragmatism as a method spurs further action rather than providing permanent solutions to problems, it should not be surprising that I do not offer a grand proposal for how Christian scholars should present their work. Adopting James's pragmatic method would, however, help scholars present their work in a number of ways. First, pragmatism reminds scholars that their work ought to have practical consequences. In some cases, directing scholars to solve problems may be enough to help them present their work as contributing to the mainstream academy. Viewing one's work as a response to specific problems could help a Christian scholar present her work as a solution to that problem. Second, focusing on problems can help remind scholars of the many audiences for their scholarship. The problems in questions are not limited to the kinds that form scholarly research projects. Students, their departments, their universities, and ultimately even larger communities face problems that scholarship might help to solve. Third, focusing on faith-based scholarship as solving specific problems faced by their communities rather than finding permanent solutions can free Christian scholars from feeling like they need to find such solutions. We need not provide a general, one-size-fits-all response to the question of why faith-based scholarship should have a place in mainstream universities. We are instead freed to promote Christian scholarship to specific audiences and institutions. To me personally, it is extraordinarily liberating to not have to work out how my academic work best represents faith-based scholarship as a whole. It is enough to devote that work to responding to the particular problems that I and my communities face.

Pragmatic Christian Responses to Pedagogical Problems

One of the perennial concerns in higher education is whether scholars should be focused on their own production of knowledge or on their students' learning. We might call this the problem of pedagogical emphasis: whether the teacher's teaching or the students' involvement should be emphasized in the classroom. Marsden's warnings about the university's loss of soul include the concern that the increasingly professionalized and specialized university chooses the former at the expense of the latter.[32] Remarkably, the "new New Atheist" de Botton's criticisms of the secular university echo Marsden's concern. De Botton writes that "The difference between Christian and secular education reveals itself with particular clarity in their respective characteristic modes of instruction: secular education delivers lectures, Christianity sermons. Expressed in terms of intent, we might say that one is concerned with imparting information, the other with changing our lives."[33] De Botton's worries that orators like Martin Luther King Jr. and other Christian preachers can produce transformation in their hearers than secular lecturers cannot. Here too we see a tension between emphasizing professors' scholarly expertise, such as their content mastery, and student-focused approaches. So Christian scholars and Newer Atheists agree that that the contemporary university must solve the problem of pedagogical emphasis. De Botton's solution to this problem involves training professors to lecture more eloquently and thus effectively.[34] But while de Botton's solution involves making lectures more sermon-like, some Christian scholars have begun to abandon the lecture in the first place.

The recent turn to teaching practices could help Christian scholars in mainstream universities respond to the problem of pedagogical emphasis. Scholars have been talking about practice with renewed vigor since the philosopher Alasdair MacIntyre's 1984 *After Virtue*. More recently, books like David I. Smith and James K.A. Smith's 2011 *Teaching and Christian Practices* prompted Christian scholars to consider the merits of using practices in the classroom. A practice, in Etienne Wenger's formulation, is an action "in a historical and social context that gives structure and meaning to what we do."[35] Playing chess is a practice because it is a specific form of social activity that requires players to learn its history (or at least its rules).[36] Through playing chess, people cultivate intellectual virtues like patience and practical judgment. Wenger and other theorists of practice think that students, including college students, could cultivate the virtues—intellectual and otherwise—through learning other practices. For example, a class could use the practice of gardening to learn about what commitment to a community involves. (Jeffrey Bilbro and Jack Baker propose gardening as a way to cultivate wisdom in their chapter in this volume.) Teaching through practices can help universities respond to the problem of pedagogical emphasis. To show how, I will consider two exemplary practices—one employed by Rebecca DeYoung in one of her classes at Calvin College and one that I have enjoyed as a part of the Conyers Scholars program at Baylor.

DeYoung's solution to the problem of pedagogical emphasis involves incorporating the practice of silence into her class on the virtues and vices. She uses this practice as a response to the vice of vainglory. Vainglory involves a disordered desire for attention and approval. It prompts people to focus on themselves and talk about themselves, especially when others' goods make them feel insecure.[37] In order to better understand the vice of vainglory, DeYoung's students spend a week practicing a specific kind of silence: refraining (as much as possible) from talking about themselves. They then discuss and write about their experiences. Practicing silence gives students two sorts of insights into the nature of vainglory. They realize how much they talk about themselves.[38] They are also encouraged to resist doing so. DeYoung's focus on the practice of silence has several pedagogical benefits. First, it helps her students learn more about the vice of envy than they would through listening to a lecture on the topic. Second, requiring her students to practice silence (or at least a certain sort of silence) frees

DeYoung from having to focus on merely her own work or on empowering her students. Instead, DeYoung and her students share the experience of practicing silence. They enter the classroom as (on one level, at least) equal co-practitioners rather than as teacher and students. So DeYoung does not need to choose between instructing her students (through lectures) and empowering them to pursue knowledge individually. By encouraging them to become practitioners, she can do both. Third, practicing silence gives DeYoung's students the experience of resisting the vice of envy. DeYoung's class thus provides students with an opportunity to be transformed. Furthermore, the class provides a context for transformation without sermonizing in a way that would prove objectionable to those in the mainstream university. DeYoung's use of the practice of silence in her class is one way that teaching practices can solve the problem of pedagogical emphasis. It exemplifies one way that Christian scholars can use teaching practices solve problems in the mainstream academy. Finally, DeYoung's use of the practice of silence does not reduce her teaching and scholarship to apologetics, or otherwise break the rules of the academic game that Marsden discusses. Although DeYoung teaches at a church-related institution, an analogous course at a mainstream university could incorporate a similar practice of silence in order to respond to similar concerns. Adopting a practice-based approach might thus be good stewardship of time in the classroom.

The Conyers Scholars program at Baylor University emphasizes a practice of hospitality that, like DeYoung's practice of silence, provides a solution to the problem of pedagogical emphasis. The Conyers Scholars are graduate students from a variety of disciplines who gather (usually monthly) to discuss texts alongside faculty mentors. Here, the problem of pedagogical emphasis is compounded by the interdisciplinary nature of the group and the graduate student status of the Conyers Scholars. Since the scholars come from different disciplines, there is additional pressure on the faculty mentors to lead and focus the discussion. However, since the scholars are graduate students, there is also more pressure to promote student engagement.

The Conyers Scholars program solves the problem of pedagogical emphasis by situating our discussion of texts in the context of our communal practice of dining together before discussing those texts. We enjoy the hospitality of one of the faculty mentors, who take turns hosting our discussion. During the meal, we talk about our lives, the courses that we're teaching, and our concerns about our graduate study. These concerns provide a shared context for discussing the texts that we read together. Instead of approaching these texts as engineers, sociologists, and philosophers, we read them as graduate students seeking insights into our present concerns. Our faculty mentors also share their concerns with us, which frees them to discuss these texts alongside us (rather than having to lead us). Now certainly our discussions don't always go well. (I am personally too often guilty of letting my philosophical commitments distract me from the concerns of my colleagues.) But our practice of eating together has, in my experience, informed the ways we read texts together—as a unified community rather than as graduate students and our mentors. For us, the practice of hospitality provides a response to the problem of pedagogical emphasis. And though the Conyers Scholars community is faith-informed, such practices need not be limited to church-related institutions. In my own teaching, I strive to introduce students to texts and allow them to attend to those texts before we move to questioning and evaluating them. By welcoming texts before (sometimes) criticizing them, we attempt to show hospitality to the authors who have come before us and from whom we learn.[39]

So far much of the reflection on practices and pedagogy has occurred in Christian contexts. But nothing prevents Christian scholars working in the mainstream university from designing their courses around practices also. Of course, such scholars will have to focus on practices and virtues that are not specific to their religious tradition. Christian scholars might, for example, focus on intellectual virtues like humility, patience, and interpretive charity rather than theological virtues like faith, hope, and charity as such. But many of the specifically Christian reflections on practices could be adapted for use in the mainstream university with few revisions. The recent work on Christian practices represents one way that faith-based scholarship can be seen as a response to problems—like the problem of pedagogical emphasis—that the mainstream university faces. Appealing to this sort of pedagogy as one way that faith-based scholarship can solve problems in the mainstream university would allow Christian scholars working in secular contexts to present their work more attractively. Instead of appealing to pluralism as an unquestioned universal good, Christian scholars could point to their contributions they make within their particular contexts. Doing so would help to insure that Christian scholars are not included in universities only to be marginalized within them.

To conclude, I want to nuance two key features of my account of pragmatic pluralism as a way to advocate for faith-informed scholarship in the mainstream university. My proposal of pragmatic pluralism is only a proposal about the presentation of faith-informed scholarship. It says nothing about the content of that scholarship. We certainly should not reduce Christian scholarship to its pragmatic accomplishments. Doing so would render it neither Christian nor scholarship. Yet emphasizing the ways faith-informed scholarship can solve pedagogical problems could help Christian scholars to present their work more attractively. This sort of public scholarship is an important kind of stewardship for Christian scholars within the academy. Christian scholarship need not always be central, but neither should faith-informed perspectives be marginalized. As Marsden reminds us, authentic pluralism includes religious perspectives. And as I have argued, authentic pragmatism prompts us to employ religious solutions to problems when those solutions present themselves. However, the differences between my account and Marsden's should not be overstated.

To Marsden's credit, *The Outrageous Idea of Christian Scholarship* anticipates my argument that we should highlight Christian scholarship's practical results. In the two chapters following the one in which he appeals to William James and the hotel metaphor, Marsden discusses ways in which Christian scholarship can "have real impact" in the contemporary university.[40] So my argument in this chapter is more of a shift of emphasis than a broad disagreement with Marsden's approach. Marsden advocates appealing to pluralism to respond to those who think Christian scholarship should have no place in the mainstream university. He then claims that we should respond to those who question the efficacy of Christian scholarship by emphasizing the positive contributions such scholarship can make. But Christian scholars should extend Marsden's second response to both sorts of challenge. It is not enough to promote Christian scholarship through appealing to pluralism alone. We should instead appeal to a pragmatic pluralism by emphasizing the ways that Christian scholarship can respond to the challenges particular communities face. These responses will vary. Yet this lack of permanent solutions is something that Christian scholars—whose hearts are restless until they rest in God—should expect.

Notes

1. George M. Marsden, "Beyond Progressive Scientific Humanism," in *The Future of Religious Colleges*, ed. Paul J. Dovre (Grand Rapids: Eerdmans, 2002), 44.
2. Marsden's advice to Christian scholars in mainstream universities has remained consistent throughout his career. Most of my discussion of Marsden's view comes from his early essay on "The Soul of the University" rather than the more well-known *Outrageous Idea* that followed it. We can use Marsden's earlier works to examine his view because Marsden has advocated for this sort of pluralism throughout his published works. For example, in his 2009 paper "Reflections Doing American History in a World of Subcultures," Marsden writes that "the convention of checking one's substantive religious identification at the door [...] neither is nor should be absolute." C.f. George M. Marsden, Doing American History in a World of Subcultures," *Reviews in American History* 37, no. 2 (June 2009): 303–314, 306–307.
3. George Marsden, "The Soul of the American University: A Historical Overview" in *The Secularization of the Academy*, 9–45, edited by George M. Marsden and Bradley J. Longfield (New York: Oxford University Press, 1992), 38.
4. Ibid., 39.
5. Ibid., 40.
6. Ibid., 40.
7. Ibid., 40–41.
8. William James, "What Pragmatism Means," in *Essays on Pragmatism,* New York, Hafner Press, 1948, 146. Quoted in George M. Marsden, *The Outrageous Idea of Christian Scholarship* (New York: Oxford University Press, 1997), 45–46.
9. Marsden, *The Outrageous Idea*, 46.
10. Ibid., 46.
11. Marsden, "The Soul," 39.
12. Marsden, *The Outrageous Idea*, 46.
13. Ibid., 53.
14. Ibid., 54.
15. Ibib., 53.
16. Susan VanZanten, *Joining the Mission: A Guide for (Mainly) New College Faculty* (Grand Rapids: Eerdman's Publishing Company, 2011), 42.
17. Ibid., 42.
18. Marsden, "Doing History," 308.
19. Alain de Botton, *Religion for Atheists* (New York: Pantheon Books, 2012), 6.

20. Ibid., 54.
21. Ibid., 58.
22. Nelson Jones, "Atheism+: the new New Atheists," *New Statesman*. 23 August 2012. http://www.newstatesman.com/blogs/religion/2012/08/atheism-plus-new-new-atheists.
23. "Atheism+—FAQ" 22 November 2012. https://web.archive.org/web/20121122044846/http://atheismplus.com/faq.php.
24. de Botton, 22.
25. Marsden, *The Outrageous Idea*, 60–61.
26. Ibid., 62.
27. Ibid., 63.
28. de Botton, 58.
29. Marsden, "The Soul," 38.
30. James, 142.
31. James, 145.
32. Marsden, *The Outrageous Idea*, 108.
33. de Botton, 54–55.
34. Ibid., 61–62.
35. Etienne Wenger, *Communities of Practice: Learning, Meaning, and Identity* (Cambridge: Cambridge University Press, 1999), 47.
36. Alasdair MacIntyre, *After Virtue* (Notre Dame, IN: Notre Dame University Press, 1984), 187–188.
37. Rebecca Konyndyk DeYoung, "Pedagogical Rhythms: Practice and Reflections on Practice," 24–42 in David I. Smith and James K.A. Smith, *Teaching and Christian Practices: Reshaping Faith and Learning* (Grand Rapids: Eerdmans, 2011), 32.
38. Ibid., 33.
39. My pedagogical strategy here is indebted to Scott Huelin, "Peregrination, Hermeneutics, Hospitality: On the way to a theologically informed general hermeneutics," *Literature and Theology* 22:2 (2008): 223–236.
40. See chapters four, five, and six in Marsden, *The Outrageous Idea*. Quote from p. 59.

CHAPTER 14

The Ecclesial Turn: Putting Stanley Hauerwas's Vision for Christian Higher Education into Practice

David C. Cramer

I first read Stanley Hauerwas's essay "Pro Ecclesia, Pro Texana: Schooling the Heart in the Heart of Texas" shortly before designing and teaching an introductory survey course in Christian Scriptures at Baylor University, where I was a doctoral student in the Religion Department.[1] In preparation for teaching the course, I also read much from the growing body of literature on pedagogical practices for Christian college and university classrooms.[2] This literature proved immensely helpful as I thought through *how* to teach the course, but it still left me with the question of *why* I should approach teaching at a Christian university any differently than I might at a secular one. By arguing that the end toward which the Christian university is oriented is neither the state nor the university but the church, Hauerwas's essay provided the missing piece: a vision of the Christian difference for the classroom.

In this essay, my goal is to put the *why* and the *how* together. I first draw on Hauerwas's essay to recount his reasons for resisting approaches

D.C. Cramer (✉)
Keller Park Church, South Bend, IN, USA

T.L. Scales and J.L. Howell (eds.), *Christian Faith and University Life*,
DOI 10.1007/978-3-319-61744-2_14

to Christian education that separate academics from the theological activity of the church.[3] I then describe how I went about attempting to put Hauerwas's vision into practice in my Christian Scriptures course by designing a course aimed at *ecclesial formation* as much as *information acquisition*, and I reflect on some lessons from my classroom experiment. While the example I offer is of a Christian Scriptures course, my hope is that these lessons might be appropriated and adapted to fit the needs of various classroom settings.[4]

Hauerwas on Teaching Christian Ethics in the University

Hauerwas presented his essay "Pro Ecclesia, Pro Texana" to an audience of mostly Christian educators at Baylor University two years after the attacks on the World Trade Center and just six months after the United States' invasion of Iraq. In light of these realities, he begins on a somber note:

> I believe we live in dark times. By "we" I mean we Christians. We live a country that I believe is quite literally out of control. Possessed by power unchecked, Americans think they can do what they want. After September 11, 2001, moreover, Americans seem ready to do anything to return the world to normalcy. By "normal," Americans mean they want to live in a world in which they feel safe no matter what the cost securing our safety imposes on the rest of the world. The American desire for security, to have our lives protected not only from the reality of death but also the recognition we will die, is clothed in the language of the highest ideals.[5]

Hauerwas argues that rather than providing an alternative to the American drive for "normalcy" and "security," Christian universities merely reinforce these American ideals and have thus failed their (mostly) Christian students. By failing in this important respect, Christian universities are virtually indistinguishable from their secular counterparts, despite Christian universities' claims to educate their students according to the standards of the gospel. According to Hauerwas, "the modern university and the modern state are by design mutually supportive projects."[6] The university is legitimated by legitimating the state. Thus, the state rather than the church becomes the locus of so-called universal values, whereas religion "is now acceptable only if it is kept private."[7] Hauerwas believes that the American university is "an extraordinarily successful system of moral formation" to the extent that it creates such unquestioned loyalty to America under the pretense of producing "critical thinkers."[8]

As an example of such moral formation, Hauerwas offers what he calls "the standard course in ethics," in which the professor is expected to offer a neutral perspective on ethical issues in order to help students think critically about these issues. Such a course begins with a number of weeks on metaethics, where the various ethical theories or systems are described and analyzed. It then switches to normative ethics, where students are asked to analyze ethical quandaries by applying the various ethical theories to highly artificial cases. Hauerwas gives the disturbing yet humorously absurd example of a group of students exploring a cave that begins to fill with water. As they try to evacuate the cave, the first to exit, who happens to be the largest student of the group, gets stuck in the only way out. After discovering a stick of dynamite and matches, the rest of the students have to decide whether to blow up their classmate in order to escape or to save their classmate and thus all drown. As Hauerwas observes, "Students love this kind of game because they understand such exercises are no threat to their lives."[9] Indeed, for Hauerwas, such courses "are designed to underwrite the presumption the students have prior to taking such courses. Students assume that ethics names that part of life in which you have to make up your own mind," and such a course "legitimates that assumption by giving students names to describe the choices they are going to make anyway."[10] Such courses are abstract and artificial by design, as they are "the outworking of the attempt of modern universities to be ahistorical institutions that can serve anyone anywhere."[11] Yet for Hauerwas, "in trying to serve anyone anywhere, it turns out that the universities turn out people educated to be willing agents of the modern state."[12] Under the pretense of training critical thinkers, universities are producing students incapable of imagining anything beyond the parameters circumscribed by the state.

While the standard course in ethics may be a particularly illustrative example, Hauerwas argues that the problem he describes is ubiquitous in the modern university, particularly in humanities courses. In an attempt to teach from a so-called neutral perspective, humanities courses tend to reinforce students' unexamined commitment to the nation state. "The attempt to make truth qua truth the purpose of the university," Hauerwas argues, "results in the failure of those at universities dedicated to the 'search for truth' to acknowledge whose truths they serve because they think they serve no one's truth in particular."[13]

Despite Hauerwas's criticisms of the modern university, his essay is not a counsel of despair. Instead, he finds a way forward in Baylor University's motto, "Pro Ecclesia, Pro Texana." While the history of

Texas—as with the history of the church—is by no means free of its own violence, Baylor's motto nevertheless resists the false universalization of the nation state by creating space for "a more determinative community that can acknowledge that such a history is ours without trying to justify such violence as necessary."[14] For Hauerwas, this community is the church—a community with a particular narrative and its own "robust intellectual tradition," which is "governed by the facts of revelation, by the language and imagery of the Bible."[15] For Hauerwas, then, the goal of a Christian university such as Baylor should be ecclesial formation as much as it is information acquisition.

Putting Hauerwas's Vision into Practice in the Classroom

Hauerwas's claim about the goal of the Christian university naturally raises the question: What would it look like for a Christian university to orient itself *pro ecclesia*? In particular, how might such an orientation impact the way an instructor approaches her students? While I do not pretend to have conclusive answers, these are the kinds of questions that I brought to my course in Christian Scriptures.

There is a standard approach to teaching courses in Christian Scriptures that closely parallels Hauerwas's description of the standard course in ethics. One begins by describing to students the various methods of biblical hermeneutics—source criticism, form criticism, redaction criticism, and so on—and then one shows how these methods can be applied to biblical passages to produce various readings of the text. Whether intentionally or not, instructors thus teach students to keep the text at an objective distance, treating it in much the same way that students treat the artificial ethical case studies Hauerwas describes: as though the text has no claim on their lives. Indeed, because of the inherently religious nature of the biblical text, instructors are sometimes more insistent that it be approached objectively so that courses in Christian Scriptures can meet the same standards of academic neutrality that are expected in other disciplines.

The standard approach to teaching Christian Scriptures is not without merit. It introduces students to the field of biblical studies as a serious academic discipline with its own methods and history, and in so doing it encourages students to consider pursuing a major in religion. In addition, maintaining an objective distance and treating the text primarily as a historical document allows students from different faiths—or no religious convictions at all—to engage with Scripture in a nonthreatening way. Nevertheless, the question for the standard approach remains: How does teaching the course at a Christian college or university differ from how it would be taught at a secular one? With this question in mind, I attempted to design the course in a way that would potentially lead to ecclesial formation without sacrificing the necessary information acquisition attained in the standard course.

I began by having the students—fifty-nine in all, mostly first-year freshman—write a brief introductory essay in which they reflected on their level of knowledge of the Bible coming into the course as well as their religious background. Regarding their level of Bible knowledge, I learned that fifteen had minimal knowledge (25%), four low (7%), twenty-four moderate (41%), three substantial (5%), and thirteen high (22%). Regarding their religious background, I found that at this historically Baptist institution only seven students self-identified as Baptist (12%), while another eighteen self-identified as Christian (31%), sixteen as Catholic (27%), ten as nonreligious or agnostic (17%), three as Church of Christ (5%), two as Methodist (3%), two as nondenominational (3%), and one as Lutheran (2%). This diversity of backgrounds complicates Hauerwas's approach, for it is difficult to orient a course for the church when a prior question might be: whose church? At a historically Baptist institution, I could not simply assume a Baptist—or even a broadly Protestant—perspective from my students.

In order to account for the varying perspectives represented in the class without simply adopting a neutral or objective approach to the biblical text, I next shared with the class my own religious and educational background and how that background would affect the way I approached the text and taught the course. I explained that I approached the text as a confessing Christian (from the Anabaptist–Mennonite tradition), but at the same time, I assured them that whether they had minimal or high knowledge of Scripture, Christian convictions or none, they would be able to succeed in the class.

Having provided some basic expectations for the course, I dove straight into the biblical text, starting week one with the opening chapters of Genesis. Instead of beginning with the method, we began with the text and let the text itself raise methodological questions. So, for example, after reading Genesis 1 and 2, we compared and contrasted the creation accounts in each of these chapters and discussed why these passages are juxtaposed with each other. In order to make the experience of reading Scripture as imaginative and immersive as possible in a classroom setting, I split the class into twelve groups of five and named each group after one of the twelve tribes of Israel. Within each "tribe," each student had a particular role: a "priest" who moderated group discussion, a "scribe" who took notes, a "judge" who made sure the group stayed on task, a "rabbi" who looked up biblical passages pertaining to the discussion, and a "prophet" who shared the group's findings with the rest of the class. By studying the text in groups, the students were able to engage not only with the text but also with the various perspectives that each student brought to the text. Baptists learned from Catholics; Methodists learned from agnostics.

Moreover, students from various disciplines realized that they could contribute something unique to the discussion, that the ability to read and understand Scripture is not limited to those like their professor who study religion as a career. Indeed, in this class of fifty-nine students, there were no declared religion majors. Of those students who responded to a question about their major, 50% were in a professional degree program, while only 16% were majoring in the humanities, another 16% were undecided, 13% were majoring in political science, and 6% were majoring in education. Yet rather than stifling conversation, the various disciplinary backgrounds of the students provided fresh ways of reading and interpreting the text that benefited class discussion as a whole. Often a student would raise a question of the text that I had never considered before, and rather than trying to come up with a quick answer, I would turn the question back to the students to see how we might come up with an answer from the diverse backgrounds and collective wisdom of the class.

It is difficult to evaluate whether my experiment with this course was a success. By the objective standards of the Religion Department, the class seemed on par with other Christian Scriptures sections. The students received about the average numbers of As, Bs, and Cs as in other sections, and their scores on the required exit exam, which tests basic biblical comprehension, were on par with other sections as well. In that sense, my approach did not deprive them of the information acquisition expected of the course.

But it is much more difficult to determine whether the course aided their ecclesial formation. For the final (extra-credit) writing assignment of the semester, I had students reflect on what they took away from the course. As with any class, there were many who were simply happy to check this required course off their list and move on. But many student responses were encouraging, including the following selections:

> As a Catholic, I only need to know the big picture stories of the Bible. It is interesting now in mass when the readings are read and I know the context to the Scripture, and that helps me understand the verse even more.… In the future, I hope I continue to read Scripture and find new meanings each time. I am glad I now know the general themes and contexts of the books of the Bible, as now I can better study Scripture both analytically and spiritually.

> In the future, I hope to maintain some of the knowledge I got from this course and help inform people about what the Scriptures really are and what their purpose is. I will also be confident enough in my Bible study groups to be able to discuss an array of different topics because of Christian Scriptures.

> When I first started this class, I was honestly afraid of failing miserably due to the fact that I had barely any previous knowledge of the *Bible*. I soon found out that this class was not meant to kill my grades, but to guide me on the path to God and learning his narrative along the way.… Now that the class is almost finished, I can honestly say my background for scripture has drastically changed and I can tell other people a brief narrative of the whole *Bible*.… Taking this class was a blessing in my life and I will definitely take what I have learned and use it for future interaction with the *Bible* and God. I will continue to reread all the books and look at popular scriptures. I will also make certain to teach my children about the *Bible*.

> I have been raised in the Christian tradition for most of my life, but over the course of this semester, my knowledge of scripture has radically grown.… I want to continue to follow God where He leads me. I want to continue to deepen my knowledge of scripture after this class ends, growing not only to increase my knowledge, but also to be a force of change in this dying and broken world.

> This class has helped me get a better understanding of scripture as one flowing story. I'd never done one study or course on the Bible as a whole, and I realize now that I didn't always see different books as even occurring at the same time. This course definitely helped me see Bible events as God's work in real history.… I want to be able to understand the

> New Testament as well as I understand the Old Testament. Because of this desire to learn and grow spiritually, I've begun to attend church on a regular basis. This is helping me to understand and learn more about the growth of the early church and how the religion was started.... Thank you for a great semester, and helping me grow both in my knowledge and understanding of the Bible, but also in my spiritual life outside of class.

> If you asked about my knowledge of the Christian background at the beginning of this course I would have told you it scared the heck out of me. If you were to ask me now, at the end of the course my answer would be a little different. It would be that having the requirement to take religion classes no longer scares me and that I truly believe that this course has helped me with my understanding.... This course will now help me with the plans I have for the future on pursing the scripture in the Bible. With being an active member in a local church and hearing the sermons this course has prepared me to understand what the scripture means and also what is happening during that time that it is written. This course has and will keep on helping me with my growth as a Christian believer.

Based on these responses, it seems that at least some of the students experienced some amount of ecclesial formation as a result of the course. And just as I assigned my students to reflect on the things they learned throughout the semester, I conclude this section by offering four lessons that I took away from the semester about how to orient a course *pro ecclesia*.[16]

Lesson One: Recognize Your Own Theological Narrative

Most guides for college instructors include general maxims about knowing yourself, recognizing your own ambitions, and understanding how your identity impacts the way material can be presented. Instructors naturally focus on the material that is important to their research, area of interest, or even the interests of their mentors. In the same way, instructors should identify their own theological narrative and consider how this narrative might inform their teaching—instead of pretending that this narrative is irrelevant and attempting to approach the course from a neutral or objective standpoint.

Many Christians who pursue graduate study, especially in fields of theology and religion, share a common contour of their religious self-understanding: a shift from fundamentalism (in some form) to a more educated position on theological matters. By recognizing this defundamentalizing narrative in their own life, instructors can guard against unintentionally undermining students' entire faith and participation in the church in an otherwise legitimate attempt to challenge students to examine their narrower belief system.

Part of the defundamentalizing narrative includes the recognition that one's particular approach to Christianity—whether Baptist or Catholic, Methodist or Presbyterian—is not the exclusive legitimate expression of historic Christianity. Instructors who have broadened their understanding of the Christian tradition can introduce their students to the various practices that compel their own participation in a manner that is both educational and formational. However, such broadening need not be at the expense of the theological and denominational particularities of both the professor and the students. If the goal of Christian higher education is ecclesial formation—including shaping students to become more rather than less faithful participants in the local church—then the theological and denominational particularities of the student must be respected even as the student is introduced to a more holistic understanding of the Christian tradition. By taking account of one's own theological narrative, the instructor is better equipped to create a classroom environment where the students' faith is not deconstructed but nurtured—even as it is appropriately challenged.

In the Christian Scriptures course, the recognition of my own theological narrative allowed me to better sympathize with students who entered the class with fairly naive—though nonetheless strongly held—views on questions like the age of the earth, the composition of biblical books, or the details of the end times. I was able to sympathize with such students when I remembered that I held some of these same views myself as a college freshman. Reflecting on my own narrative thus helped me to approach these questions in ways that would challenge the students without at the same time unintentionally leading them to abandon their faith.

Lesson Two: Establish Common Ground with Students

By recognizing one's own theological narrative, the instructor is able to establish common ground with students. Establishing common ground with a diverse group of students is not easy. Given such diversity, common ground cannot be assumed at the outset but must be established in the context of the classroom.

In attempting to establish common ground with my students, I found the work of David I. Smith particularly helpful. Smith explains the vital role played by the student's imagination in shaping the learning community. He notes that as a course begins, expectations and procedures are emphasized that contribute to how the student begins to think about the course and the institution as a whole. From the patterns of interaction there gradually emerges a repertoire of expectations and norms. These expectations and norms can themselves serve as common ground between the instructor and students, as everyone together engages in what Smith calls the "jointly constructed enterprise" of education.[17]

While most university courses provide detailed methodological instruction at the outset, I found that taking an inductive approach in the Christian Scriptures course helped to create the sense that instructor and students were sharing in a collective pursuit. Rather than presenting lectures on how to read the Bible (thereby assuming that students do not already read it or that they will readily accept any new frame of reference), I allowed principles of biblical exegesis and hermeneutics to be drawn out of careful attention to the text itself. I invited students through their roles in their respective "tribes" to discover hermeneutical insights in the manner they were discovered in the first place. Such an approach locates students as active participants in formulating new points of reference for receiving instruction, thereby lowering the risk of alienation and discontinuity, as any student who understands her church congregation to be participating in the reading and teaching of Scripture can identify with such processes.

Lesson Three: Model "Religious Reading" in the Classroom

By establishing common ground with students through the shared experience of encountering the text, the instructor is able to model what David I. Smith describes as the practice of "religious reading." This practice is marked by the charitable reception of texts and the subsequent shared interpretation that can lead to personal transformation. Rather than "using" a text for certain ends, such as gaining a skill or passing an exam, the reader receives the text with reverence and is willing to be changed by the text. Smith notes that while Christians are accustomed to describing the reading of Scripture in this manner, there are many other materials that are worthy of such an approach. Indeed, the Christian virtues of charity and humility inculcated in this practice of reading are essential not only to engagements with Scripture but to serious engagements with any text.[18] Learning to read with charity and humility gets to the heart of a curriculum oriented *pro ecclesia.*

The practice of religious reading in the classroom is not at all diminished by the ecclesial diversity noted above. Since the purpose of a course at a Christian university is most often not to present a religiously uniform selection of content in the first place, the instructor can instead use the survey of materials selected to encourage students to learn the discipline of religious reading. A Catholic student reading John Wesley or a Baptist student studying Flannery O'Connor will be encouraged to engage these texts with reverence. The classroom can be a place where frank and honest conversations about difficulties with and refinements to this style of reading will shape the student *pro ecclesia* despite the apparent lack of a common *ecclesia.*[19]

Modeling religious reading of texts enables an instructor to overcome a temptation to present herself as the first (and perhaps only) trustworthy source of religious knowledge the student has yet had access to. Some students are prone to overconfidence in a knowledgeable and articulate instructor, and some instructors are prone to relish such attention. A course constructed around an instructor's attempt to properly interpret carefully selected texts on behalf of her students encourages this misguided approach. Focusing instead on a shared practice of religious reading of diverse texts can help to remind both student and instructor that participation in religious life outside of the classroom is the primary goal. An instructor who models this type of submission to the text furthermore communicates that she is not to be taken as a demagogue. Appropriately referring questions to figures of authority outside of the classroom is both a product of the ecclesial diversity common in Christian universities and a component of the type of charitable, humble engagement an instructor would do well to demonstrate. Respecting the churches and traditions that students come from and turn to afterwards is an important part of shaping a course *pro ecclesia.*

Lesson Four: Practice Interdisciplinary Engagement

Just as religious reading is not diminished but enhanced by the ecclesial diversity represented in the classroom, so too can it be enhanced through interdisciplinary engagement. A temptation common throughout Christian academia is to isolate the various bodies of scholarship from one another, and instructors often choose to refine their courses to reflect not only their own area of expertise within the field but also standard pedagogical practices of the discipline. A course oriented *pro ecclesia*, however, will resist this narrowing.

As Hauerwas has noted in his reflections on the demarcation of Christian ethics as a field within the study of religion in general, the division of the curriculum into various disciplines may serve the purpose of placing theology into the wider context of a modern university, but it does not necessarily lend itself to ecclesial formation.[20] The division suggests to both the university and to its students that the academic search for truth in God takes place in a manner far different from the practices and experience of religious communities that have never organized themselves in a similar fashion. While it may serve the needs of the university to organize along disciplinary lines and to narrowly define the content of a course, such balkanization does not reflect the nature of the church.

Since a narrow presentation of content does not reflect life within the church, neither does it prepare students to move more deeply into participation in that life. Students who have learned the basics of the historical-critical method, for example, will be unable to provide much else than a (hopefully) respectful critique of a sermon unless they have been guided into deeper reflection on the nature of discourse about God. Courses oriented *pro ecclesia* should provide a theological account of the practices being performed that can unify otherwise seemingly disparate disciplines and methods. Without such a unifying theological account, the particular skills learned in a college course could be corrosive of, rather than beneficial to, students' participation in their church contexts.[21]

Conclusion

Christians in America still live in as dark of times as when Hauerwas first presented his essay at Baylor in 2003. We live a society that caters to the basest instincts of the American public, scapegoats the most vulnerable among us for its collective ills, and justifies almost anything in the name of safety and security. Perhaps most troubling of all is that large percentages of Christians in America seem to equate American values with the standards of the gospel, which suggests that Hauerwas's analysis of the failures of Christian higher education might be on the mark. But rather than simply criticizing, Hauerwas offers a vision of a powerful alternative. He writes that "any university shaped by the story of Christ is also a university that is peopled by those who would rather die than lie."[22] It is my contention that the Christian university is incapable of developing such people on its own. It will always be dependent on the church, the body of Christ, to form its people through its own teaching, preaching, practices, and common life. Nevertheless, the Christian university does have a significant supporting role to play in this formation. Rather than hindering ecclesial formation, it can be a place that fosters it. And given the present state of both the church and society, there is clearly much work for the Christian university to do.

Notes

1. Hauerwas's essay was first presented at the Pruit Memorial Symposium on The Schooled Heart: Moral Formation in American Higher Education, 30 October 2003, Baylor University, Waco, Texas (video available at: http://www.baylor.edu/player/index.php?id=112554&gallery_id=5428). This speech was later published as "*Pro Ecclesia, Pro Texana*: Schooling the Heart in the Heart of Texas," in *The Schooled Heart: Moral Formation in American Higher Education*, ed. Michael D. Beaty and Douglas V. Henry (Waco, TX: Baylor University Press, 2007), 103–114; and again as "Pro Ecclesia, Pro Texana: Schooling the Heart in the Heart of Texas," in Stanley Hauerwas, *The State of the University: Academic Knowledges and the Knowledge of God* (Malden, MA: Blackwell, 2007), 122–136. All subsequent references are to this latter text.
2. See, for example, Joel Boehner, "Praying for Change: The Ignatian Examen in the 'Remedial' Classroom," *Journal of Education & Christian Belief* 16 (2012): 215–227; Darin H. Davis and Paul J. Wadell, "Educating Lives for Christian Wisdom," *International Journal of Christianity & Education* 20 (2016): 90–105; Ashley Woodiwiss, "From Tourists to Pilgrims: Christian Practices and the First-Year Experience," in *Teaching and Christian Practices: Reshaping Faith & Learning*, ed. David I. Smith and James K. A. Smith (Grand Rapids: Eerdmans, 2011), 123–139.
3. See, for example, Stanley Hauerwas, "How 'Christian Ethics' Came to Be," in *The Hauerwas Reader*, ed. John Berkman and Michael Cartwright (Durham, NC: Duke University Press, 2001), 37–50; Hauerwas, "On Keeping Theological Ethics Theological," in *The Hauerwas Reader*, 51–74.
4. My thanks go to a peer reviewer who explained how my approaches do—and sometimes do not—translate into her context as an English professor.

5. Hauerwas, "Pro Ecclesia, Pro Texana," 122.
6. Ibid., 125.
7. Ibid., 126.
8. Ibid.
9. Ibid., 128.
10. Ibid., 129.
11. Ibid.
12. Ibid.
13. Ibid., 134.
14. Ibid., 135.
15. Ibid., 125.
16. Special thanks to Matthew Porter, who helped me to articulate these four lessons.
17. David I. Smith, "Recruiting Students' Imaginations: Prospects and Pitfalls of Practices," in *Teaching and Christian Practices*, 214–215.
18. David I. Smith, "Reading Practices and Christian Pedagogy," in *Teaching and Christian Practices*, 44–46.
19. As but one example, I had this approach modeled in seminary, when my Calvinist professor had us read and appreciatively engage the revivalist writings of Charles Grandison Finney, despite my professor's clear personal penchant for Jonathan Edwards.
20. Hauerwas, "How 'Christian Ethics' Came to Be," in *The Hauerwas Reader*, 37–50.
21. Incidentally, while I appreciate the turn toward the use of "Christian practices" in the classroom, as is well articulated in the work of David I. Smith, James K. A. Smith, Craig Dykstra, Dorothy C. Bass, and many others, this last point offers something of a critique of the working assumption of some who have appropriated this literature that practices can be "Christian" in any meaningful sense without being tied into a larger theological context, such as that provided by the church.
22. Hauerwas, "Pro Ecclesia, Pro Texana," 135.

CHAPTER 15

Rising from the Rubble: The Vital Significance of Christian Research Universities in the Twenty-First Century

L. Gregory Jones

We are living through challenging times, especially in higher education. The economic crisis of 2008 in the USA exposed weaknesses and fault lines in colleges' and universities' business models. Concerns continue to rise about such issues as the cost of higher education, the difficulties of student indebtedness and drop-out rates, and whether undergraduate degree programs are preparing students for the issues and opportunities of the twenty-first century—a concern increasingly expressed by employers as well as graduates. Parents are frustrated with whether their children are receiving adequate value in the education and formation they receive. Add to this the reality that tenure-track jobs are decreasing and the expectations of faculty and students seem to be increasing, and the word "challenging" may understate the reality of what people are feeling.

Yet the problem is not really with higher education itself. It is not as if other "industries," or other "vocations," are remarkably more stable.

L. Gregory Jones (✉)
Duke University, Durham, NC, USA

T.L. Scales and J.L. Howell (eds.), *Christian Faith and University Life*, DOI 10.1007/978-3-319-61744-2_15

Indeed there is good reason to believe that we are living through a time in which tectonic plates are shifting underneath us, and it is difficult to find anywhere solid on which to stand. The challenges are difficult in any industry, in any vocation.

Could we be on the fault lines of the end of one age, and the beginning of another? The great Czech poet, playwright, and former president of the Czech Republic Vaclav Havel noted in a speech in Philadelphia in 1994, "I think there are good reasons for suggesting that the modern age has ended. Today, many things indicate that we are going through a transitional period, when it seems that something is on the way out and something else is painfully being born. It is as if something were crumbling, decaying and exhausting itself—while something else, still indistinct, were rising from the rubble."[1]

There is much that feels like rubble, and little that seems to be rising yet. And, though we may have successfully hidden it from view, when we are honest with ourselves, modern universities are part of the rubble. Not universities per se, but modern versions of them. While universities have not been in the news as much as Wall Street and Washington, we ought to own our share of culpability for the messes we are in.

If modern universities are part of the rubble, what kind of higher education might rise from that rubble—however indistinct it may appear at present? It will be a form that is both familiar and new, a form that combines the best of the past with creative edges designed to address the needs of tomorrow. It will be a form rooted in "traditioned innovation," a practice that continually retrieves and reinterprets the past for the sake of faithfulness in the future.[2]

This form is the twenty-first century "Christian Research University." The form returns to some of the most fundamental insights of medieval universities, thus retrieving the best of our traditions of higher education. Rowan Williams illumines core insights that undergirded such universities in a 2004 sermon commemorating the benefactors who founded the University of Oxford.[3]

Williams argues that these universities were marked by a deep sense of purpose, one rooted in the conviction that the world ultimately makes sense through the work of God. This conviction set the university in the context of a coherent narrative that begins with God's Creation of all that is, and concludes with a vision of the fullness of God's Reign.

Yet Williams rejects the canard that medieval universities were thus focused on "abstract contemplation." He notes that medieval universities served a quite practical purpose: the formation of leaders for the broader culture. He writes about the university:

> This was in large part an institution designed to give a professional formation to the clergy who would shape the policy of a kingdom; and that formation – so far from being in any way dilettantish – assumed that to govern a kingdom you needed to know how language worked, what the difference was between good and bad arguments, and how you might persuade people to morally defensible courses of action. You needed the tools of thought; and when you had acquired them, you could proceed to the other things you needed to know – the proportions and relations of the world, mathematics, music and the stars. Beyond that, specialisation set in; but when you had completed all these minor preliminaries, at least you had the techniques, the 'arts', of thinking. And when you proceeded to acquire the material you needed for medicine or law or the teaching and governance of the Church, you would have established a formidable common vocabulary and common method connecting you to all the other qualified technicians of thought in Europe.

At the heart of medieval universities, then, is a combination of a coherent purpose shaped by a vision of God and God's Reign and an intensely practical focus on forming leaders capable of wise and just governance and public discourse.

Yet Williams observes that these two dimensions are precisely what modern universities have lost. Having lost the positive vision shaped by God's overarching Creation and, through the redemptive work of Christ, a promised Consummation of that Creation, modern universities are left with skepticism that too easily becomes cynicism. And we lose sight of a vision of a wise and just society and the practices that sustain it. Practically, the loss of these dimensions means we no longer think of education "as a formation in the kind of reasonable argument and decision that will make someone a sure guide to others."

Williams' analysis is not an exercise in nostalgia, nor is he engaging in a fantasy in which "the Church" might again order entire cultures and societies or even simply universities. Such an era is gone. Rather, Williams retrieves these insights in order to point toward a new, if also re-newed, vision of higher education. It is a vision in which religious commitments, the intellectual life, and the cultivation of public discourse and public life co-exist in mutually enriching ways.

It is a vision that a "Christian Research University" is exceptionally well suited to serve. The rubble of modernity contains those universities that have lost their overarching purpose, separated from the larger narrative of God, and in so doing have too-often turned even their "practical" functions into skepticism, suspicion, and cynicism that undermine public life. What would it take for a "Christian Research University" to rise from the rubble, and what kinds of practices of stewardship will be required to sustain it as it rises?

Each of the key words—Christian, Research, and University—is crucial to the overall vision. In what follows I sketch some key components of each of those words and why they mutually inform and illumine each other. I then return at the end to the stewardship that will be needed to sustain such a university.

What Does a Twenty-First Century Christian Research University Entail?

My description here is necessarily brief and perhaps even cryptic, pointing toward key components that underlie a more robust vision and description that would require more extensive analysis. I also note that I am describing something of an ideal type rather than any university or set of universities. At the same time, however, it should also become apparent that there exist universities around the world that are better suited to rising from the rubble than others, drawing on their own traditions to nurture the innovation needed for the twenty-first century in their contexts. There also likely will be new Christian Research Universities created in the twenty-first century, especially in the majority world, that I hope will draw on the best of the past in higher education to create new patterns of what the world needs.

Christian

Many of the world's leading universities, along with countless numbers of liberal arts colleges, have been founded as "Christian" institutions of one sort or another. Many of them now distance themselves from their founding, which has led to a burgeoning literature that diagnoses and often laments the current state of affairs in the context of "secularization" and a loss of identity and purpose. My intention here is not to enter into those debates, but rather to identify three key reasons why the term "Christian" is crucial for twenty-first century higher education.

First, it offers a distinctive answer to the question of "why" universities exist at all. Williams's analysis points to the impoverishment of modern universities that seem only able to answer questions of "what" and "how," answers that often devolve into issues of who has the power to make decisions in the university. Answering questions of purpose, the "why," provide a different framework for addressing the "what" and the "how" that must also be addressed. "What" and "how" issues are important, but absent a larger trajectory of purpose they tend to become "only" questions of power between traditionalists and advocates for change.

The term Christian points to that transcendent purpose for the institution, calling everyone involved to attend to the *telos*, "the end," of God and God's Reign. This calls for a distinctive vision of leadership, one shaped by Christ's pattern and focused on such virtues as humility and wisdom. It also orients thinking, focusing on how to honor the past while discerning the most faithful and imaginative way forward: to be a people who bear witness to the Holy Spirit who, by conforming us to Christ, is "making all things new." The end helps discern and clarify what needs to be preserved and what needs to be jettisoned in order to be faithful. It encourages the practice of "traditioned innovation"—envisioning the future by honoring and drawing on the church's past—rather than merely ceaseless change.

Yet there is a caution here. Simply claiming the term "Christian" does not imply any clarity about the purpose of the higher education practiced in the institution. Indeed, at least part of the loss of a "Christian" higher education in the USA in recent years is the result of the loss of Christian imagination by Christians ourselves. Charles Taylor's magisterial book *A Secular Age* displays the predicament in broad sweep: he argues that, at the beginning of modernity, there were very few genuine atheists because virtually everybody, believers and nonbelievers, took for granted that there is a God. The debates were about how, if at all, God is engaged with the world. By contrast, at the end of modernity, in our current context, the default assumption for Western people, believers and unbelievers alike, is secularist, even atheistic, because even believers tend to live and act as if there is no God.[4]

Too many contemporary "Christian" colleges and universities live and act as if secularity is the dominant framework. It is, as Taylor suggests, a defining feature of our "age" in Western culture. There are specific manifestations of this secularity that create mission drift: desires for respectability that lead schools to pattern themselves after more prestigious secular institutions such as Harvard, pressures from accrediting bodies, and broader cultural influences.[5] The deepest problem, though, is that Christians, and Christian institutions, have diminished—if not entirely lost—our "Christian imagination" for the larger story of the world that begins with God's Creation and concludes with the consummation of Creation in the fullness of God's Reign. Education, and Christian higher education in particular, needs to be understood in the light of this larger story that draws us into questions of the classical transcendentals of Truth, Goodness, and Beauty.

This suggests a second key reason why the term "Christian" matters for twenty-first century higher education: the centrality of faith for central questions of education and formation. In the conditions of modernity, faith has too often been understood to be a "private" matter that might inspire someone's interior life, but it was largely assumed to be irrelevant to "public" matters.

In response, Christians in recent decades have focused on multiple strategies to re-connect "faith" to various dimensions of education and formation. We have typically done so through the conjunction *and*: faith and learning, faith and work, faith and leadership, faith and entrepreneurship.[6] Such efforts are a half-step in the right direction, but ultimately tempt us to settle for the half-step and thus also distort our imagination. The "and" leaves each of the terms unquestioned, and then explorations begin about whether there might be connections.

The adjective Christian in the term "Christian Research University" calls, instead, for us to see how faith "animates" everything in our lives—including our teaching and learning, our research, our work, our leadership, our approaches to innovation and entrepreneurship. In this perspective, faith is not held at a distance from the activities of life but is instead its vital force, providing the imagination, passion, and commitment that leads to transformation.

The notion of "faith animating" moves beyond efforts to import faith as an afterthought, as if faith "christens" anything to which it is connected. To say that faith animates our vision of higher education (or anything else) suggests something richer and more challenging: faith is not just one more thing—faith is *the* thing. In this way, faith inspires, directs, and works in and through our lives. A Christian research university is the advanced educational component of a Christian way of life. It flourishes only as a part of a larger institutional ecosystem that animates faithful Christian life.

This "faith animating" perspective also involves a shift in how Christian institutions recruit, form, and nurture their students, staff, faculty, and administrative leadership. The primary focus shifts from "exterior" criteria (e.g., whether people go to church, or whether they assent to a creed or a "statement of faith," or whether their research focuses on "Christian" topics) to criteria that assess how a person's faith animates their life—especially their sense of vocation, their daily life, their teaching, and learning. This may be more challenging to discern at the outset in some ways, and yet it also invites ongoing growth and discernment as well as commitment to the larger Story of God.

The third reason why the adjective "Christian" is important in this context is closely related: the focus on how "faith animates" all that is, orienting us to the Story of God, transcends denominations or even "orders" within Catholicism. This point has both a sociological and a theological dimension. The sociological point is that denominational identity is declining precipitously in twenty-first century America. There are more people who identify as "nondenominational" of one sort or another, and even those who identify with a denomination often do so loosely because they have been members of other denominations at other points in their lives. It seems that most protestant Christians in America are "congregationalists" now. It is not practical, even for self-interested reasons, for most Christian institutions to continue to think of themselves as serving exclusively, or even primarily, a specific denominational constituency. While it is possible that denominations might discover a resurgence, it is unlikely that they will recover a primary loyalty sufficient to shape an overall identity.[7]

The theological point is that we need to focus on an ecumenical future in faithfulness to God and the larger narrative of God's creation, redemption, and promised consummation of all that is. John 17 calls us to such a future, not defined by the "ecumenical movement" of the twentieth century that, despite good intentions, was too often shaped by modern assumptions and goals. Rather, it is a call to embrace "Christian" witness in the context of an "evangelical-catholic" future. To be sure, institutions founded by particular denominational traditions will continue to bear, at their best, the "distinctives" of those traditions. At the same time, though, they need to be open to the broader Christian family in ways that continually press them theologically to embrace the fullness of classical Christian witness. There will likely continue to be disagreements about the heart of the Gospel and its implications, but it is likely that those disagreements will be re-framed more by what is shared in common.

Christians need strong and robust colleges and universities to form faithful, effective, and wise leaders across diverse vocations in the twenty-first century. And American culture needs Christian institutions that nurture and form wise people who help to lead in the renewal of public life and public discourse.

Research

Many institutions of higher education exist as liberal arts colleges, and a significant subset of those colleges place a primary, if not exclusive, focus on teaching rather than research. Indeed, the phenomenon of a "research" university is typically understood as a modern phenomenon, with its origins conventionally being traced to the University of Berlin at the beginning of the nineteenth century and, in the USA, the emergence of Johns Hopkins University at the dawn of the twentieth century. In this sense, the "research" university is described over-against liberal arts colleges, and the activities of research are described in contrast to a focus on education and formation.[8]

There is little reason to value a "research" institution in the modern vein, especially when it is set over-against liberal arts emphases, including both teaching and the importance of the formation of students' character. There is significant frustration that modern research universities have had a decreasing impact in educating and forming students well. Even so, there are important reasons to emphasize "research" as an integral component of a Christian university in the twenty-first century. I highlight three reasons here.

First, research and teaching at their best are two sides of the same coin. The best teachers discover in their interactions with students important questions that require further investigation and research. Similarly, the best researchers want to share their discoveries and insights with others, especially students whom they can mentor. We need to develop new and re-newed understandings of both excellent research and outstanding teaching so that they are seen as mutually enriching rather than as competitors for a faculty member's time, energy, and focus.

These new and re-newed understandings will likely challenge contemporary definitions of both research and teaching, and also imply better ways to assess and evaluate faculty productivity and impact. Advances in digital technology are already offering new challenges and opportunities both for research (e.g., for collaboration with other scholars, as well as for dissemination of findings) and teaching (e.g., for engagement with students in new patterns other than a modern classroom). In the future, we are likely to see far more nuanced understandings of research and teaching that are mutually reinforcing in virtuous spirals for faculty and students, undergraduate and graduate/professional, alike. Such a research university will combine the strengths of modern research universities and modern liberal arts colleges in a rich interplay of education and formation.

Second, a research university offers a scale and scope that equips it well to address the grand challenges and "wicked problems" of the twenty-first century (e.g., poverty, health, water). Wicked problems require engagement of multiple approaches simultaneously, because focusing only on one angle often can make the overall problems worse rather than better. Research universities tend to have multiple schools that can bring diverse perspectives and resources to bear on those challenges and problems. No single discipline or school is capable of addressing these major issues alone, and modern universities have often made problems worse by suggesting they are "hard" problems that can be solved by new research by a specific discipline rather than "wicked" problems that require collaborative efforts from diverse perspectives.

Take, for example, health. We now recognize that issues of health are not only about advances in the sciences in fighting disease and unlocking patterns of DNA, important as those disciplines are. We also are more and more aware of the social determinants of health, which bring multiple disciplines and schools into the research and education that needs to be undertaken. Even schools of music and education, which seem to be quite distant from modern definitions of "health care," are in distinctive ways integral to the cultivation of health. This requires both re-discovery of insights that our pre-modern forbears actually recognized better than we do, and the discovery of new knowledge from cutting-edge research.

This points to the third reason why research universities are important. Their scale makes it possible to hold together the conservation of wisdom and the discovery of new understandings. Once again, modern universities tend to make these oppositional, often with the prejudice toward new knowledge (the paradigm of the Ph.D. dissertation) rather than the conservation of wisdom received from the past. Yet our forbearers often understood in ways we have forgotten the interrelationships that cultivate insight, wisdom, and positive impact.

Each of these three reasons point to the integral role of "research" to a vibrant twenty-first century university. It is the Christian dimension, though, that drives these understandings of research into a more holistic understanding than they typically have had in modern universities. The Christian dimension points toward emphases that focus on education and formation together, addressing challenges and solving problems rather than preserving academic turf, and holding together wisdom and discovery. But that also requires that we continually deepen and broaden the interactions of what we mean by "Christian" and what we mean by "Research" as we articulate the significance of a Christian Research University.

University

In many ways this seems to be the most obvious of the three terms, a descriptor of educational institutions that offer both undergraduate and graduate and professional degrees. Many colleges now aspire to the description of a "university" because of the appearance of greater prestige. Yet, given that many modern institutions have difficulty in answering the question of "why" they exist, it is by no means certain what constitutes them as a "university" rather than a "polyversity." What, after all, holds together the diverse schools, departments, programs, and athletic endeavors of a typical modern institution of higher education? Is the central administration of a contemporary university more than the "holding company" for a variety of independent and sometimes competing enterprises?

I highlight three reasons why it is important to emphasize the term "university" for twenty-first century higher education. First, a university requires sufficient clarity about its purpose that it can articulate to itself and to others why the various dimensions of its enterprise are integral and not merely contingent or the result of historical accident. One of the crucial tasks for any excellent organization is to be able to determine what it will NOT do because it is outside the scope of its purpose. Insisting on the determinative significance of being a "university," rather than some other kind of organization, will enable those entrusted with the governance of a university to make wise decisions and cultivate a healthy organizational identity.

Second, a university that has a clear sense of purpose will also cultivate coherence across its diverse schools, departments, programs, and athletic endeavors. This coherence will continually press all constituents of the university to be "rowing in the same direction," propelling the ship forward in positive ways. Such coherence will always be somewhat contested, and yet the contested coherence will enable research to focus on grand challenges and wicked problems rather than just sustaining independent and often competing enterprises. This coherence will be rooted in, and also nourish, "opposable" thinking rather than "oppositional" mindsets.[9] Opposable thinking requires people to hold ideas in tension until creative solutions can be found, rather than seeing them as fundamentally opposed to each other. Such coherence recognizes, for example, that the arts and design are as important to solving problems as are the Science, Technology, Engineering, and Math (STEM) fields, and vice versa.[10]

Third, a university that understands its purpose, cultivates coherence, and has significant scale will be more sustainable than will smaller institutions. The business models of modern higher education are problematic, and in some instances, irretrievably broken. They are too dependent on escalating tuition revenues and increasing levels of student indebtedness (that are in turn dependent on government subsidies for that student debt). The problems with the economic models of higher education are especially evident in small liberal arts colleges, unless they are blessed with a significant endowment (and even then the challenges are substantial). But a coherent university can draw on a wider range of potential partners to cultivate new business models for sustainability because they will have more diversified sources of revenue. This includes new ways of relating to partner organizations, such as businesses and other organizations that need well-prepared leaders for their organizations as well as partners in research.

What will make this vision of a university with clear purpose, coherence, and sustainability possible? The interrelations of the terms Christian and Research with that of a University. This is not to say that the only model of a university that can have purpose, coherence, and sustainability will be one that is Christian and committed to a broad vision of Research. However, it is the case that the greater the clarity, and the depth of insight, about what it means to have a Christian focus as well as a Research identity will enhance the ability to sustain the vision of a University in the twenty-first century.

In order to sustain such a vision of a Christian Research University, we will also need a new and re-newed vision of stewardship of the academy. What would that entail?

Stewards of A Christian Research University

Higher education in the twenty-first century will need new and re-newed patterns of relationships in order to flourish. This will require a commitment to stewardship, along the lines that the editors of this volume outline in their Introduction to this volume. Serving as "stewards" of the mysteries is integrally tied to practices of traditioned innovation. We will need continually to depend on, and carry forward, the best of our traditions as we encourage innovation that helps us address the grand challenges and wicked problems of the twenty-first century.

I highlight here, albeit briefly, key commitments that will be entailed for a diverse set of stakeholders in the flourishing of a Christian Research University:

Intrinsic Institutional Partnerships

Modern colleges and universities increasingly have seen themselves largely as self-sustaining entities that engaged in various agreements with other constituencies. These agreements have largely been extrinsic to their identity, such as potential employers of graduates or funders of research or scholarships. By contrast, a Christian Research University of the twenty-first century will need to cultivate partnerships that are intrinsic to its identity. Intrinsic partnerships are such where both parties' identities become enmeshed with each other. This will be important for diverse organizations, including Christian churches as well as businesses, other employers, and educational institutions (K-12 as well as other colleges and universities). Such intrinsic partnerships will require universities to think in new and re-newed ways about their governance, their recruitment and placement, and their funding models.

The distinctiveness of a Christian Research University will involve multiple overlapping partnerships, some of which will align closely with the larger purpose of the institution while others will not. For example, there will be core partnerships with a variety of Christian institutions, including congregations, colleges and universities, and businesses. Yet there will also be important partnerships with organizations that will only partially overlap with the university's Christian purpose. This might include secular businesses that are co-invested in particular curricula or programs, as well as various government and non-governmental (NGO) entities.

Stewarding the mission of a Christian Research University will require ongoing discernment about these intrinsic partnerships in order to ensure that the mission is continually renewed, deepened, and extended rather than being allowed to drift. This stewardship also depends on "ecosystem" thinking, recognizing that there are a variety of institutional partnerships necessary for the whole environment both to survive and flourish.

Faculty and Staff

The role of faculty and staff in this vision will be more distinctive than in the current model of an "industry" of higher education. Both faculty and staff will need to be aligned with the distinctiveness of a Christian Research University. This carries with it mutual obligations and expectations, in which the University is as invested in the people it recruits and retains as are the faculty and staff.

Such a commitment also encourages different mindsets as well as funding models for the formation of faculty and staff through doctoral education and leadership development. This is not simply a challenge to be addressed by a Christian Research University understood as a siloed organization, but points toward the crucial emphasis on developing and sustaining ecosystems of intrinsic institutional partnerships as well.

Students

A stewardship model for a Christian Research University will entail a new and re-newed description of "students." In modern universities, students are those enrolled in degree programs. After graduation, the relationship with alumni is primarily extrinsic, focused especially on raising money to sustain the institution for the future. By contrast, on this view the relationship of a Christian Research University to its constituents is a lifelong commitment to learning and growth. At various points the "student" may be enrolled in a degree program, a program for certification, or other continuing education. But the ongoing investment of a Christian Research University is in lifelong relationships with its constituencies, and offering ongoing opportunities for learning and growth. This is especially important given the pace of change in the twenty-first century, and it is intrinsic to the formation and education and research to which Christians ought to be committed in our witness to the Reign of God.

Doctoral Study

Doctoral students exist in a crucial, if also ambiguous, space in a Christian Research University. They are crucial because doctoral studies exist at diverse intersections that matter for the renewal of higher education: teaching, learning, and research; focused research in disciplines and cultivation of transdisciplinary strategies; preparation for leadership in the future at different kinds of institutions and sustenance and renewal at the current institution; and stewardship of one's own field while pressing questions that might transform it.

The ambiguities of doctoral study in the midst of "the rubble" of modernity make it profoundly disorienting. Yet it is also filled with promise. The key is to cultivate networks of relationships to provide support as well as to encourage asking the large questions that need to be addressed. These questions need to be addressed about one's own vocation as well as about the broader changes that are occurring on the landscape of higher education (as well as the church and other institutions). The better these questions are addressed during the time of doctoral education, the more promising the future leadership of Christian higher education will be.

Conclusion

Even though there is a great deal of confusion, anxiety, and despair about the current predicament of higher education as well as its future, there is significant room for encouragement and hope. We do not need to scrap what currently exists in order to start over, nor do we need to invent radically new approaches. Rather, by practicing traditioned innovation, we can discover new and re-newed approaches that will offer the wisdom and leadership the world needs for the twenty-first century: a vision of a Christian Research University. It will require a lot of collaboration, courage, and commitment, and yet there are institutions poised for leadership based on their current identities. In addition, there are other institutions emerging in the majority world that might provide even more transformational leadership than we currently can foresee.

The key is to recognize that there is rubble in higher education (as well as in the rest of modernity), and that there is a pressing need for new and re-newed forms of higher education to rise from that rubble. A vision of a Christian Research University is well positioned, even if somewhat "indistinct" currently, to lead that rise.

Further, as Williams's sermon suggests, such a vision is important for far more than higher education itself. Indeed, the sustenance of public life, and the coherence of public discourse, and thus human flourishing, depends in no small measure on the emergence and vitality of institutions such as a Christian Research University. It is a daunting challenge, and also a life-giving vocation worth devoting one's best energies to serving as stewards.

Notes

1. Vaclav Havel, "The Need for Transcendence in the Postmodern World," delivered in Independence Hall, Philadelphia, PA, July 4, 1994. Accessed online on November 12, 2016, at http://www.worldtrans.org/whole/havelspeech.html.
2. For further description of the idea of "traditioned innovation," see L. Gregory Jones, *Christian Social Innovation* (Nashville, TN: Abingdon, 2016). Short reflections on the topic can also be found by searching for L. Gregory Jones or C. Kavin Rowe in the web magazine *Faith & Leadership* (www.faithandleadership.com). Kavin Rowe's reflections are particularly valuable in illuminating "traditioned innovation" as "a biblical way of thinking."
3. Rowan Williams, "Oxford University Commemoration Day Sermon," June 20, 2004, accessed via the web on November 25, 2016, at the following address: http://rowanwilliams.archbishopofcanterbury.org/articles.php/1637/oxford-university-commemoration-day-sermon. Quotations from this sermon are cited from this location.
4. See Charles Taylor, *A Secular Age* (Cambridge, MA: Harvard University Press, 2007). A valuable popularization of Taylor's argument can be found in James K.A. Smith, *How (Not) to be Secular* (Grand Rapids: Eerdmans, 2014).
5. For a diagnosis and prognosis related to "mission drift," see L. Gregory Jones, "Overcome Mission Drift by Practicing Traditioned Innovation," *Faith & Leadership* (November 17,

2015), https://www.faithandleadership.com/l-gregory-jones-overcome-mission-drift-practicing-traditioned-innovation.

6. As one of the founders of the web magazine *Faith & Leadership*, as well as a participant in other groups focused on "faith and …", I have been an active part of the predicament I am describing.
7. My point here is primarily about Protestant Christianity. I note, however, that this issue has already had to be confronted by Catholic orders in the context of faculty and administrators, and the loyalty of Catholic laity to specific orders. For example, the extensive network of Jesuit colleges and universities have increasingly turned to laypeople, and even non-Catholics, for diverse leadership roles in their institutions.
8. See, for example, Julie Reuben's analysis in *The Making of the Modern University* (Chicago, IL: University of Chicago Press, 1996).
9. See Roger Martin, *The Opposable Mind* (Cambridge, MA: Harvard Business Review Press, 2007).
10. This has led some to emphasize "STEAM" (the A referring to the Arts) rather than "STEM" in thinking even about solving technical problems.

CHAPTER 16

Afterword: Vocation, Stewardship, and Teaching: A Hopeful Response

David I. Smith

In a recent, much-shared online article about how he approaches the task of helping first-year students adjust to college, Keith Parsons, a philosophy professor, reports that he had been warned that the students would be "apathetic, incurious, inattentive, unresponsive and frequently absent, and that they would exude an insufferable sense of entitlement."[1] While graciously admitting that many do not fall under this description, Parsons goes on to relate that his advice to first-year students includes the nuggets that it is "no part of my job to make you learn. At university, learning is your job—and yours alone," and "I get paid the same whether you get an 'F' or an 'A'." Pedagogy, he continues, will be heavily based on lecturing since he feels under no obligation to cater to students' "conditioned craving for constant stimulation." Parsons turns to a particular metaphor for the situation of new students. When entering the academy, they are "in a sense going to another country, one with a different culture and different values," and so must face the harsh challenge of adapting to unfamiliar rhythms whether they like it or not.

D.I. Smith (✉)
Calvin College, Grand Rapids, MI, USA

T.L. Scales and J.L. Howell (eds.), *Christian Faith and University Life*, DOI 10.1007/978-3-319-61744-2_16

The present book opens with the same metaphor. It begins with an evocation of the challenging task of learning the "values and habits" of "the academy," a place akin to "a foreign land" where the neophyte must painstakingly learn the proper ways of navigating. From there, however, the paths diverge, and this is not just because of the focus on graduate education and the preparation and vocation of new faculty. Perhaps one might characterize Parsons' picture of professors as exhibiting its own insufferable sense of entitlement; it seems to display minimal room for intellectual humility. His account of professors who need to invest little in their students' growth rhetorically sets faculty over against students, expertise over against pedagogical investment, and authority over against care. In the preceding chapters in this volume, this picture is replaced by a focus on vocation, stewardship, and hospitality, on the intentional cultivation of students' capacity for wise, virtuous engagement, on the professor's responsibility to think through carefully how his or her faith and values might shape a relationship to a discipline, to the material taught, to students, to the trajectory of a career. Here, the responsibility and engagement of students and professors are not a zero-sum game, and the attempt is made to sketch an academic world driven more by love of neighbor than by *ressentiment*. I like this version better.

It is true that the academy has its own demands, and that learning to work with them is a necessary ingredient of success. The research paper, lecture, or conference presentation are not the same practices as the sermon, the tract, or the blog post. There are challenging disciplines, methods, literatures, and norms of self-presentation to be mastered. And yet, as is evident at various junctures in the preceding chapters and already in this one, talk of "the" academy is an oversimplification. There is no universal agreement concerning the goals, methods, priorities, boundaries, practices, past, or future of "the academy." Parsons and I both belong to the academy, yet I find his prescriptions for the most part wrongheaded, objectionable even. Joining "the academy" as a Christian, is not a matter of joining an enterprise in which all the key positions and practices are already worked out to everyone's satisfaction. Submitting to learning the norms and practices currently prevalent in one's discipline is a necessary step, but it is also normal to see and seek space for alternative paths, just as getting off the beaten track and finding the surprising corners and niches can be a perfectly valid impulse when visiting a foreign country. Working as a Christian in the academy involves working with scholars of various beliefs and commitments and learning to communicate in ways that the denizens of one's particular guild find compelling. Yet the understandable desire to achieve respectable participation can lead us to imagine that the possible dance steps are more tightly choreographed than they in fact are. The ideological, social, and pragmatic diversity within "the academy" means (as Karl Aho's essay notes) that there is room to move, room to carve out an identity that is animated by faith, that dares to think non-standardized thoughts and try more promising practices, and in so doing witnesses to the possibility of a different future academy.

When I first joined the more particular realm of Christian higher education, I think I came with a somewhat naive expectation that I would find it to be more finished and ready. Surely, given the depth and scope of the Christian tradition, the flurry of activity in recent decades (around 10,000 peer-reviewed articles and counting)[2] attempting to define and exemplify the "integration of faith and learning," and the strong sense of mission that animates many Christian campuses, there would be a pretty clear template by now. We would at least have the main parameters wrapped up, and would be able to focus on pushing forward the boundaries. What I discovered (for both good and ill) was a much more open-ended conversation still underway, peppered with gaps, disagreements, cliques, reinventions of the wheel, sharp insights, and shoddy rehashes. There were some widely shared points of reference, but there was also a lot of terrain still contested (including the notion of "integration of faith and learning" itself). The Christian academy was as partially woven as the academy at large. I mention this not to lament; the frayed edges are at least in part a normal feature of the attempt to think and act out of a complex and internally diverse tradition in a continually changing intellectual, institutional, and social landscape. If the project were about getting all the right answers nailed down and then repeating them ad infinitum, it would not last long. I mention it rather to underline that in Christian conversations about the academy too, there is space to move.

The essays in this volume exhibit a variety of attempts to find room to move, to find the places where a Christian tether might enable a fresh arc, rather than offering only a tired academic routine with added religion. There are too many specific themes and contexts in these essays to respond to them one by one. Instead I will focus on what I take to be one heartening sign of movement, on a question that emerges from the conversation, and on one way in which we might want to push things further than this conversation has done.

Faith and Teaching

In order to identify the particular movement that I have in mind, and to pinpoint why it might be needed, let's take a closer look at one of the statistics quoted by Nathan Alleman, Perry Glanzer, and David Guthrie in their chapter on how faith can animate teaching. Alleman, Glanzer, and Guthrie surveyed 2309 faculty at 48 Christian colleges and universities, and, among other things, asked: "Does your theological tradition influence the following areas of your teaching?" in relation to five aspects of teaching.[3] Three of these areas produce positive results. 79% of faculty feel their theological tradition influences the "foundations, worldview, or narrative guiding the course," 78% agree that it influences their "motivations for or attitude toward the class," and 84% affirmed that it influenced their "ethical approach." When the focus is on framing intellectual perspectives, then, roughly four out of five faculty affirm that their theological tradition plays a role in their approach (between 5 and 9% answered "don't know," and between 12 and 16% denied any influence).

The two remaining areas were "course objectives" and "teaching methods," which move us more squarely into the realm of concrete pedagogical decision-making. 48% agreed that their theological tradition influenced their objectives (43% denied an influence), and 40% saw an influence on their teaching methods (an identical 40% denied an influence). Perhaps most tellingly, the 20% figure for "don't know" in answer to the question about teaching methods is more than double any other area of uncertainty, with the "yes" and "no" responses evenly divided around it. It seems reasonable to conclude that among Christian academics at large, there is a great deal more confidence in the possibility of relating faith to perspectives and philosophies than to pedagogical practices.

The three more affirmatively answered questions might be taken as resonating with the perspectival, worldview-oriented focus of much of the literature on "integration of faith and learning." The results in these areas seem to suggest that faculty at broadly evangelical institutions have largely internalized the general argument in that literature that a Christian worldview can justifiably and meaningfully frame academic knowledge claims. In other words, the results pertaining to teaching methods do not seem to come from a sample of educators who have failed to engage with the project of connecting faith and learning. The same faculty who have by and large embraced the idea of drawing upon faith commitments at the level of worldview, vision, and ethics are the ones who show a clear majority that either sees no connection to teaching practices or does not know whether there might be such a thing. This is not particularly surprising. The factors suppressing scholarly attention to teaching and learning have been well documented,[4] and the amount of attention given to questions specifically focused on teaching and learning in the explicitly Christian scholarly literature over the past four to five decades is demonstrably marginal.[5] The fostering of expertise in tracing out presuppositions, perspectives, worldviews, intellectual histories, and the like in faith-informed ways has not yielded a strong set of tools for describing how faith animates the practical wisdom involved in pedagogical decision-making.[6] This has affected our ability to address pedagogical questions with adequate nuance.

Power Spots

An example may help make this claim more concrete. In his classic account of his ethnographic research at an urban Catholic junior high school, Peter McLaren describes the point at which he began to speculate that every teacher had a "power spot." He describes the "power spot" as the place in the classroom to which the teacher tended to retreat when he or she felt threatened or unsure. It was the place that represented their authority in some way and reinforced their feeling of being in charge. The pull towards that spot was not conscious, and the actual location varied from teacher to teacher—it might be behind a lectern or beside a desk or out in front of the class—but they all seemed to have one. In fact, McLaren noticed that when teachers exchanged classes, they would tend to go to the power spot of the teacher whose class they had taken over. One day, a teacher asked McLaren to briefly take over his class while he was busy preparing a projector in another room. McLaren found himself in charge. He describes what ensued:

> I wandered around the room, watching the kids do their seatwork. As soon as I approached [the teacher's] power spot the noise began to dim. But when I actually entered the power spot, one of the kids shot up his hand:

Are you the teacher now?

"Well, not exactly," I said.

Cause I wanna know if I can get a drink.

Sure, go ahead.[7]

Despite the likelihood that neither the teachers nor the students could have clearly articulated what was going on, it seems there was a physical location in the room that meant *I am the teacher, I am in charge, and I am about to exert my authority.* Merely standing in that spot affected the noise level, led a student to construe McLaren as the teacher, and pushed McLaren into taking on the behaviors expected of the teacher role even though he denied actually being the teacher. This is one small example of the bodily rituals of the classroom. The meaning of pedagogical behavior is carried not just in words, but in positions and postures, in a kind of bodily memory, the material underpinning of what happens.

With some prompting, I have found college students well able to describe other instances of this kind of thing. One group of students described to me being in a class in which the professor was clearly trying to get discussion going, but it never seemed to really take off. I wonder whether the professor left class dejected about his or her ability to lead discussion, or about the apparently unresponsive group of students they had to face this semester. Looking back, the students came to the conclusion that the main problem was the furniture. There were about twice as many chairs in the room as there were students, and they often ended up sitting a couple of empty chairs away from the next person. Discussions across empty chairs are awkward. The teacher who does not intentionally organize the furniture begins at a disadvantage, for teaching happens in material time and space.

Taking this aspect of teaching and learning seriously opens up questions different from the ones most commonly pursued in discussions of faith and learning. Consider prayer. Since becoming part of Christian higher education, I have experienced a number of discussions among faculty about the role of prayer and devotions at the start of class. Is it an appropriate way to frame learning as Christian and invite God's presence, or perhaps a cheap or manipulative move, visibly performed piety that does not actually change anything that follows or create any interesting Christian intellectual perspective on the content studied? In other contexts, especially in K-12 education, prayer in schools has been hotly debated, especially in North America, as a potent symbol and proxy for whether a theistic or a humanistic frame reigns in schools. If we return to McLaren's observations about the power spot, a different kind of question emerges: if we do decide to pray at the start of a class, where should we stand? What might it mean if we pray while standing in the power spot?

The answer to this depends in part on the wider culture of our classroom and our institution. In other parts of his account, McLaren traces how, in the Catholic school that he studied, "the interdictions, elicitations, preachments and imprimaturs of the teachers took on greater force when teachers were seen to dispense both the wisdom of Moses and the tables of multiplication."[8] Religious symbols and rituals found their meaning within a larger school culture that emphasized obedience and conformity. Devotional practices such as prayer reinforced, and to some degree collapsed into, the school's mechanisms for controlling student behavior. Students were seated in straight rows facing the large metal desks of the teachers, a layout designed to inhibit social interaction.[9] One teacher felt that as it was practiced in the school, "prayer was really just a technique to get students to settle down before the lesson."[10] How might praying from the power spot help to construct this sense of what prayer is? As McLaren emphasizes, the meaning of gestures and rituals is not a given, but emerges as part of an interwoven context of use. If we pray publicly, in a classroom, it does not necessarily follow that we have led students in inviting God into our midst. Again, where should we be if and when we pray? And do we even think of physical location as one part of the faith language of the classroom, part of the "integration of faith and learning"?

Signs of Change

It is heartening to see signs in this volume of emerging Christian faculty who are willing to engage with and begin to develop questions about Christian higher education that have this kind of pedagogical specificity. Beyond the taxonomy offered by Glanzer and his colleagues, such questions recur in the remaining chapters. How might we go about constructing a culture of vocation in universities (Davis)? How might we enable students to internalize a different definition of freedom (Griffis)? What might gardening add to higher education pedagogy (Bilbro and Baker)? How does changing the question on an exam transform the learning that emerges from literary study in the direction of practical wisdom (Schwehn)? What does creative and faithful reading look like, and how does it relate to pedagogical formation (Moser)? What might Augustine have to teach us about dialogic pedagogy (Howell and Scales)? How might practices of prayer and fellowship inform doctoral education (Scales and Howell)? What effect might a hospitable pause mid-semester have on learning (Rodeheffer)? How does humility relate to learning (Echelbarger)? How does enacting embodied practices form our faith (Childress)? How does a concern for justice inform education of citizens (Hunt and Chavez)? How can a Christian pragmatism give us pedagogical options beyond merely increasing the eloquence of our lecturing (Aho)? What kinds of pedagogical practice might remain academic while fostering ecclesial formation (Cramer)? How does the work of the Christian research university relate to character formation (Jones)? These are all questions about how we teach as much as they are questions about what we should think or believe. They are not the only questions addressed by the preceding chapters, but they do provide a recurring thread that is a welcome sign of progress in expanding questions of faith and learning beyond matters of what truth is and how we know and into the arena of how we teach and learn.[11]

Amend or Reform?

Having noted this welcome trend, I turn to a question that arises from it. The question can be conveniently framed by two comments in Mark Schwehn's characteristically fine essay on Christian practical wisdom. Schwehn notes (and I entirely concur) that "if we are serious about seeking to cultivate practical wisdom in our students as a primary aim of a college education, we must above all else reform our pedagogy."[12] A little later, after describing an instructive example of the results of a specific pedagogical change, Schwehn concludes that "this account of the purpose of the liberal arts did not require me radically to change my classroom teaching at all," but merely to "amend slightly but significantly what I hoped to accomplish."[13] There seems to be a little tension here: *reform above all else* and *amending one's hopes slightly* sound like rather different levels of aspiration.

There are perhaps good reasons for this tension. There are always things we should want to keep, even in the midst of reform. There are often sound reasons to reassure readers that they need not abandon everything they know in order to take a meaningful step in a fresh direction, and to show that a proposed modification, especially one that touches on Christian faith, will not pull down the pillars of the academy and plunge us into chaos. Small changes are, moreover, the most realistic kind, and attempting to question all of our practices at once is a good prelude to bidding our sanity farewell. Focusing on a very specific moment in our pedagogy and asking what would change if we shifted it a little is a wise and admirable strategy. As Schwehn notes, "adjusting the course of the Queen Mary ocean liner by one degree at the beginning of a journey of 2000 miles"[14] can yield a new destination.

Yet I also sense a punch pulled. What if the best destination for us to arrive at required a two-degree correction? Or three? Or five? Schwehn quite rightly notes that changing the question asked in a literary assignment is likely to change the learning that takes place, to yield essays that "could not and would not have been written"[15] until the right question was asked. Make a specific change to pedagogy and there is a shift in the kind of learning that is invited. As I have wrestled with similar questions in the context of literature teaching, I have found that the same is true of other changes. If I arrange the chairs in straight rows, or in a circle or a tight cluster, or if I remove the chairs altogether and have us sit on the floor, different conversations ensue. If I insist that students read certain texts more than once, or slowly, or together with another person, or aloud, or repeatedly across the course of a week, and if I connect these changes explicitly to a shared exploration of what patience, charity, and humility have to do with the act of reading, different kinds of learning ensue. If I have students read one another's interpretive responses to texts in conjunction with research on different kinds of readers, and if we then discuss which of us are the wrong readers for the current text and what we might have to learn from one another, different learning ensues. If I stand or sit, if I talk a lot or a little, if I leave longer or shorter silences, if I refuse to step in and lecture when students have not prepared well, learning goes differently. If I switch the final exam and the final class, so that the semester ends not with judgment, but with deliberation on what we have learned and wish to carry forward, the final thoughts of the students in the class are different. If I assign not only reading but practices that require students to try out ways of engaging with their wider community that might help them engage with what the reading is addressing, learning changes. And so on.[16] What bearing might any of these changes, and others besides, have on the teaching of Christian practical wisdom? Schwehn's course adjustment is a valuable one, but also just one moment in a larger set of navigational conversations that should continue to progress beyond Schwehn's essay and the others that accompany it here. I point to the rhetorical tension in Schwehn's essay, then, not to fault Schwehn for how he proceeds, but to make the suggestion that his small step (and the others in other chapters) might indeed be just a small, incremental part of something more disruptive and far-reaching if diligently pursued. I hope that as the small suggestions accumulate, at least some of them will be developed further, and might lead to a robust questioning of which of the habits of the foreign country that is the academy it is really fruitful to accept. I take this to be integral to the vocation of Christian scholars and their stewardship of the academy.

Gaps

Finally, I think that one significant gap in the conversation represented here requires comment if this book is to be addressed to Christian faculty and doctoral students at large. It will hardly have escaped the attention of many readers that the conversation here is basically a humanities conversation. The social sciences make a brief appearance in a couple of chapters, the natural sciences and professional disciplines are scarcely mentioned. This is, I take it, in large measure simply historical accident—this is the book that this group of scholars were able to write, and perhaps a different group should work to supplement it in those other areas. I also concur with the general sense that if we are to think well about our Christian identity in any discipline, then some engagement with theology, philosophy, and literature has to be at least part of the picture, if for no other reason than that a great deal of significant reflection on what it means to be Christian has been, and continues to be, hammered out in those disciplines. And yet, with the rise of social investment in Science, Technology, Engineering, and Mathematics (STEM) disciplines continuing unabated, I suspect that warning about the dangers of trying to solve everything with technical rationality and pointing to the deep formative import of engagement in the humanities may prove to be a limited strategy if it cannot also communicate an appreciation for what technical rationality is good at, and offer a compelling account of what scientists, engineers, psychologists, and other more empirically oriented colleagues will gain *in terms of their own work* from reading Augustine or pondering the nature of humility or practicing hospitality. Without this kind of engagement, the conversation will end up sounding from one substantial end of the disciplinary spectrum more like a monologue (or more like imposition than hospitality), and I hope that as the conversations represented here are carried forward, their interdisciplinary scope will also be strengthened and deepened. The broad cultivation of stewards of the academy and faithful service demands no less.

Notes

1. Keith M. Parsons, "Message to my Freshman Students," Huffington Post, May 14, 2015, updated May 14, 2016, retrieved June 28, 2016, http://www.huffingtonpost.com/keith-m-parsons/message-to-my-freshman-st_b_7275016.html.
2. David I. Smith, Joonyong Um, and Claudia D. Beversluis, "The Scholarship of Teaching and Learning in a Christian Context." *Christian Higher Education* 13, no. 1 (2014): 74–87.
3. See p. 169.
4. See, for example, Mary T. Huber and Pat Hutchings, *The Advancement of Learning: Building the Teaching Commons* (San Francisco, CA: Jossey-Bass, 2005).
5. See Smith, Um, and Beversluis, "The Scholarship of Teaching and Learning," for details, including a breakdown by discipline and by decade.
6. I discuss this at greater length in David I. Smith, *Christians, Teaching* (Grand Rapids: Eerdmans, forthcoming 2018).
7. Peter McLaren *Schooling as a Ritual Performance: Toward a Political Economy of Educational Symbols and Gestures*, 3rd edition (Latham, MD: Rowman & Littlefield, 1999), 112–13.
8. Ibid., 190.
9. Ibid., 197.
10. Ibid., 231.
11. I trust that it is clear that this is welcome not because those other questions are not important, but simply because they are not sufficient.
12. P. 81.
13. P. 85.
14. P. 84.
15. P. 85.

16. I have explored some of these changes and their results in "Reading Practices and Christian Pedagogy: Enacting Charity with Texts," in *Teaching and Christian Practices: Reshaping Faith and Learning*, eds. David I. Smith and James K.A. Smith (Grand Rapids: Eerdmans, 2011), 43–60. See also David I. Smith, John Shortt and John Sullivan, eds., *Teaching Spiritually Engaged Reading* (Nottingham: The Stapleford Centre, 2007).

Index

T.L. Scales and J.L. Howell (eds.), *Christian Faith and University Life*,
DOI 10.1007/978-3-319-61744-2

Zeitfracht Medien GmbH
Ferdinand-Jühlke-Straße 7
99095 Erfurt, Deutschland
produktsicherheit@kolibri360.de